The JOY *of* Publishing

Fascinating Facts, Anecdotes,

Curiosities, and Historic Origins

about Books and Authors,

Editors and Publishers,

Bookmaking and Bookselling

Nat
Bodian

The JOY *of* Publishing

by Nat Bodian

Open Horizons FAIRFIELD, IOWA

Published by Open Horizons Publishing Company
209 S. Main Street, P. O. Box 205
Fairfield, IA 52556-0205
(515) 472-6130; Fax: (515) 472-1560
E-mail: OpenHorizons@bookmarket.com

Printed and bound in the United States of America

Cataloging in Publication Data

Bodian, Nat. G., 1921-
　The joy of publishing.

　Bibliography: p.
　Includes indexes.
　1. Publishers and publishing. 2. Authorship.
3. Booksellers and Bookselling— United States.
4. Book industries and trade. 5. Advertising—Books.
I. Title
ISBN 0-912411-47-3

Preface

My Lifetime Love Affair with Books

This work culminates a lifetime love affair with books and the people involved in writing, creating, publishing, and circulating them. While my formal career in the world of books spanned just three decades, my interest in and passion for books started in the early years of my life at a neighborhood library near my home. *The Joy of Publishing* reflects this lifetime infatuation.

The contents of this volume encompasses the entire world of books. Its aim is to provide a panoramic view of the fascinating writing and publishing process, both contemporary and historic, but with a slight twist. That twist is the influence of my early background as a journalist. It is this background that prompted the writing of the more than 300 entries, not only to entertain and enlighten, but also to highlight the offbeat, unusual, and landmark happenings in the community of the book.

The *Joy of Publishing* was triggered by a comment to me from the editor of a publishing newsletter to which I'd been a substantial contributor for many years. In addition to my regular articles on book marketing and bookselling, I'd often sent the newsletter short pieces about books and their histories that were offbeat or unusual.

Once, the editor acknowledged my contribution by noting that at the rate I was contributing these captivating pieces soon I would have enough to fill a book. Why not? I thought. So, the work on *The Joy of Publishing* began. With selected earlier newsletter contributions as a starting point, I went to work in earnest starting with research of virtually every book available on book publishing. Exhausting that source, my search next led to books by and about publishers and famous editors. Finally, I turned to biographies and autobiographies of literary greats.

A large part of *The Joy of Publishing* is based on research. I read through hundreds of books—both old and newly-published—and years of newspaper book review supplements. I then connected facts with information gleaned from innumerable encyclopedias, dictionaries, and literary references as well as from publishing industry and library resources.

I am indebted to many individuals, libraries, and organizations who responded to my requests for information or assistance. While all cannot be individually acknowledged, I would like to cite a few here who were of special help.

These included Richard Morris, who during his tenure as executive director of COSMEP, the International Association of Independent Publishers, was a continuing source of encouragement and inspiration; Howard Cady, former consultant for William Morrow and Company; Mike Bradstock, University of Canterbury Press, New Zealand; Debra Kaufman, library director at Perkin Elmer; Ed Langlois, Camera Ready Composition Company; Nadine Siegel, librarian at the American Booksellers Association; Sidney Landau, editorial director, Cambridge University Press; Al Bodian, former staffer at *The Village Voice*; Les Bodian, former editor at Prentice-Hall; Helen Morris, Random House; Shirley Horner, a former book editor at *The New York Times*; Herman Estrin of the New Jersey Literary Hall of Fame; and the reference staff at the Cranford Public Library.

One pleasant outcome of my research for *The Joy of Publishing* was the volume of useful material emanating from books I myself had authored in earlier years for the book industry and from articles I had written for various book industry publications.

A further enhancement in writing *The Joy of Publishing* was the opportunity to reminisce over my 30-year career as a book marketer and to draw a number of entries from my experience with special book projects.

Here, then, for all who love books in general and for all authors, publishers, booksellers, librarians, wholesalers, literary agents, rights buyers, book reviewers, literary critics, journalists, translators, and educators, is a heartfelt and joyous contribution that I hope will bring as much pleasure to you, the reader of *The Joy of Publishing*, as it did to me in creating it.

Nat G. Bodian
Cranford, New Jersey

Short Contents

Contents

Chapter 2 — Editor and Publisher Lore and Legends, 59

Chapter 3A — Book Publishing Origins, Firsts, and Curiosities in the 20th Century, 77

Chapter 3B — Book Publishing Origins, Firsts, and Curiosities in the 19th Century, 93

Chapter 3C — Book Publishing Origins, Firsts, and Curiosities in the 18th Century, 109

Chapter 3D — Book Publishing Origins, Firsts, and Curiosities in the 17th Century and Earlier, 117

Chapter 4 — Landmark Advances and Events in Bookselling, 125

Chapter 5 — Book Reviews and Reviewers, 137

Chapter 6 — The Evolution of Bookmaking, 143

Chapter 7 — Book Titling, Tidbits, and Trivia, 153

Chapter 8 — Book-Word Origins and Curiosities, 163

Introduction

A Celebration of the Book!

The Joy of Publishing is a celebration of the book. It is intended for all who love or have a curiosity about books and about the people who write, create, edit, distribute, and deal with them.

In *The Joy of Publishing*, I have presented a wide-ranging collection of hundreds of human-interest stories and little-known facts, curiosities, and anecdotes about books that reflect my life-long passion for books as well as an ongoing interest in the people involved in their creation and dissemination.

In the opening chapter, you will find anecdotes, recollections, and behind-the-scenes revelations about scores of widely-known and best-selling authors and their contributions to the world of literature. Chapter 1 talks about their dreams, their idiosyncrasies, their approaches to creativity, and little-known facts about their literary beginnings and growth.

In Chapter 2, you'll discover fascinating entries about great publishers and fabled editors who made literary discoveries and developed techniques that led to their success. You'll also read about the founding of some of the leading publishing houses, about great book editors and their idiosyncrasies, about the breaking of racial barriers in publishing and the emergence of black publishing, and about the world's great book fairs.

The third chapter, **Book Publishing Origins, Firsts, and Curiosities,** is actually four chapters combined into one and arranged by century. It deals with the historic development of the book and the origins of many of the world's best-known reference classics.

In the Chapter 3 portion dealing with the 20th century, you'll read how Emily Post got started with her book on *Etiquette*, how the Book-of-the-Month Club originated, the book that led to the U.S. Pure Food Act, the birth and development of the paperback revolution, and numerous interesting characteristics of various authors whose books became No. 1 bestsellers.

In the Chapter 3 portion dealing with the 19th century, you'll learn about dozens of publishing innovations including the origin of the detective mystery and the invention of Sherlock Holmes, the birth of *Grimm's Fairy Tales*, and the origin of *Bartlett's Quotations, Who's Who*, and *Webster's American Dictionary*. You'll also learn about the novel that started the anti-slavery movement in the United States, how Mark Twain made publishing history with a manuscript, how Jules Verne invented a world of the future, and how the George Washington cherry tree story was created.

In the Chapter 3 portion dealing with the 18th century, you'll learn how Benjamin Franklin published America's first novel, the origin of the *Encyclopedia Britannica*, the first dictionary printed in the United States, and the origin and history of *Gray's Anatomy*.

The Chapter 3 portion covering the 17th century and earlier provides details on the origin of numerous famous books, including the first American almanac, the first dictionary in the English language, the earliest Latin dictionary, the first printed book in the New World, the world's oldest publishers, the first North American college press and library, and a listing of legendary authors and historic works that were banned or censored.

The success of the book in America is largely associated with the growth of the bookselling trade. The fourth chapter deals with **Landmark Advances and Events in Bookselling**, beginning with the earliest record of trade in books and history's first recorded bookseller. It goes on to discuss America's first book fairs, the banning of books in Boston, early publishers as retail booksellers, and the first U.S. traveling book salesman. Included in this chapter is the origin and purpose of the American Booksellers Association and a behind-the-scenes visit to the world's largest and most unusual bookstore.

As books often sell on the strength of their reviews, the fifth chapter on **Book Reviews and Reviewers** describes in detail the kinds of book reviewers, what goes into a good book review, what influences the reviewers, and some anecdotes involving various book reviewers. A highlight of this chapter is a first-ever published study of reviewer opinions on book writing quality.

How books got started and grew to their present format is told in interesting detail in Chapter 6 on **The Evolution of Bookmaking**. It deals with such facets of the book as the origin of paper, bookbinding, the title page, endpapers, printed illustrations, the thumb index, the book jacket, and the plastic book jacket cover. There is also a fascinating behind-the-scenes look at how present-day book jackets are created.

The key to success for many books often lies in its title. How do authors arrive at their book titles and how can a simple title change transform a so-so book into a bestseller? These are among the many topics discussed in Chapter 7 on **Book Titling Tidbits and Trivia**. This chapter presents many interesting anecdotes and curiosities involving various book titles, some adapted from an earlier book on titling by the author.

Chapter 8 on **Book Word Origins and Curiosities** is a treat designed to entertain the curious reader, inform the would-be author, and answer nagging questions for the publishing professional, bookseller, librarian, and book reviewer. It starts with the origin and meaning of *book* and goes on to treat the origin and meaning of various book parts and words. It explains, for example, the difference between a book's preface, foreword, and introduction, the difference between a *novel* and a *novella*, and the difference between an *impression* and an *edition*. It also explains why a coffee table book has nothing to do with coffee or tables, and how Baedeker became the accepted term for guidebooks. Included among the numerous chapter entries is a complete guide to biblio words.

In the growth of bookselling and the book industry in the United States, publishers over the years have tried numerous innovative approaches for promoting their books, from skywriting to subway poster advertising. Chapter 9 tells about the introduction of many of these innovative approaches, including the first book review supplement and the early use of book jackets for advertising. There are numerous anecdotes on book promotion exploits.

The author's career as a book marketer spans some thirty years. In Chapter 10, **Some Personal Publishing Recollections**, the author recalls some interesting publishing projects and authors with which he was associated, including the first *Neiman Marcus Christmas Catalogue* and a famous dictionarist's strange source of inspiration.

Publishing Miscellany is the eleventh and concluding chapter. It offers a collection of strange, interesting, fascinating, and otherwise unusual bits of book trivia that can be read and enjoyed by every book lover.

As I said earlier, *The Joy of Publishing* is a celebration of the book. While these eleven chapters are meant to fascinate and entertain, I hope they also provide you with a deeper understanding and appreciation of the book and its role as an enriching contribution to life and learning.

Chapter 1

Author Anecdotes, Recollections, and Revelations

When McGraw Trusted Irving:
The Publishing Hoax of the Century

One of the greatest and most widely-publicized publishing hoaxes of this century took place in 1971-1972 when author Clifford Irving contracted the sale of the memoirs of the reclusive billionaire, Howard Hughes, for a reported one million dollars for book and magazine rights.

The McGraw-Hill Book Company acquired world publishing rights. Then *Life* magazine bought the rights to serialize the book in three installments and, at the same time, Dell Publishing Company bought the paperback rights. It was rumored in the publishing industry that the *Life* and Dell rights purchase cost $500,000.

The colorful and legendary Howard Hughes (1905-1976) had, among other things, founded the Hughes Aircraft Company, owned controlling interests in RKO pictures and in Trans World Airlines, and had discovered and introduced such famous movie personalities as Jean Harlow and Paul Muni.

Hughes was widely known for his aversion to publicity and at the time of the hoax had been in complete seclusion since 1950. However, when publicity broke on the Irving contract with McGraw-Hill, Hughes went public.

As the *New York Times* of February 27, 1972, reported, "In one of the most extraordinary news conferences on record, a man identified as reclusive billionaire Howard Hughes conversed for nearly three hours over a 3,000 mile telephone circuit from his present retreat in the Bahama Islands with seven reporters assembled in Hollywood, CA." Hughes said in the interview that he had never met Clifford Irving or even heard of him until recently.

When the scandal broke in 1971 and a trial was held, the manuscript and letters concerning the book, supposedly written by Hughes, were found to be fraudulent and forged. Following a subsequent trial, Irving served a prison sentence as did his wife. McGraw-Hill recouped most of its advance, which Irving's wife had deposited in a Swiss bank account. Irving's wife also served time in a Swiss prison for that offense.

In July 1972, Grove Press vice president, F. Jordan, reported in the *New York Times* that his company would publish Irving's account of his attempts to swindle McGraw-Hill of $850,000 and that the first printing in September was set at 750,000 copies.

After the event, Curtis Benjamin, a former chairman of the McGraw-Hill Book Company, lamented in *A Candid Critique of Book Publishing*,[1] "Who would have believed that when the company [McGraw-Hill] moved into its new skyscraper in 1972, the name of the bank that leased the first floor facing the Avenue of the Americas would prominently label that side of the building as The Irving Trust Company?"

Biggest Advance In Publishing History
Made Tom Clancy a Multimillionaire

The biggest single book advance in publishing history went to bestselling author Tom Clancy in the summer of 1992 when Putnam Berkeley agreed to pay him between $13 and $14 million as an advance against an uncompleted new work, *Without Remorse*. Clancy's history-making deal with Putnam Berkeley, at a time when other publishers were struggling to stay profitable, was paid a year in advance of the August 1993 publication date and, reportedly, was only for North American hardcover and paperback rights. Book industry experts estimated Clancy's income from *Without Remorse* would easily top $20 million since Clancy had retained all other rights, including foreign rights, movie rights, audio rights, and video rights.

At the end of 1995, Putnam signed Clancy to a reported eight-figure deal for a four-volume series to be titled *The Commanders*, which will tell the behind-the-scenes stories of the four military leaders who ran the Desert Storm operation. The first book in the series will be published in 1997.

A number of Clancy's books have been converted into blockbuster movies, with rights selling in the seven figures. In the past, the appearance of a Clancy movie usually propelled the paperback of that title back onto the bestseller lists. Some of Clancy's earlier successes included *The Sum of All Fears, The Hunt for Red October, Red Storm Rising, Patriot Games, The Cardinal of The Kremlin,* and *Clear and Present Danger*. Clancy's best-selling techno-thrillers have already sold more than 50 million copies.

It is interesting to note that Tom Clancy's first bestseller, *The Hunt for Red October*, was published by a small specialty publisher, The Naval Institute Press, when larger publishers rejected the manuscript as too technical.

Truman Capote's Advice to Would-Be Writers

Truman Capote (1924-1984) made his impressive literary debut at the age of 24 with *Other Voices, Other Rooms*. His best-known literary effort was his 1966 nonfiction novel *In Cold Blood*, a breathtaking account of a series of murders by two men in Kansas. It sold 4,243,338 copies in cloth and paper editions. Here is Capote's advice to writers:

I attended schools in New York City and Greenwich, Connecticut. The reading I did on my own was of greater importance than my official education which was a waste. It ended when I was seventeen when I obtained a job at The New Yorker magazine sorting cartoons and clipping newspapers. It was not a very grand job; still, I was fortunate to have it, especially since I was determined never to set a studious foot inside a college classroom.

I felt that either one was or wasn't a writer, and that no combination of professors could influence the outcome. I still think (26 years later) that I was correct, at least in my own case. However, I now realize that most young writers have more to gain than not by attending college, if only because their teachers and classroom comrades provide a captive audience for their work. Nothing is lonelier than to be an aspiring artist without some semblance of a sounding board.

Orwell's *Animal Farm*: Too Hot to Handle

George Orwell's *Animal Farm* is firmly established in world literature as a 20th century classic. Yet, when written more than half a century ago in the winter of 1943-44, it was considered by a number of publishers as too hot to handle.

Animal Farm tells a satirical tale of how the domestic animals stage a successful revolution against Farmer Jones only to fall under the much worse tyranny of the Communist pigs. While told as a fairy story for children, it ingeniously traced the Bolshevik revolution, depicting the ruling Communists and Stalin. The expulsion of the pig Snowball, was Trotsky. The pains of Boxer in building the twice-destroyed windmill were those of the Russian people under the Five Year Plans. The ending where animals look from men to pigs and cannot tell one from the other referred to the wartime Teheran Conference of 1943 where the three government leaders—Churchill, Roosevelt, and Stalin—toasted each other as allies.

Orwell had submitted his completed *Animal Farm* manuscript to the English publisher Victor Gollancz. He promptly turned it down, saying he feared it would endanger Anglo-Soviet relations. Orwell then submitted it to Faber and Faber, where it was turned down by T.S. Eliot. Then, the manuscript went to publisher Jonathan Cape who also rejected it as a slur on Britain's gallant Soviet allies. In a final try, Orwell went to publisher Frederic Warburg, who reviewed the manuscript and accepted it without hesitation.

Published in early 1945, *Animal Farm* received mixed reviews from the critics. But from the day of publication, sales of the book took off and the book went on to become an international bestseller. The list of all time bestsellers through 1973[2] showed *Animal Farm* had sold in excess of 7 million copies through that year, and the book continued to sell at the rate of over 150,000 copies a year.

Orwell (whose real name was Eric Arthur Blair) died in 1950 at the age of 47. He is regarded as a prophet whose work posthumously has become part of 20th century folklore. Numerous writers, particularly Russian and including Alexander Solzhenitsyn, were later in their written works to describe various situations under Communism as Orwellian. The greatest tribute to Orwell came from numerous East European intellectuals who hailed Orwell's surprising understanding of life under Communism despite the fact that he had never visited a Communist country.

Hemingway Gave Budding Publisher a Rule for Life

Charles Scribner, Jr., who headed the Scribner publishing firm for many years until it became a part of Macmillan Publishing Company, recalls this rule for life given him as a young man by Ernest Hemingway, who was a close friend of his father (Charles Scribner, 1890-1952) and the publishing firm's top author at the time: "Always do sober what you said you'd do when you were drunk. That will teach you to keep your mouth shut."[3]

Damon Runyon: Literature's Most Colorful Writer

One of the most colorful writers in American literature was the journalist and short story writer Damon Runyon (1884-1946). His individualistic writing style relied heavily on constant use of the present tense and on the Broadway slang of the early decades of this century. His writings appeared for decades in the *New York American*, Hearst syndicated features, and numerous magazines.

Collections of his short stories were made into dozens of books of which nineteen were still in print at the time of this writing. Most of his books were successful in the bookstores and many of them were successfully translated into Hollywood movies and Broadway stage plays—among them *Hello Dolly, Little Miss Marker, The Big Street*, and *Bloodhounds of Broadway*.

Although basically a journalist, his short stories sold regularly and well and, often after 15 or 20 had been published, were collected and published in book form. His first book in 1931 was called *Guys and Dolls*. A second book in 1934, Runyon wanted to title *More Guys and Dolls*, but he was overruled by his publisher who titled it *Blue Plate Special*. More than half a century later, these two titles are still in print, and a later collection of Runyon short stories, after his death, picked up the title *More Guys and Dolls*.

Eight years after Damon Runyon's death, in 1946, LaRocque DuBose, a French scholar, made a study of Runyon's use of non-literary words[4] and found that in 51 short stories, Runyon had used 750 non-literary words, of which fully half were colloquial or slang. So heavily was Runyon's writing laced with slang words and expressions that in a 1930's list of America's top ten coiners of slang, Runyon's name was included. The list was compiled by W.J. Funk of Funk and Wagnalls, dictionary publishers.

In 1935, when Runyon's third collection of short stories was published in the volume *Money from Home*, the *New York Times* reviewer opined "They are grand, entertaining reading ... full of Broadway wisecracks and hard-boiled comedy. Many of the yarns end up with the whip-snap finish which makes critics compare Runyon to O'Henry." After a later collection was published, another *Times* reviewer wrote "the characters are too thin for any long life" but he found "Mr. Runyon's big shots, gunmen, chorus girls, chiselers, dopes, and hangers-on to have a frankness which is neither pseudo-romantic nor brutal."

Damon Runyon died of cancer on December 6, 1946. In the concluding paragraph of Runyon's biography *A Gentleman of Broadway*,[5] biographer Edwin P. Hoyt wrote, "He was conscious as he was taken to the hospital.... He wrote a few notes.... He asked that his name be carved on the tombstone above Ellen's [his first wife] grave.... He asked that his ashes be scattered over Broadway.... Early in the evening he died. A week later Eddie Ricken-backer flew slowly above Broadway in a big transport plane, scattering Damon's ashes above the busy thoroughfare. The Gentleman of Broadway was home."

John O'Hara: Suffered Hunger in Early Years

John O'Hara is best remembered for his great novels. But he also enjoyed a career as a newspaper and magazine reporter and publicist before achieving fame as a novelist. His big novels include *Appointment in Samarra, Butter-field 8, Pal Joey, A Rage to Live, From the Terrace,* and *Ten North Frederick.* His early life was far from easy. In 1928, at the age of twenty-three, O'Hara came to New York City from Pottsville, Pennsylvania, where he'd been a reporter for his hometown paper, *The Pottsville Journal.* He'd also sent articles to magazines without success.

His first two years in New York City were difficult with short stints as reporter for the *New York Herald Tribune,* reporter for *Time* magazine, re-porter for *Editor & Publisher,* rewrite man for *New York Daily Mirror,* and movie critic for *New York Morning Telegraph.* At one time during this pe-riod, he was literally starving, going without anything to eat for three days.

By 1934, six years after arriving in New York, O'Hara had written and published numerous short stories and he was already author of a highly suc-cessful first novel, *Appointment in Samarra,* published in 1934. He was now doing research for his second novel, *Butterfield 8.*

O'Hara's *Butterfield 8* was a factually-accurate, but fictionalized, account that grew out of the newspaper headlines of the day. It was about a beautiful young woman whose body had been found on a Long Island beach in June of 1931. An autopsy had revealed that she'd been drugged and sustained injuries before drowning. She was twenty-five, drank heavily, and had been a high-class prostitute. Her death, at first, was thought to be a suicide. But, as evidence unraveled, the theory was developed that she had been thrown from a ship. The case was never solved.

O'Hara had seen the woman around New York City in various speakeasies and, after her death, obtained access to her diaries. As he read them, he became convinced that the information in the diaries, together with the extensive newspaper coverage, provided ready-made material for a novelized treatment. He proceeded to write *Butterfield 8*.

The first draft went quickly and he completed the work on August 5, 1935, although the final version was later to undergo considerable deletion of sexual material that the publisher felt would be found objectionable by the reading public. *Butterfield 8* was published by Harcourt, Brace, on October 8, 1935, to mixed reviews. However, word of mouth had spread the news that this was a very sexy book and sales got off to a fast start. The first printing of 15,000 was sold out within two days of publication, and the publisher did a quick second printing of 10,000 additional copies. Despite this early success, O'Hara's records later showed he drew a total of only $8,502.53 from his Harcourt, Brace royalty account in 1935, and that amount covered three books.

By coincidence, the bindery that bound O'Hara's *Butterfield 8* was simultaneously binding a life of John Wesley, the founder of Methodism, and several hundred copies of *Butterfield 8* were accidentally bound in the covers of the Wesley book.

From publication until 1975, forty years later, *Butterfield 8* sold a total of 3,577,729 copies, according to the book *Eighty Years of Best Sellers*. It was also an Oscar winning movie for Elizabeth Taylor in 1960.

E.E. Cummings: Examination of His Creative Process

One of the most gifted poets in the early and mid-twentieth century was E.E. Cummings (1894-1962). The Harvard-educated poet, critic, novelist, and painter had twelve volumes of verse published and was known for his extensive use of slang, dialect, and the rhythm of jazz. The moods of his verse were alternately satirical and tough or tender and whimsical. Until the 1930's, Cummings writings were characterized by the lower-case signature preference "e. e. cummings" and this lower-case preference is used in the Cummings entries in various encyclopedias and bibliographies.

Here, from Richard S. Kennedy, Cummings' biographer, is an explanation of Cummings' creative process as described in *Dreams in the Mirror: A Biography of E.E. Cummings*.[6]

Throughout his career, Cummings would spend his time sitting at the typewriter or with pencil in hand, setting down images, sayings, fleeting concepts, reminiscences, observations about his friends, thoughts from books he had read, slogans, parodies, streams of association, patterns of correspondence, typographical manipulations, and at some point a creative spark would catalyze some of this linguistic doodling and a form would emerge: a poem would "write itself." It could be rewritten, revised, or polished, perhaps a great many times, but the original burst of creative coalescence was the essential act.

Banning and Burning Helped Popularize Joyce's *Ulysses*

Largely because of a book that fanned public ardor by being banned as obscene in most countries, the Irish writer James Joyce (1882-1941) has emerged as one of the most influential authors of the twentieth century.

If any writer can ever lay claim to the description of struggling author, Joyce filled the bill. He lived in extreme poverty during many of the years he labored over his masterwork *Ulysses*. His labors spanned seven years, from 1914 to 1921, while he lived in Zurich and Paris. All told, Joyce's writing had occupied 20,000 working hours in 2,500 eight-hour days, some episodes having been rewritten as many as nine times.

While in Zurich, he gave private lessons in English to support himself. Later, he lived off grants, partly in support of his work and partly because of such eye diseases as iritis, glaucoma, and cataracts. Joyce was said to have written some of his best work when his health was at its worst.

Initially, Joyce's *Ulysses* was published serially in the New York avant garde publication, the *Little Review*. The serialized publication ran from 1918 to 1920 at which time it was banned by a prosecution launched by the Society for the Suppression of Vice. The notoriety Joyce received from this action generated worldwide interest in *Ulysses*.

By the time *Ulysses* was completed, because of its reputation as obscene, publishers in England and the U.S. would not touch Joyce's major masterpiece. Joyce finally succeeded in having *Ulysses* published in Paris on February 2, 1922, by Sylvia Beach, proprietor of a bookshop called Shakespeare & Co. There followed a brisk trade of book collectors smuggling copies of the Paris edition into England and America, where *Ulysses* was promptly banned on publication. In 1923, at Folkestone harbor in England, 499 copies of *Ulysses* were seized under the Customs Act of 1867 and burned. In 1929, the British courts officially ruled that *Ulysses* was obscene.

It was not until an American judge's ruling in 1933 that the ban was lifted on public sale of *Ulysses* in England and America. A partial reading of Judge John Woolsey's 1933 judgment on *Ulysses* follows: "... my considered opinion, after long reflection, is that while in many places the effect of *Ulysses* on the reader undoubtedly is somewhat emetic, nowhere does it tend to be an aphrodisiac. *Ulysses* may, therefore, be admitted to the United

States." As a consequence of the 1933 U.S. court ruling, the first unabridged and uncensored edition of *Ulysses* was published in the U.S. in 1934.

The book *Ulysses* explores the stream of consciousness of two men, Bloom, a Jewish advertisement canvasser, and Dedalus, a scholar/philosopher, during a single day in Dublin—June 16, 1904. In *The Truth About a Publisher*, Sir Stanley Unwin, the British publishing sage wrote of *Ulysses*: "a few pages of Joyce at his best is worth a stroll around Dublin and many a pint of Guinness at any Dublin watering hole."

Born in Dublin, Joyce wrote only about the Irish. His first book, written at the age of twenty-five, was *Chamber Music*. In 1914, his book *Dubliners* was published after a nine-year delay resulting from Joyce's refusal to excise certain portions as demanded by his publisher.

See also Chapter 2 — A 1920's Profile of Joyce's Publisher: Shakespeare & Company.

Robert Frost: Pulitzer Defends Old Age from Undertakers

In 1943, the three members of the Advisory Committee of Columbia University responsible for recommending to the Board of Trustees a winner of the Pulitzer Prize in Poetry unanimously agreed that Robert Frost's *A Witness Tree* deserved the coveted award more than any other American book of poetry published in 1942. However, two of the three Committee members— Bliss Perry and Wilbur Cross—also felt that the three Pulitzer prizes Frost had won earlier were all that any poet should receive in a lifetime. They, therefore, voted as a majority that the award go to the second book under consideration.

The third member of the Committee, Louis Untermeyer, disagreed. In his minority report on the Committee's recommendation, Untermeyer explained the Committee's predicament and urged the Board of Trustees not to penalize Frost because of prior winnings. The Board agreed and took the unprecedented step of overriding the majority vote of the Advisory Committee and awarded the prize to Frost's *A Witness Tree*.

Frost, on learning he had won a Pulitzer prize for the fourth time at the age of 69, was quoted as having made this remark: "What I like best about it is that it defends my old age from the undertakers." A week after learning of the award, Frost, still in a happy frame of mind, had this to say in a letter to Professor George Wicher at Amherst College:[7]

> Prizes are a strange thing for me to have come by, who have hated competition and never wanted to be anybody's rival. I could never have written a single poem if I had to have even in a remote corner of my mind the least thought that it might beat another poem. Poetry is "too high for rivalry." It is supposed to differ in kind rather than degree. Still I can accept the fate of prize winners with fortitude and if my victory pleases my friends, I do not care too much if I annoy my enemies.

Earlier Frost Pulitzer Prizes were in 1924 for *New Hampshire; A Poem with Notes* and *Grace Notes*, in 1931 for *Collected Poems*, and in 1937 for *A Further Rage*. The Pulitzer Prize for Poetry is one of five annual prizes awarded for American Literature. The Poetry prize is awarded for the finest annual volume of American poetry. the award was established in 1922.

See also Chapter 2 — How a Publisher Moved to Nail Down Its Most Coveted Author.

H.L. Mencken: Had Bad Word for Virtually Everyone, Drove A Hard Bargain

H.L. Mencken (1880-1956) was a newspaperman, editor, and critic as well as author of numerous highly-regarded books. In the *American Mercury* (1924-1933), which Mencken co-founded with George Jean Nathan and edited, he specialized in debunking articles on the shames of the day. He also excelled at framing insults at almost everyone. Despite his irreverence for virtually all causes and things, Mencken once told his biographer, Edgar Kemler, a Washington newspaperman, "Make it clear I am a baptized man and a fanatical lover of the flag."

At one point in his journalistic career, Mencken had written a hoax on the origin of the bathtub, "A Neglected Anniversary," which was accepted as true even after he openly admitted he'd made up the entire story. Some thirty years after his bathtub story, in January 1947, he signed a contract with a Canadian film maker for its movie rights that reflected the irreverent character of the man.

In exchange for the film rights, the Canadian film maker was to furnish Mencken with two cases of Labatt's ale a month for the rest of his life. Also, he made it part of the contract that he would not be required to return either the empty bottles or the cartons in which they were shipped. Further, the agreement called for a board of arbiters. The cinema company was to be represented by a Canadian committee. Mencken was to be represented by the Governor of Maryland. And, in the event this worthy should be "inebriated or otherwise incapacitated," the Chief Justice of the United States was to serve in his place.

Sixteen years before his death, in a statement to the Associated Press in 1940, "for use in my obituary," Mencken wrote: "My writings have had only one purpose: to attain for H.L. Mencken that feeling of tension relieved and function achieved which a cow enjoys on giving milk. Further than that, I have had no interest in the matter whatsoever. It has never given me satisfaction to encounter one who said my notions had pleased him."

Mencken authored numerous books spanning more than half a century, including *George Bernard Shaw* (1905), *The Philosophy of Friedrich Nietzsche* (1908), and *In Defense of Women* (1917). His most important work was *The American Language*, originally published in 1919, revised in 1921, 1923, and 1936, and with supplementary volumes in 1945 and 1948.

Pearl S. Buck: Creative Approaches of Prize Winner

Pearl S. Buck (1892-1973) was the daughter of American missionaries who spent her youth in China and later returned there to teach at a university in Nanking. She devoted a good part of a distinguished literary career writing about Chinese life and making the East understandable to the West.

She is best remembered for a trilogy of novels about China—particularly the first, *The Good Earth*, published in 1931. It won the Pulitzer Prize in 1932 and went on to sell five million copies. The other parts of the trilogy were *Sons*, published in 1932, and *A House Divided*, published in 1935.

Ms. Buck moved back to the United States in 1935, and in 1938 she was awarded the Nobel Prize for Literature. After becoming a Nobel Laureate, she continued writing books for more than thirty years.

Here, based on an interview,[8] are some of Ms. Buck's creative approaches as she once outlined them:

> My intellectual activity is based on regular hours of work, on a vivid, almost photographic memory, on a quiet way of living, and the enjoyment of human beings.
>
> I find that my creative impulses arise from the circumstances of my daily life and experiences. These I do not use immediately, but they lie in my mind; after meditation and reflection, gradually certain themes and characters appear and come to the foreground.
>
> Usually the catalyst for any new period of creation is a special experience, sometimes very brief and seemingly slight, which, nevertheless, arouses my emotions and crystallizes my thinking along certain lines.

Robert Benchley: Views on Writing Reflect Sparking Wit

Robert Benchley (1889-1945) was a highly-talented American humorist who, in addition to his numerous books, achieved fame as a motion picture actor, drama critic, and screen writer. A witty conversationalist, he was also a member of the famed Algonquin Round Table.*

Known equally well for his motion picture short subjects and for his humorous essays, Benchley's skit, "The Treasurer's Report," was the basis for one of the first all-talking motion pictures. Benchley appeared in forty-six movie shorts. One of these, "How to Sleep," won him an award from the Motion Picture Academy of Arts and Sciences in 1935.

* The Algonquin Round Table was a group of writers who gathered daily for lunch at the Algonquin Hotel in New York City in the 1920's and lasted until nearly the end of the decade. Many of its members went on to great success, not only as writers and authors, but also on Broadway and in Hollywood. Some Roundtable members were: Marc Connelly, Edna Ferber, George S. Kaufman, Ben Hecht, Ring Lardner, Charles Macarther, Herman J. Mankiewicz, Alice Duer Miller, Dorothy Parker, Robert E. Sherwood, Donald Ogden Stewart, James Thurber, and Alexander Woollcott.

His various essays were collected in fifteen books. Some of these were: *20,000 Leagues Under the Sea, or, David Cooperfield* (1928), *From Bed to Worse* (1934), *My Ten Years in a Quandary and How They Grew* (1936), *Inside Benchley* (1942), *Robert Benchley Beside Himself* (1943), *One Minute, Please* (1945), and the posthumous *Chips Off the Old Benchley* (1949).

Here, from various works, are some Benchley thoughts on writing professionally that are also examples of his sparking wit:

It took me fifteen years to discover that I had no talent for writing, but I wouldn't give it up because by that time I was too famous.
— from *Robert Benchley*, by Nathaniel Benchley, 1955

The biggest obstacle to professional writing is the necessity for changing a typewriter ribbon.
— from *Chips Off the Old Benchley*, 1949

I do most of my work sitting down; that's where I shine.
— in R.E. Drennan's *Algonquin Wits*, 1968

P.G. Wodehouse: A Prolific Writer's Working Habits

P.G. Wodehouse, who lived to be ninety-four, was one of the most prolific writers of the 20th century. His more than ninety books sold in excess of thirty million copies. He also devoted a considerable amount of his time to writing short stories and collaborating on Broadway musicals and Hollywood movies.

At his home in Remsenburg, Long Island, Wodehouse did his writing at a plain wooden desk in a pine-walled study overlooking the back garden. The only furnishings on his desk were a dictionary, a knife for cleaning out pipes, and his bulky Royal typewriter which he had used since 1934.

A book published in his 92nd year described Wodehouse's writing regimen, which he said he had used for some forty years. He did his first draft in longhand with a pencil. Then he sat down at a Royal typewriter and did a moderate amount of revising and polishing as he typed.

He once tried using a dictating machine. But, when he had dictated the equivalent of a page, he played it back. It sounded so unfunny that he turned off the machine and returned to his pad and pencil.

Wodehouse's output, even after the age of ninety, on a good working day was about 1,000 words. In younger years, it averaged closer to 2,500 words. His most productive day, he once told a biographer, was in 1933, when he turned out the last 8,000 words of *Thank You, Jeeves*.

See also Chapter 9 —Introduction of Publisher Jacket Blurb Sparks Wodehouse Book Sales.

Lindbergh: The Most Fussy of Authors, Living or Dead

Charles Scribner, Jr., succeeded his father as president of Charles Scribner's Sons in 1952 and held that position until 1986. He was the fourth Charles Scribner to head the respected family-owned firm, which had been established in 1846. In his charming memoir of his life at Scribners, *In the Company of Writers,*[9] he talks about working with author Charles A. Lindbergh, whose *Spirit of St. Louis* Scribner published in 1953.

In his book, Scribner recalls a mild disagreement with the famed aviator as they lunched together in New York: "I suddenly said to myself, 'You're talking to a man who flew a single-engine plane alone across the Atlantic Ocean!' ... I hoisted the white flag immediately."

Writing of Lindbergh as a Scribner author, Scribner says, "Lindbergh could be very difficult. He was the most fussy of authors, living or dead. He could measure the difference between a semicolon and a colon to make sure each was what it ought to be. To him every detail in the book had as much significance as if it were a moving part in his airplane."

Father of the Western Started Out as a New York Dentist

Graduating from dental school in 1896, he had established a small practice in the early 1900's in an office on West 74th Street in New York City. Nights during the winter of 1902-1903, he sat at his kitchen table in a dingy, rented room and, by the light of a flickering oil lamp, he wrote his first book. In the spring, the book—about one of his Ohio ancestors—was finished.

He submitted it to Harper & Brothers; they quickly rejected it. Submissions to four other publishers produced the same result. Finally, he accepted financial help from a young female patient and had the book printed himself. Not only was he his own publisher, but he was also his own distributor, taking the book to bookstores and to reviewers. He clipped the reviews, showed them to his dental patients, and told them at what stores the book could be purchased. The book never earned back the money it had cost to print. But the author never stopped writing.

While his second novel was making the rounds of publishers, he worked on his third, *Spirit of the Border*. After several rejections, *Spirit* was accepted by the publishing firm of A.L. Burt & Company. With publication of his first book by a "real" publisher, the 32-year-old author closed his dental office in 1904 to devote his fulltime energies to writing. *Spirit of the Border* became a bestseller. And in 1905, the author married the young patient who financed his first book.

His name was Zane Grey. He is now universally recognized as the father of the western story. During his lifetime (he died on October 23, 1939), Grey produced 89 novels, of which more than 56 were westerns. They sold over 100 million copies and resulted in more than 100 movies—some of them remade 2, 3, and 4 times.

Two of Gray's westerns, *Riders of the Purple Sage* and *The U.P. Trail*, are widely believed to be the two best westerns ever written by anyone. Both reflect Grey's rare gift—the ability to see the romance in frontier America and to put it down for all America to read.

Faulkner Writes About a Writer's Responsibility

William Faulkner, one of the great American novelists of the first half of the 20th century, was widely praised for his technical virtuosity and his brilliant stylistic effects. Winner of the 1949 Nobel Prize in Literature and the Pulitzer Prize in 1955 for *A Fable*, Faulkner had little formal education and ended his schooling at the end of his second year in high school.

Born in New Albany, Mississippi, in 1897, he worked at various jobs before establishing himself as a writer with his first novel, *A Soldier's Pay*, in 1926. He died at the age of 65 in 1962. In his later years, in addition to his novel writing, he also wrote a play, *Requiem for a Nun*, in 1951 and acted as a movie script doctor in Hollywood, polishing up ailing scripts.

In the year Faulkner received the Nobel Prize, he described his philosophy in his essay, "A Writer's Responsibility," in the spring 1950 issue of *Paris Review*:

> The writer's only responsibility is to his art. He will be completely ruthless if he is a good one. He has a dream. It anguishes him so much he must get rid of it. He has no peace until then. Everything goes by the board: honor, pride, decency, security, happiness, all, to get the book written. If a writer has to rob his mother, he will not hesitate; the *Ode on a Grecian Urn* is worth any number of old ladies.

Practicing Physician and Pulitzer-Winning Poet:
His Life and Work Habits

William Carlos Williams (1883-1963) is widely regarded as a "patron saint" of American poets and the most widely-imitated poet of this century. The poet, essayist, and novelist from Rutherford, New Jersey, influenced and inspired other poets through his abandonment of conventional rhyme and meter to reduce the barrier between the reader and his consciousness of his immediate surroundings.

Williams's twenty works of poetry won national and international recognition. His *Pictures from Breughel* won the Pulitzer Prize for American Poetry in 1963. His *Paterson, 1, 2, 3, 4* (1946-51) was included in *The Modern Movement: 100 Key Books From England, France, and America 1880-1950* (Cyril Connolly) where Williams joined other authors on the list selected from the same period, including Dylan Thomas, Albert Camus, Ezra Pound, and George Orwell.

Of Williams's Pulitzer Prize winning *Paterson*, Robert Lowell wrote in his review in *The Nation*: "No poet has written ... with such a combination of brilliance, sympathy and experience, with such alertness and energy."

For all his activity as internationally renowned author of books of poetry, plays, essays, and prose, Williams also enjoyed a full and flourishing medical practice in his hometown of Rutherford, New Jersey, where he practiced after completing medical studies in pediatrics in 1909.

How was it possible for a fulltime practicing physician to maintain both a medical practice and a full and fruitful life as poet and author? Williams explains it himself in the foreword to his autobiography:[10]

> As a writer, I have been a physician, and as a physician a writer. Five minutes, ten minutes can always be found. I have my typewriter in my office desk. All I needed to do was to pull up the leaf to which it was fastened and I was ready to go. I work at top speed. If a patient came in at the door while I was in the middle of a sentence, bang would go the machine—I was a physician!

Some Other Famous Authors Who Were Doctors

William Carlos Williams was one of the more recent of many illustrious authors who were also doctors of medicine. The nineteenth century romantic poet John Keats was educated to be a surgeon. Oliver Wendell Holmes was both a doctor and a professor at the Harvard Medical School. W. Somerset Maugham was a doctor trained at St. Thomas's Hospital in London. The author of the medical classic *Principles and Practice of Medicine*, William Osler, was famous as a physician. England's Poet Laureate from 1913 until his death in 1930, Robert Bridges, was also a doctor of medicine.

90-Year-Old Award-Winning Poet Has Plans for His Future

In his acceptance speech for the 1995 National Book Award, 90-year-old Stanley Kunitz made it a point to thank his publisher, W.W. Norton, for having "enough confidence in my work and, to put it delicately, my life expectancy, to offer me a three-book contract."

Kunitz won the 1995 National Book Award for *Passing Through: The Later Poems, New and Selected.* During his 70-year writing career, Kunitz has garnered numerous honors for his poetry, including a Pulitzer Prize in 1959 and a National Medal of Art. A native of Worcester, Massachusetts, and a long-time resident of New York's Greenwich Village, the Harvard graduate was the first official New York state poet.

Kunitz writes his ideas in a notebook and then transfers them to typed pages on a manual typewriter, sometimes typing until 3 or 4 in the morning. "In youth," Kunitz told a *New York Times* reviewer (November 30, 1995), "poems come to you out of the blue.... But at this age, one has to dig."

Despite Bond Successes, Fleming Book Killed by Censors

In the fall of 1960, when Ian Fleming was enjoying great success with his early James Bond novels, he was commissioned by the Kuwait Oil Company to visit Kuwait and then write a short book describing the transformation of life in the small sheikdom since the discovery of oil there.

After two weeks in Kuwait and two weeks of writing, the manuscript was delivered to the Kuwait Oil Company for a fat fee. The book, titled *State of Excitement*, failed to clear Kuwait government censorship and was never published. Fleming had his copy of the book bound and retained it. *State of Excitement* was the only Fleming book every banned.

T.S. Eliot: Nobel Laureate and Unabashed Fan of Groucho

T.S. Eliot (1888-1965), one of the major poets of the 20th century and winner of the Nobel Prize in Literature in 1949, had dined with kings and queens and won numerous literary awards over his lifetime, but he had a weakness. He was an unabashed fan of the comedian, Groucho Marx. Eliot had written Marx a fan letter and when Marx responded, they exchanged photographs and continued their correspondence for many years, culminating with a visit to Eliot's London home by Marx and his wife.

A friend of Eliot's once remarked to an interviewer that Eliot had placed Groucho Marx's photograph alongside those of Goethe, Yeats, and Valery so that all were noticeable to visitors in his office. He especially admired Marx's movie *A Night at the Opera*.

A highlight of their growing friendship was a visit by the brash comedian and his wife to Eliot's Kensington Court Gardens quarters toward the end of his life. Eliot was highly pleased that the London newspapers had reported the visit with a photograph of Marx. Despite his frail health, Eliot hosted the visit and poured the wine. He found that he and Marx were in immediate harmony, especially in their mutual liking of puns, cigars, and cats.

Agatha Christie:
How She Created Her First Book and Character

Dame Agatha Christie (1890-1976) was the author of eighty-seven novels, the majority of them about detectives. Her books have sold over 300 million copies worldwide and been translated into thirty-seven languages.

Her first novel in 1920, *The Mysterious Affair at Styles*, introduced her eccentric and egotistic Belgian detective, Hercule Poirot, who reappeared in about twenty-five novels and many short stories before returning to Styles, where in *Curtain* (1975) he died. Here, in her own words, is how the great lady of detective fiction launched her writing career and created her first character:[11]

It was while I was working [as a nurse during World War I] I first conceived the idea of writing a detective story.... I began considering what kind of a detective story.... Since I was surrounded by poisons, perhaps it was natural that death by poisoning should be the method I selected.

There would naturally have to be a detective ... someone like Sherlock Holmes.... He would have to also have a friend as a kind of butt or stooge.... We had a colony of Belgian refugees living in the parish. Why not make my detective a Belgian? ... I allowed him to slowly grow into his part.

Safire's Novel So Big, He Provided Reading Guidelines

When William Safire's novel about Abraham Lincoln, *Freedom*, was published in August 1987, it included a special author's note from Safire: "If it deals with war or politics, it is fact; if it has to do with romance, it is fiction; if it is outrageous and obviously fictional, it is fact."

The 3,300-page manuscript was so large, Safire's publisher, Doubleday, employed two copy editors working in tandem to coordinate the stylistic details. The most time-consuming aspect of their work was verifying that every word used in the dialog was in use in the America of the 1860's.

When the manuscript was converted into book pages, a binding problem arose. Binding facilities available to Doubleday in the United States were able to do books up to 2½" thickness; Safire's book was thicker. The solution: A section was removed from the book bringing it down to the required thickness.

His Books Did Not Sell Well,
But Thoreau's Wisdom Sparkled and Inspired

Henry David Thoreau (1817-1862) is recognized as one of the major figures in American literature. Throughout most of his life, the Harvard educated author, poet, and essayist earned what little money his life required by working as a surveyor and handyman. At one time he was resident handyman and caretaker in the home of his friend, Ralph Waldo Emerson.

His best-known book, his second, was *Walden* (1854), an account of his life in a shack in the woods at Walden Pond from July 4, 1845, to September 6, 1847. Despite its later fame, *Walden* sold only 2,000 copies in the five years after publication.

Thoreau was a convinced abolitionist who lectured against slavery. His most famous essay "Civil Disobedience" (1849) espoused the doctrine of passive resistance. It was later to serve as an inspiration for such men as the Indian nationalist leader Mahatma Gandhi.

Thoreau was keen of mind and wit up to the very end of his life as this anecdote illustrates: Just before his death, Thoreau was asked whether he had made his peace with God—Thoreau is said to have calmly replied that he was not aware that they had ever quarreled.

Curiously, Thoreau's tombstone at Sleepy Hollow cemetery in Concord, Massachusetts, the city of his birth, is marked simply "Henry."

Herman Wouk's Prior Life as a Radio Comedy Writer

Herman Wouk, best known for his Pulitzer Prize winning *Caine Mutiny* (1951) and such subsequent bestselling works as *Marjorie Morningstar* (1955), *Winds of War* (1971), *War and Remembrance* (1978), and *Inside, Outside* (1985), had another life prior to becoming a novelist. He was a researcher and writer of humorous material for the late radio comedian Fred Allen.

His early material for his books most likely came from his experiences during World War II. He had been a communications officer aboard a destroyer-minesweeper and later an executive officer aboard another ship of the same class.

Prior to his Naval service in World War II, Wouk had attended Columbia University. Upon his graduation, he was employed for five years by the vastly popular radio comedian, Fred Allen. Here is how the comedian described Wouk's employment with him in a letter to Book-of-the-Month Club in 1947:

> [He] helped me conjure up humorous matter for my radio program. He contrived jokes (The cannibal had a sweet tooth. He always ate a Good Humor man for dessert.) ... (A doughnut is a cookie with an enlarged pore.). He interviewed people with odd occupations (a lady blacksmith, a worm salesman, a man who sniffed around subway stations to trace leaks, a window washer at the Empire State Building).
>
> He also wrote sketches (The G-String Murder, or Murder at Minsky's; Mountain Justice, or The Judge Who Knew His Gavel Was Broken So He Didn't Give a Rap).

Wouk's first novel, *Aurora Dawn*, written when he got out of the Navy, was published in 1947 when he was thirty-two. It had a sale of about 30,000 copies and was also a Book-of-the-Month Club selection. A year later, in 1948, Wouk's second novel, *City Boy*, was published and despite fair reviews sold only about 6,000 copies.

By the time Wouk had completed his third novel, *The Caine Mutiny*, the publisher of his first two books, Simon & Schuster, quickly turned it down, as did Alfred Knopf. The Pulitzer-Prize winning novel was subsequently published by Doubleday and sold over a million copies in the first 23 months after publication.

Kipling's Advice and Shortening Formula
for Lengthy Manuscripts

Rudyard Kipling (1865-1936) was a novelist, short-story writer, and poet who is chiefly remembered for his celebration of British imperialism, his tales and poems of British soldiers in India and Burma, and his tales for children. In 1907, he became the first English writer to win the Nobel Prize for Literature.

Kipling began his writing career as a journalist at the age of 17 in Lahor, India, where he joined the staff of the *Civil and Military Gazette*. He wrote many stories about life in British-ruled India. These stories were collected and converted into successful books, which were widely popular both in India and in England. In 1889, he returned to England and continued his writing career from there.

Kipling was said to have displayed an extraordinary ear for language and a precise use of spare, vivid imagery. He spoke of his writing style in the waning years of his life in the mid-1930's in an autobiographical work, *Something of Myself*. In it, Kipling commented on his sparse writing style by revealing that he was inclined to make the first draft of his stories two or three times longer than their published form and then review them periodically for improvement.

Here, from *Something of Myself*, written in 1934 and 1935 and published posthumously in 1937, is how Kipling told about his writing procedures:

> In an auspicious hour, read your final draft and consider faithfully every paragraph, sentence and word, blacking out where requisite. Let it lie by to drain as long as possible. At the end of that time, re-read and you should find that it will bear a second shortening. Finally, read it aloud alone and at leisure. Maybe a shade more brushwork will then indicate or impose itself. If not, praise Allah and let it go, and 'when thou hast done, repent not.' ... I have had tales by me for three or five years which shortened themselves almost yearly.

While *Something for Myself: For My Friends Known and Unknown* was his official autobiography, Kipling also wrote about his early life in *Stalky & Co.*, in his short story "Baa, Baa, Black Sheep," in the early chapters of *The Light That Failed*, and in his books dealing with his travels, including *From Sea to Sea* and *Letters of Marque*.

Some of the best pictures of Kipling and his life did not occur in books by and about him, but rather in the letters and biographies of many of his famous contemporaries, including: Sir Arthur Conan Doyle, Ford Madox Ford, Sir H. Rider Haggard, Henry James, William James, T.E. Lawrence, Joel Chandler Harris, Irvin S. Cobb, William Lyon Phelps, T.S. Eliot, James Joyce, William Butler Yeats, S.S. McClure, Edgar Wallace, Mark Twain, and Dean Howells.

Philip Roth on Writing as a Profession

For Philip Roth, author of twenty books and two-time winner of the National Book Award, writing is as much discipline as talent. Roth, when working on a book, works every day, seven days a week. Roth does his writing at his studio, some twenty paces from his home near the Housatonic River in Connecticut. He writes every day from 9:00 a.m. to 2:00 p.m.

I go to work like everyone else, and I sit there and do it. Once I'm writing, I don't want to go anywhere. When I'm finished writing about 2:00 p.m., I drive to a little town nearby, pick up the newspapers and the mail, and have lunch. Then I'll exercise, swim, or walk for three or four miles.

At about 5 or 5:30, I usually go over what I've done for another two hours before sitting down to dinner. At night I usually read. I go to bed early.

In a number of Roth's writings, he has kept alive his memory of his boyhood in Newark and nearby New Jersey towns. His nineteenth book, *Patrimony*, which Roth called the "awful adventure of my father's death," mirrored life in the Newark-area Jewish community during the first half of the 20th century and did it so well that it won the New Jersey Historical Society's 1992 award for significant contributions to New Jersey history. *Patrimony* also won a National Book Critics award.

Roth's first National Book Award was for *Goodby, Columbus* in 1959 when he was twenty-six. The novels that followed, *Letting Go* (1962), *When She Was Good* (1967), and *Portnoy's Complaint* (1969) established Roth as one of the leading writers of his generation. His 1995 novel, *Sabbath's Theatre*, won him his second National Book Award.

Here's how Roth views the task of writing:

Writing to me is problem solving. Every day there are a series of problems I have to solve. I solve them as best I can and that leads to new problems. Completion consists of joining all the problems together. That's what constitutes a solution. Writing is a profession in which it is very easy to fail.

Edith Wharton and Henry James: Recollection of a Remarkable Friendship

A close and enduring friendship existed between Henry James (1843-1916), a major figure in the history of the novel, and Edith Wharton (1862-1937), the noted novelist and short story writer. James had guided Miss Wharton through her literary pursuits, and Miss Wharton's autobiography is remembered by many for its picture of Henry James.

James had attended Harvard Law School, but was determined to write. In 1871, at the age of twenty-eight, he had his first novel published. However, despite the many books that followed, his most fruitful writing period was in the years after the turn of the century.

Shortly after the turn of the century, he wrote three novels in rapid succession and then toured the United States, returned to England, and wrote a travel book, *The American Scene*. In the years following, he devoted his energies to writing critical prefaces and, where needed, revisions for the reissue of his works in the New York edition (1907-1909), a project that ran to twenty-six volumes.

In his book *Dukedom Large Enough*,[12] David A. Randall of the Scribner Rare Book Department tells about a letter from Edith Wharton to Charles Scribner about Henry James during that period:

> She wrote that James had just received his year's royalty account from Scribners (this was around 1912) and was violently depressed, not because of the money but because of the evident lack of interest in his books. Would Scribner's, therefore, deduct a considerable sum from her next royalty report and transfer it to his? Absolute secrecy was to be observed and no one but CS himself was to handle the matter.

Born in New York City, James was educated in the U.S. and England. He chose to live in England and became a British subject a year before his death in 1915. In 1976, half a century later, he became one of the few Americans to be immortalized in the Poet's Corner of Westminster Abbey.

Gore Vidal on Being a Famous Novelist

Gore Vidal, author of biographies of Abraham Lincoln and Aaron Burr, is also a novelist whose work includes such novels as *Myra Breckinridge, Duluth, Empire, Two Sisters*, and *1876*. Here, from his book *Screening History*,[13] are some of his thoughts about being a famous novelist:

> There is no such thing as a famous novelist now, any more than there is such a thing as a famous poet. I use the adjective in the strict sense. According to authority, to be famous is to be much talked about, usually in a favorable way. It is as bleak and inglorious as that.

> Yet 30 years ago, novels were actually read and discussed by those who did not write them or, indeed, read them. A book *could* be famous then. Today the public seldom mentions a book, though people will often chatter about the screened versions of unread novels.

> Contrary to what many believe, literary fame has nothing to do with excellence or true glory or even with a writer's position in the syllabus of a university's English Department.... If what he has written is known only to a few other practitioners, or to enthusiasts, then

the artist is not only not famous, he is irrelevant to his time, the only time that he has; nor can he dream of eager readers in a later century, as Stendhal did.

You Don't Fool Around, Fool Around, Fool Around With Gertrude Stein

One of Bennett Cerf's favorite literary anecdotes concerned his good friend and a loyal Random House author, Gertrude Stein (1874-1946). The American author, who lived an expatriate's life in Paris most of her adult years, published many of her books through Random House. Although widely talked about, they sold poorly until her first big literary success, *The Autobiography of Alice B. Toklas*, which came out in 1933, twenty-five years after the appearance of her first book.

On one occasion, in the pre-World War I years, when Miss Stein's saying from her 1913 book *Sacred Emily* was being quoted all over the country, "A rose is a rose is a rose is a rose is a rose," publisher Cerf was about to send her a royalty check. It was pitifully small and, to ease the pain, Cerf made out the check to "A Stein is a Stein is a Stein" and mailed it.

Back came the check from Miss Stein with this note: "Dear Bennett, cut out the nonsense and send me a proper check immediately. Love, Gertrude."

Isaac Singer: U.S. Novelist and Nobel Prize Winner Who Wrote Only in Yiddish

With a fear of what the future might bring, Isaac Bashevis Singer immigrated from the town of Radzymin in Poland to the United States in 1934 and settled in an upper Broadway neighborhood of New York City. Singer was the son and grandson of Hasidic rabbis and himself was trained as a rabbi at the Warsaw Rabbinical Seminary. But once in America, the life he chose for himself was to be a writer.

During his early years in New York, Singer supported himself as a writer in Yiddish for *The Jewish Daily Forward*. A year after his arrival in the U.S., he also had his first novel published, *Satan in Goray*. Eight years after his arrival, Singer became an American citizen.

For all of the years Singer thrived as writer and novelist, all of Singer's written efforts were in Yiddish, although once he became familiar with the English language, he carefully supervised all translations.

Singer was awarded the Nobel Prize for Literature in 1978. In his Nobel lecture, he said:

> To me, the Yiddish language and the conduct of those who spoke it are identical. One can find in the Yiddish tongue and the Yiddish style expressions of pious joy, lust for life, longing for the Messiah,

patience, and deep appreciation of human individuality. There is a quiet humor in Yiddish and a gratitude for every day of life, every crumb of success, each encounter of love.

His earlier books were moving and penetrating depictions of life in Poland that reflected Polish-Jewish cultural traditions. In his later years, some of Singer's books drew inspiration from the cafeterias and coffee shops of the upper Broadway Manhattan neighborhood that he frequented. Singer died on July 25, 1991, eleven days after reaching his eighty-seventh birthday.

John Gunther:
The Author Who Lived to See Himself in Lower Case

John Gunther's numerous *Inside* books solidly established his reputation as an author who surveyed various lands and painted a broad picture of conditions therein. As a consequence, he was surprised to find his name was being lower-cased in various writings. In a 1951 review of one of Gunther's books, Charles Poore in the *New York Times* coined the word "guntherize" with a small "g" and the usage of the word became fairly common.

Subsequently, a book reviewer in *Harper's* magazine called Chester Wilmot's book on Europe a "guntherian symphony." Then, another *New York Times* article appeared calling for something to be "re-guntherized."

"I must admit," Gunther later wrote in one of his books, "I had never thought to see myself in lower case."

Linus Pauling's Cure for Cancer Backfires

In 1970, Linus Pauling wrote the bestselling and widely-acclaimed book *Vitamin C and the Common Cold*. It triggered a nationwide craze for the vitamin that lasted for many years. The scientist, who had 16 years earlier won the Nobel Prize for Chemistry, had also convinced himself that vitamin C was a cure for cancer as well. Research supporting this claim was later reported in a book Pauling co-authored: *Cancer and Vitamin C*.

Pauling and his wife, Ava Helen, began taking large daily doses of the vitamin in reinforcement of Pauling's cancer cure theory. However, ten years after starting the daily megadoses of Vitamin C, his wife died—of cancer.[14]

Michener as Beginner:
Suffered Rejection and Discouragement

When a textbook editor at Macmillan returned to work after Navy service in World War II, he convinced the Macmillan trade department to publish a book of connected war stories he'd written. Macmillan released it in 1947 with little fanfare. When he approached Macmillan with his second book, a novel, George Brett, the head of Macmillan turned the textbook editor down telling him he didn't have much future as an author and should stick to his Macmillan editorial job and not waste his time. Brett also told the author/editor he didn't approve of publishing the work of Macmillan employees.

So the editor took his novel to Random House where he promptly signed a contract for *The Fires of Spring*. Two weeks later, his first book of short stories won the 1948 Pulitzer Prize for fiction. It was *Tales of the South Pacific*, and author James Michener was on his way to literary fame and fortune.

Thirty-four more Michener titles were to follow in the next forty-seven years, including *Hawaii* in 1959, *Chesapeake* in 1979, *The World Is My Home* and the novel *Mexico* in 1992, his partly autobiographical *Literary Reflections* and a book of short stories titled *Creatures of the Kingdom* in 1993, and another novel *Recessional* in 1994.

Discovery of Margaret Mitchell and *Gone with the Wind*

When Macmillan publisher Harold S. Latham traveled to Atlanta in 1933 to search for possible new authors, a local librarian turned him on to a former newspaper woman who had been writing a book. The young Atlanta native admitted to Latham that she'd been working on a book off and on for the past seven years but told him, "I hadn't any intention of letting you or any publisher see it. I only wrote it for my own entertainment."

"I shall never forget her," Latham later recalled, "a tiny woman sitting on a divan in the lobby of the hotel where I was staying. Beside her was the biggest manuscript I have ever seen, towering in two stacks almost up to her shoulders."

Although the book lacked an opening chapter and she had written several other chapters in more than one version, Latham went out to purchase a suitcase to contain the manuscript and hauled it back to his offices at Macmillan in New York. Scanning the manuscript on the train, Latham recalled, "I was convinced I had something really important."

After editors at Macmillan had read the manuscript with great enthusiasm, Latham wrote, "We then had to convince the author that she had written not merely a publishable novel, which she really seemed to doubt, but a more than ordinarily significant one."

The book was *Gone with the Wind*, published in 1936. The author was Margaret Mitchell.

The book sold a million copies in its first six months and went on to win the 1937 Pulitzer Prize. It remains one of the bestselling novels of all time, as well as a Hollywood movie classic.

Miss Mitchell (Mrs. John R. Marsh) never wrote another book. She died in 1949 at the age of 49, struck by a car while crossing Atlanta's Peachtree Street to attend the Arts Theatre.

Success of First Novel Prompts Maugham
to Abandon Medicine and Become a Writer

W. Somerset Maugham, the great English novelist and playwright, lived to be ninety-one and enjoyed a long and distinguished writing career. He is best remembered for *Of Human Bondage*, a partially autobiographical novel that sold nearly three million copies and was made into a movie three times in 1934, 1946, and 1964.

While it was published in 1915, Maugham had actually written *Of Human Bondage* under another title in 1898, but put it aside when his publisher refused him a 100 pounds advance royalty. The original title had been *The Artistic Temperament of Stephen Carey.*

Maugham was raised by a clergyman uncle after having lost both parents by the age of ten. After he had completed public school in Whitstable, England, his uncle had wanted Maugham to go into either law or the ministry. However, since Maugham stammered when he talked, he was unsuited for either occupation. Consequently, he was sent to London to study medicine in St. Thomas Hospital.

In his second year of medical studies at the age of twenty-one, Maugham was working as an obstetric clerk in the Lambeth slums of London. His term of duty as obstetric clerk lasted three weeks during when he attended sixty-three confinements. He used this experience to start his writing career.

Writing later about his experiences as an obstetric clerk, Maugham said you had to be on hand day and night. You took lodging immediately opposite the hospital. If you were wanted in the night, the porter came across the street and woke you. You dressed and went to the hospital where you found waiting the husband or perhaps the small son of the patient with the card that the woman in labor had obtained earlier from the hospital.

You were taken to grim houses where the families lived and shown into a stuffy room in which two or three women, the midwife, the mother, and the "lady as lives on the floor below" were standing round the bed on which the patient lay. "This is the material I used for my first book. I exercised little invention. I put down what I had seen and heard as plainly as possible."

Maugham's first novel was *Liza of Lambeth*. It was published in 1897 when the 23-year-old medical student was completing his fourth and final year at medical school. The appearance of *Liza of Lambeth* created a sensation and appalled the conventional society of his day. Considered to be in bad taste and shocking, it became the subject of a sermon by a bishop in Westminster Abbey.

The novel was also the turning point in W. Somerset Maugham's life. The first edition sold out. Maugham's publisher, Fisher Unwin, told him a second edition was to be produced at once. This happened at the time Maugham's uncle and sponsor died—an event which provided the financial means that enabled Maugham to decide that he would abandon a career in medicine and become a writer instead.

How Graham Greene Found Cure for the Flu

The eminent English novelist, Graham Greene, has had a long string of literary successes since publication of his first novel, including such bestseller list toppers as *The Human Factor, The Power and the Glory*, and *The Quiet American*. And a high percentage of his novels have been successful films as well, including *The Ministry of Fear, The Third Man*, and that classic spoof of his spy novels, *Our Man in Havana*.

The Oxford-educated author's greatest thrill, however, was the acceptance of his first novel, which, incidentally, helped cure an illness as well, as this autobiographical anecdote from Greene's *A Sort of Life*[15] indicates:

> It was the winter of 1928. I was married and happy. In the evenings I worked at *The Times*. Mornings I worked on my novel.
>
> One day that winter, I was in bed with a bad attack of flu.... I'd sent copies of my manuscript to Heinemann and The Bodley Head about ten days before. I was now resigned to a long delay.
>
> The telephone rang in the sitting room.... My wife came in and told me, "There's a Mr. Evans wants to speak to you."
>
> "I don't know any Evans," I told her, "Tell him I'm in bed. Tell him I'm ill."
>
> Suddenly I remembered that Evans was the chairman of Heinemann, and I ran to snatch the telephone.
>
> "I've read your novel," he said, "We'd like to publish it. Would it be possible for you to look in here at eleven?"
>
> My flu was gone in that moment and never returned.
>
> Nothing in a novelist's life later can equal that moment—the acceptance of his first book.

Famed Golfer and Lefty Author
Is Righthanded in *Lefthander's Golfbook*

Bob Charles is New Zealand's most famous golf professional and, among other things, the first lefthanded golfer ever to win the British Open. He is also the author of *The Bob Charles Lefthander's Golfbook*.

When the *Lefthander's Golfbook* was published in 1984 by Reed Methuen, a New Zealand publisher based in Aukland, it featured an illustration on the page facing the book's title page showing golfer Charles and his parents, all holding golf clubs and ready to tee off. The illustration was captioned to point out that all three of them were lefthanders.

The punch line: The picture was printed back to front, converting the trio into righties, and nobody at Reed Methuen picked it up in proof.

"I hasten to add," postscripts Mike Bradstock who contributed this entry, "that it was not until shortly afterwards that I joined the staff of Reed

Methuen." Bradstock is currently managing editor of the Canterbury University Press in Christchurch, New Zealand.

After Twelve Turndowns, Lowry's Persistence Paid Off

Author Malcolm Lowry was not deterred in 1941 when his manuscript for a novel was returned by his agent. The agent explained he'd tried twelve different publishers and all had turned it down. Four years later, in 1945, Lowry went back to his agent. He'd considerably rewritten his book over the previous four years and he asked the agent to please try again. This time the agent scored, placing the novel, *Under the Volcano*, with Reynal & Hitchcock, who published the book in 1947.

The book got rave reviews with the *Saturday Review of Literature*, which called it a work of genius. Although hailed by many as the finest novel of the year, it went out of print after a short time. With continued demand, J.B. Lippincott, who'd turned it down in 1941, reissued the book in 1965.

In the 1984 book by Anthony Burgess, *Ninety Nine Novels*, which presented the author's list of the best novels published in English since 1939, *Under the Volcano* was included. In the book, Lowry joined the company of such notables as Ernest Hemingway, W. Somerset Maugham, J.D. Salinger, Ian Fleming, Vladimir Nabokov, and John O'Hara.

Said Burgess of Lowry and his other selectees, these "novelists have added something to our knowledge of the human condition, have managed language well, have clarified the motivations of action, and have expanded the bounds of imagination."

At this writing, Lowry's *Under the Volcano* is still in print in three editions, a hardcover with Harper and a trade paperback and mass-market with New American Library. Listed in *The World's Best Books*,[16] it was also made into a Hollywood movie in 1984.

Pyromania Writer Follows Own Story Line and Goes to Jail

In 1990, John Orr, a 40-year-old California native, wrote a novel, *Point of Origin*, about a pyromaniac. The novel told the story of an arson investigator who started fires in various cities while attending arson conventions there. Two years later, in October 1992, Orr, a fire captain and arson investigator in the Los Angeles suburb of Glendale, was sentenced to prison for setting fires in the same cities as the protagonist of his novel.

According to U.S. Attorney Patrick Henly, in an August 2, 1992, Associated Press dispatch, Orr's crime was remarkably faithful to the story line in his novel. He started fires in Fresno, Bakersfield, and Tulare during and after attending an arson investigator's convention. Henly added that other details of Orr's novel, including the means of starting the fires, bore "uncanny, striking similarities to evidence in the trial."

Jack London:
Giant of World Literature Lived Big, Died Young

In 1913, Jack London was the highest paid, best known, and most popular writer in the world. Yet, he managed always to live beyond his income. Three years later, in 1916, having written fifty books in seventeen years, he was dead of a drug overdose at the age of forty, reportedly a suicide.

London had lived a wild and adventurous life of excesses. He had been many things, including an oyster pirate and later a member of the government patrol that sought out such pirates, a merchant seaman, a tramp, and a rancher. He'd ridden the rails, spent time in jail, participated in the Alaska gold rush of 1897, and sailed his own boat to the South Pacific.

London had quit school at the age of fourteen to seek out adventure. At nineteen, he crammed a four year high school course into one year and managed to gain acceptance to the University of California at Berkeley. After a year, he ended his college education to seek gold in the Alaskan Klondike.

London's start as a writer came a year after his return from the Alaska gold rush. He had returned home to Oakland in broken health and virtually penniless. All he had to show for the Alaskan gold adventure was a log of his experiences and $4.50 in gold dust. He had sold some of his Alaskan stories to various magazines for as little as $5.00 each. In 1900 he received an offer from Houghton Mifflin to publish a collection of his Alaskan stories in a book under the title, *The Son of the Wolf.*

Publication of his first book brought London notoriety and demands from magazines for more of his adventure stories. He resubmitted some of his earlier rejected manuscripts and they were accepted.

London's most famous book, and the one that catapulted him to fame, was *The Call of the Wild.* Published in 1903, this classic story of the sled dog, Buck, has gone through numerous editions and been translated into eighty-three languages.

During his lifetime London had always complained that he had little imagination and that he had to take his plots from his personal experiences or from newspaper reports. Yet, approximately eighty years after his death, most of his books are still in print, not only in English, but in scores of languages all over the world, and Jack London continues to be a figure of prime importance in world literature.

Dr. Seuss, Bestselling Children's Author,
Started with Insecticide Cartoons

Dr. Seuss is the pen name of Theodor (Ted) Seuss Geisel, a native of Springfield, Massachusetts, and the bestselling children's author of all time. When he died in 1991 at the age of 87, his Dr. Seuss books had won him a 1984 Pulitzer Prize for fiction and had sold more than 200 million copies.

What turned Dr. Seuss into the world's bestselling children's author?

It started in 1928 when Geisel, using the name Dr. Seuss, had a cartoon published in the January issue of *Judge*, a magazine of social humor. In it, a knight in armor, sprawled on a bed and about to be attacked by a snarling dragon, cries out, "Darn it all, another Dragon. And just after I'd sprayed the whole castle with Flit!"

Flit was a popular insecticide produced by Standard Oil and when the wife of the advertising agency executive who handled the Flit account for Standard Oil saw the cartoon in a magazine at her hairdresser's, she fell in love with it and showed it to her husband. The result was a contract for Seuss that lasted for 17 years and a creature-of-the-month ad campaign for Flit that made "Quick, Henry, the Flit!" a part of the American vernacular and won the Seuss campaign a place in the history of advertising.

So how did Dr. Seuss go from drawing cartoons for an insecticide to writing and illustrating children's books? He'd found that his advertising agency contract did not allow other commercial illustrating endeavors, so he turned to writing and illustrating children's books as an out.

Seuss's first children's book, published in 1937, was *And to Think That I Saw It on Mulberry Street*, based on a building on Mulberry Street in his home town. So famous had the book become over the next half century that when the Greek revival building on Mulberry Street in Springfield, Massachusetts, was demolished in late December 1992, the city's Historical Commission called the demolition unforgivable and city officials declared they would seek to establish a Seuss museum and make the site part of a Seuss walking tour.

Publication of the first Dr. Seuss book did not come easy. After twenty-seven rejections from publishers, Geisel ran into a Dartmouth schoolmate, Mike McClintock, on Madison Avenue in 1936. Geisel told McClintock he had written a book "that no one will publish" and "I'm lugging it home to burn." Just hours before, McClintock had been hired as juvenile editor at Vanguard Press, and he quickly whisked Geisel up to meet Vanguard's president, Ted Henle, who agreed to publish the book.

"But," Henle told Geisel, "you'll have to give me a snappier title." The manuscript had been offered as *A Story That No One Can Beat*. Geisel substituted the Mulberry Street title and the rest is publishing history.[17]

Seuss books, from the first in 1937 through the forty-sixth in 1990, have dominated the children's book market in the English-speaking world and have been translated into twenty other languages. A late 1970's list of the bestselling children's books of the 20th century had these five Seuss books in the top five places: *Green Eggs and Ham* (1960), *One Fish, Two Fish, Red Fish, Blue Fish* (1963), *Hop on Pop* (1963), *Dr. Seuss's ABC* (1963), and *The Cat in the Hat* (1957). Some other well-known Seuss books have been *How the Grinch Stole Christmas* (1957), *Hunches in Bunches* (1982), and *The Butter Battle Book* (1984).

In addition to winning the Pulitzer Prize in 1984 "for his contribution for nearly half a century to the education and enjoyment of America's children and their parents," Seuss also was awarded eight honorary doctorates. Near the end of his life, he was getting nearly 1,500 fan letters every week.

Author Is Overnight Celebrity after 50-Year Writing Effort

It took Helen Hooven Santmyer fifty years to get her novel written and published before she became an "overnight" celebrity as an author. The story of a small Ohio town was originally published in 1982 by Ohio State University Press as a 1,348 page novel.

Two years later, it found its way to a major publishing house where in 1984 it was reprinted and released with modest expectations. But then the Book-of-the-Month Club made ...*And Ladies of the Club* a club selection. Suddenly its octogenarian author became page one news in *The New York Times*, and No. 1 on the *Times* bestseller list.

"Happy End for Novelist's 50-Year Effort," said the *Times* headline after which the *Times* described the novel about "life in small town Ohio, begun more than 50 years ago by an author who is now 88 years old and lives in a nursing home."

The *Times* story led to substantial nationwide press including radio and television coverage. Book-of-the-Month Club officials said ...*And Ladies of the Club* enjoyed greater media coverage than any previous selection in the Club's history.

...*And Ladies of the Club* told the story of a small Ohio town on graduation day, 1868, when two girls of a female college graduating class joined other local women and formed a club to discuss literary subjects. It then detailed the lives of the club members through the years ending in 1932 with the death of the last founding member.

Helen Hoover Santmyer, who was too old and sick to enjoy her late found fame and notoriety, died in February 1986, three months after her 90th birthday in Hospitality Home East, Xenia, Ohio, a town on which she had based the setting of her novel.

Canada's Mordecai Richler:
It's Time to Stop Writing When a Novel Gets Boring

Mordecai Richler, Canada's most widely-known and controversial novelist, is best known for his 1959 work, *The Apprenticeship of Duddy Kravitz*, which reflected his early years growing up in the poor Jewish section of Montreal. Later made into a successful Hollywood comic-drama starring Richard Dreyfuss, it projected Richler to international fame.

Richler's first major work of nonfiction, published in April 1992, was *Oh Canada! Oh Quebec! Requiem for a Divided Country*. The highly controversial work alienated virtually everyone in Canada, both in and out of Quebec, and prompted one member of Canada's Parliament from Quebec to demand that Canada's House of Commons ban the book as hate propaganda.

Asked about his favorite novel, Richler told one reporter, "Your favorite novel is always the next one you're going to write. I always start off dreaming of perfection. I never achieve it, but that's the way you start out."

Of novels already published, Richler says, "You always go back and read one of your novels and you'll find passages that make you cringe. There are passages that please you, but there are some that you say, 'Oh my god, I could have done that better.'"

Richler says he rewrites an awful lot. He also does a lot of editing. Speaking of his 1991 novel, *Solomon Gursky Was Here*, Richler says that he trimmed some 40,000 words out of the finished manuscript before it was published as a 413-page novel. Recalling *Gursky*, Richler said, "It took me five years to write. But you reach a point where it's boring to work on it. At that point you can only do a novel harm, so you turn it in. It's finished."

What You Need to Be a Writer: Larry Brown's Thoughts

Born to a Mississippi sharecropper in 1951, Larry Brown had failed English in his senior year at high school so writing did not come easily to him. In the late 1970's he had to teach himself how to write. After numerous rejections, he made the literary magazines with his short stories and ultimately has had five books published—*Facing the Music* in 1988, *Dirty Work* in 1989, *Big Bad Love* in 1990, *Joe* in 1991, and *On Fire* in 1994. In recent years, he has also been a faculty associate at the Bread Loaf Writers Conference in Middlebury, Vermont.

In an October 11, 1991, interview in *Publishers Weekly*, this former firefighter and ex-Marine expressed the following thoughts in reviewing his long apprenticeship as a writer before achieving success:

There's no such thing as a born writer. It's a skill you've got to learn just like learning how to be a bricklayer or a carpenter. You've got to write a number of words before you can write anything that can be published, but nobody is able to tell you how many words that is. You will know when you get there, but you don't know how long it will take.

Giving Birth to a Novel: A Comparison with Childbirth

"Childbirth, my researches into that activity have convinced me, is sheer delirious joy by comparison with the task of wrenching a novel from the brain and transferring it to paper."

So wrote Kenneth Roberts in *I Wanted To Write* (1949). Journalist and author of numerous historical novels, Roberts compared novel writing to childbirth:

> Like expectant mothers who are frequently afflicted with nausea during pregnancy, the novelist is afflicted with nausea during the entire period of his labors. He is acutely conscious at all times—even when asleep—of the burden within him, powerless to rid himself of it, and unable to obtain relief by the use of drugs or stimulants.

> It's true that writers seem to be gluttons for punishment, and by choice, remain at their desks, despite their sweating and groaning, for twelve or fourteen hours at a stretch.... It's true, too, that the author whose screams of agony have tortured those about him during his delivery will immediately, woman-like, put himself in a position certain to result in another long period of suffering.

> But for the sake of those who want to write, I cannot too often emphasize the unfortunate truth that while there are many rapturous moments during some of the preliminaries to childbirth, there are none whatever before or during the birth of a novel.

Planning the Great American Novel?
Eight Literary Greats Tell How They Did It[18]

James Michener

"I work hard hours and rewrite everything three or four times. Even when it's hardest, I don't think about quitting." Michener has said that other authors wouldn't write a book his way. "My books are very long, very involved, and very arbitrary. For example, in *Chesapeake* I spent forty pages on geese, and maybe you don't need it. I spend a lot of time building background and maybe you don't need it. But that's the way I work."

F. Scott Fitzgerald

"Every Saturday at one o'clock when the week's work was over [officer's school], I hurried to the Officers' Club and, there in a corner of a roomful of smoke, conversation, and rattling newspapers, I wrote a 120,000-word novel on the consecutive weekends of three months. There was no revising. There was no time for it. As I finished each chapter, I sent it to a typist."

Taylor Caldwell

She usually worked from midnight to dawn. Once started, she wouldn't stop writing until what she had in mind for that work session was completed to her satisfaction. She did a lot of research and travel. She sometimes destroyed entire pages or rewrote them a number of times.

Arthur Haley

Research on a book usually took a full year, followed by six months on an outline, which was usually about forty to fifty pages in length. Then, another eighteen months for the actual writing—all done in longhand. Then the material was typed. Daily goal: just 600 words. Some of the work was rewritten four or five times.

Nora Lofts

She put in a long day at her writing desk, working from 6 a.m. until 1 p.m. and then from 4:30 until 7:30 p.m., sticking to this schedule every day, year after year.

Frederick Faust

His daily quota of fiction was 4,000 words. He began as near 7 a.m. as possible and was usually through by 10 or 11 a.m. then he researched or went sightseeing the rest of the day.

John O'Hara

He was a night author who wrote many of his bestselling novels in the small hours of the morning.

Alice Munro

"When I start the first draft I write fairly slowly, about 700 words a day. Then, when I get on to the second draft, I write maybe twice that many, and so on until when I'm doing the final draft, I just work 12, 14 hours a day."

Author Amasses America's Bumper Sticker Philosophies

In 1995, Oregon graphic designer Carol Gardner turned her unusual hobby into an attractive coffee-table book that made its way into the bookstores during the Christmas season. Ms. Gardner collects unusual bumper sticker messages and then interviews and photographs their owners. After years of tracking America's fender philosophers in various western states, she had her collection published by Beyond Words Publishing as *Bumper Sticker Wisdom—America's Pulpit Above the Tailpipe*.

Her book of bumper sticker philosophies includes a wide collection of oddball and often humorous sayings, together with mini-interviews with the people who plaster their cars with such messages. These people turned out to be cowboys, nudists, mechanics, abortion foes, Elvis freaks, and even a scientist. Some samples from *Bumper Sticker Wisdom* follow:

Enjoy Life—This is Not a Rehearsal

I'm Pink, Therefore I'm Spam

So Many Pedestrians ... So Little Time

Single Mormon Seeks Several Spouses

Happiness Is Seeing Your Boss' Picture on the Back
of a Milk Carton

The Road to Hell Is Paved with Republicans

It's Bad Enough Driving Sober. Don't Drive Drunk.

Support Your Local Belly Dancer

Howard Garis: Wrote 500 Uncle Wiggley Books

How many books can an author write on the same subject? Howard Garis (1873-1962) proved the sky's the limit during his long career with the *Newark Evening News* when he penned enough stories about Uncle Wiggley—a rabbit hero—to fill about 500 books. The East Orange, New Jersey, newsman first wrote his stories for his paper—more than 15,000 of them—one a day for many years until he retired in 1947.

Eminent Author's Legacy:
Shelving More Valuable Than Library

The eminent British scientist Sir Arthur Schuster (1851-1934), co-author of *Britain's Heritage of Science* (1917), had been responsible for numerous important theoretical works in the field of optics.

A little over a decade after his death, at the end of World War II, his library, complete with oak bookcases and shelving, was offered for sale in a catalog. Many of the items in his library were autographed and/or contained marginal notes and comments that would be valuable to an historian of science. But the just-ended wartime period had caused great shortages of shelving and library materials. Hence, when the U.S. state university bought the scientist's library, it adapted the bookcases and shelving for its use but destroyed or discarded their contents.

Shortest Book Author Name Ever: The Author's Own Story

The book with the shortest author name ever came about in a curious way. The author, a young single woman, lived and worked in New York City as a book publicist. Working evenings at home over a six week period, she wrote a book about sex. She made it clear to her publisher that when the book was published she would remain anonymous. She gave these reasons:

First, she didn't want to be known as a sex book author when sending children's books to review editors. Second, she didn't want her old high school classmates back home in Kansas City to be reading about her sexual experiences. And, third, she feared that as a known sex book author, she might attract all sorts of crazies to her doorstep.

Her publisher agreed; her name would be kept secret. Both author and publisher agreed anonymous authorship might even make the book more saleable. So they searched for a pseudonym. "Why not a letter?" the publisher suggested (a mysterious Dr. X had just written a book titled *Intern*).

The author agreed that a letter would be great. So they searched for an appropriate letter. "A" for anonymous was out—too common, and "Z" belonged to Zorro. They finally settled on "J", which was the first initial of the author's legal first name, Joan. Later, she was to write about the selection, "I was the proud possessor of a pen letter."

So the book with the author named "J" became the book with the shortest author name on record. And the book with the shortest author name, *The Sensuous Woman*, went on to sell nearly nine million copies, making "J" one of the bestselling woman authors in history.

In 1984, the author of *The Sensuous Woman* wrote another book that started with these three sentences: "'J' was born in New York City in the spring of 1969. Joan Theresa 'Terry' Garrity came into the world some thirty years earlier.... We are one and the same person."

Prolific Belva Belts Out Bestsellers on 1945 Manual

With thirteen bestselling novels published in sixteen years, Belva Plain, the prolific novelist from Short Hills, New Jersey, still crafts her creative efforts on a 1945 Olympia manual typewriter. Why? "Because," she told an interviewer on October 23, 1995, "it has brought me luck." Even so, Mrs. Plain writes big books. *Evergreen*, her first book published in 1979, had 598 pages and weighed four pounds.

The Star-Spangled Author: F. Scott Fitzgerald

F. Scott Fitzgerald (1896-1940), famed for his novels and short stories of the 1920s (*The Jazz Age*), was named after Francis Scott Key, a distant cousin of his paternal grandmother and author of the poem that became our national anthem, "The Star-Spangled Banner." His full name was Francis Scott Key Fitzgerald. "*The Jazz Age* author delighted in the historical connection," says the *Wall Street Journal* (September 13, 1995), "and used many of his ancestors as models for characters in his books."

What Happened to Orwell's *1984* in 1984?

When the British novelist George Orwell (1903-1950) wrote the political satire *Nineteen Eighty-Four* in 1948, he pictured the horrors of totalitarianism pursued to the limit in a distantly future year. By 1973, Orwell's *Nineteen Eighty-Four* had entered the record books as the twenty-second biggest selling book in American bestseller history, with 8,147,624 copies sold.

What happened to Orwell's book in the year 1984? By late January of 1984, the novel *Nineteen Eighty-Four* was the fastest-selling book in the U.S., according to the *New York Times*, selling 50,000 copies a week for several weeks, in three softcover editions and one hardcover edition.

What Will Happen to Stephen King's Royalties in 1996?

Stephen King's newest novel, *The Green Mile*, due for publication in 1996, is likely to bring him about a third more royalties for the first 96 pages of his book than for the last 96 pages. Here is why:

Signet, a division of Penguin USA, will publish King's 1996 paperback original in 96-page monthly installments, with each installment priced at $2.99, starting March 1996.

Studies by the author of this book have shown that books sold serially historically have a sales decline from one serial segment to the next. Consequently, depending on the number of months from the first installment to the last, it is likely that King's royalties from the last portion of *The Green Mile* may be as much as a third less than from the first installment.

Strange Truth about Author
Whose Book Launched a National Political Career

Barry Goldwater, a former U.S. senator from Arizona and the 1964 Republican presidential candidate, won fame as an author for his controversial 1960 bestselling book, *The Conscience of a Conservative*, which is still in print. But a 1995 biography by Lee Edwards, *Goldwater: The Man Who Made a Revolution*, revealed that Goldwater never wrote the book and, most likely, never even read it before it was published.

The book was actually written by Goldwater's speechwriter, Brent Bozell. The 1995 Edwards book relates how when Bozell brought the manuscript to Goldwater, he gave it a cursory once over and then told Bozell, "Looks fine to me. Let's go with it."

When Clifton White, who headed the Draft Goldwater (for president) Committee, wrote in his memoir that Goldwater never even saw *The Conscience of a Conservative* before it was published, Goldwater is said to have responded that *Conscience* was a collection of his speeches. Yet Bozell had written all those speeches.

Queen of Romantic Writers Still Enchants at 94

In a November 1994 television interview, Barbara Cartland, the British-born "Queen of Romance," reported that, even at the age of 94, she was still averaging one new romance novel every two weeks. Since 1925, she has written more than 600 novels. The *Guinness Book of Records* once called her the world's bestselling author with over 600 million copies in print.

Her writing style is unique among contemporary authors. While reclining on a chaise lounge in her library in England, with a rug tucked around her feet and her pet Pekinese cuddled next to her, she dictates a chapter a day to a stenographer who visits daily.

"Dictation is why my books sell so well," she once told an interviewer. "When you dictate, you have to tell your story in nice, short paragraphs. My readers detest long paragraphs."

In a *New Yorker* profile, Ms. Cartland once said, "My readers want to read about ladies being made love to gently in the moonlight.... My books are an escape from the depression, boredom and lack of romance in modern life."

At 94, Ms. Cartland is far from being the oldest published author. According to the *Guinness Book of Records*, Alice Pollock had her first book, *My Victorian Youth*, published in 1971 at the age of 102 years and 8 months. She died that same year.

Chapter 2

Editor and Publisher Lore and Legends

Publishers Capitalize on British
Infatuation with TV Commercials

The British take their television commercials seriously. This is evidenced by the success of two books published in the early 1990's that originated in television commercials.

In a 1990 British television commercial, an elderly country gentleman was shown going down a list in the *Yellow Pages* and calling various bookstores. He was trying to track down a fictitious rare book called *Fly Fishing* by one J.R. Hartley. When he finally located a bookstore that has a copy, he asked the bookseller to hold the copy for pickup. Asked his name, the caller replied: "J.R. Hartley."

After the commercial began airing, such was the demand on bookstores and rare book dealers for this make-believe book that publisher Stanley Paul engaged a fishing expert to write such a book using *Fly Fishing* as the title and inventing the life, memoirs, and fishing tips of an 85-year-old Oxford graduate who had become an acclaimed fisherman. When Paul published the book in 1991, it became an instant bestseller and was also picked up for republication in the U.S. by Harper-Collins.

A second TV commercial-turned-book that went over big with British readers was *Love Over Gold*, published early in 1993 by Gorgi Books. *Love Over Gold* was subtitled *The Untold Story of TV's Greatest Romance*.

The TV commercial, which dealt with Nescafé Gold Blend, a leading brand of instant coffee, had been airing on British television for years as an ongoing serial. In this commercial, a romance developed between a handsome couple, based on their mutual interest in Nescafé Gold Blend. The commercial romance caught the British imagination to such a degree that in

1993, with the flirtation in its fifth year, one leading newspaper ranked the TV romance just below Charles and Diana in the British public interest.

When the male hunk said "I love you" in a December 1992 commercial, the news made page one of Britain's biggest-selling tabloid. At that point, the publisher Gorgi commissioned a writer to develop a novel based on the TV romance. This novel was published with a 150,000-copy first printing in 1993 as *Love Over Gold*.

The Gorgi book, which provided backgrounds for the commercial's two characters, described their meeting thus: "The heroine runs out of coffee and knocks at his door."

Love Over Gold included an order blank for a video of all the coffee commercials. The British are said to prefer instant coffee ten to one over brewed coffee, which may help explain the wide popularity for the Nescafé Gold Blend commercial.

Book Foreword So Convincing, Publisher Abandons Book

In 1990, Dover Publications asked Martin Gardner, the internationally respected author of numerous books and articles on science, numbers, and puzzles, to write a foreword for an upcoming reprint of a book it had issued earlier in 1976. The earlier printing had been a backlist bestseller for Dover over many years.

Gardner was surprised by Dover's request. It was widely known that he held the book's author, Aleister Crowley, a notorious British occultist (1875-1947), in great contempt and considered him a fraud and a faker. But he agreed to write the foreword if Dover would give him permission to critically attack the author's work. Honoring Gardner's unusual request was probably a first in the history of book publishing, but Dover agreed to Gardner's condition, taking into account the prestige the Gardner name would lend to the reprint.

The reprint edition had already been typeset and was in galley proofs by the time Dover's top brass got around to reading Gardner's powerful blast: "So totally without merit it did not deserve even the first printing."[1]

Officials at Dover realized that on the one hand Gardner's foreword might seriously harm the book's sales; on the other hand, Dover realized that reissuing the book without the foreword—after reading Gardner's respected opinion—might harm Dover's hard-won reputation as a leading publisher of distinguished books on science.

The decision was made: Dover abandoned the book entirely.

Publisher Tries Unique Solution to Author Royalty

How does a publisher deal with a complaining author when the author is his mother? The late Stanley Rinehart, head of the publishing firm Farrar &

Rinehart, came up with a unique answer. The complainer was his mother, Mary Roberts Rinehart, whose novels were among the bestselling works published by his firm.

During a conversation, his mother told him, "I understand that my books sell very well, but in spite of that I cannot recall when I received any money from your company."

Rinehart checked and found that very large royalty checks were mailed to his mother regularly and that one would be upcoming shortly.

He was very troubled by his mother's complaint and finally, in the middle of a sleepless night, got an inspiration. He bought a big strongbox and filled it up with thousands of crisp new dollar bills which he delivered to her on Christmas Day. His mother called him all excited and thrilled with the "gift." She had paid no attention to the royalty checks she had received; they meant nothing to her. But the dollar bills—that was real money!

A Publisher's Sage Advice to All Would-Be Authors

If you think you have a book in you, or have already written one and you're preparing to approach a publisher with your manuscript, you should heed the advice of the revered British publisher, Sir Stanley Unwin, who once offered the following advice to would-be authors:

> Your manuscript may be your "baby" but a publisher may find a dozen new babies on his doorstep every morning ... and he has hundreds, or even thousands, of older children overrunning his warehouse and clamoring for his undivided attention.
>
> So a publisher doesn't have much time to spend on yours. If you want your manuscript to impress a publisher, take extra care with it.... It may not matter if the pages are a bit dog-eared, but take extra pains with your spelling and your capitalization.
>
> The extra time you devote to manuscript preparation is worth more to an author than a longer interview with a publisher, or a letter of introduction.

How Medical Publishers Convert
Reluctant Doctors Into Authors

One small corner of the vast book industry is the little understood field of medical publishing, which differs from virtually every other aspect of book publishing in a number of striking ways:

- Most authors do not want to write the books they do.
- Most successful specialists who do write books could probably make much more money seeing patients.

- Most authors give little or no thought to royalties as their reason for writing.
- Most authors, no matter how successful their book, attract little attention and remain relatively unknown in the book reading world outside their specialty.

So why would any successful doctor write a clinical medical book? In many instances, the really successful medical books have been written by doctors who, because of their reputation, have been sought out by medical publishers' representatives and sold through persuasion that they will be making an important contribution.

The most common appeal to a successful doctor is the humanitarianism of the practitioner. The doctor is sold on how valuable his or her experience will be to other, younger physicians. For instance, one medical editor was able to convince a doctor he was pursuing with this remark: "Doctor, don't you realize that every copy of your book would save at least one life?"

Another medical editor snared a famed professor as an author by asking him if, out of love for his profession, he'd look over the outline of a book in his specialty and give the world the benefit of his wisdom by deleting, augmenting, or amending the outline. He would then be invited to contribute a preface to the book reflecting his changes.

The professor, of course, found great fault with the outline. He suggested additional chapters and the deletion of others. His criticisms turned to interest ... his interest to involvement ... and his involvement to commitment. He wound up writing the book.

Medical publishers are also known to compete for medical talent. When President Eisenhower suffered his heart attack during his second term in September 1955, an alert medical publisher immediately wired the publisher's field representative calling on the institution where Eisenhower's attending physician was based. He asked the rep to investigate whether the president's doctor would be interested in writing a book about diseases of the heart.

Cash Cows and Slow Movers:
Largest University Press Pays Its Way

University presses are known to publish scholarly research that commercial publishers avoid because of limited sales prospects. Not so with America's largest university press, the University of Chicago Press, which was founded in 1890. Turning out 250 new titles a year, this college press has been profitable for many decades, aided not only by a carefully selective program, but also by publishing good texts and references with year-after-year sales potential.

Among the press's largest cash cows is the more than 50-year-old *Manual for Writers of Term Papers, Theses and Dissertations*, which currently sells over 10,000 copies every month—over four million copies since its first publication. Best known among writers is *The Chicago Manual of Style*, published since 1906 and now in its 13th edition with annual sales of more than 25,000 copies. Also big is the translation from the Greek classics, the *Iliad*, which sells an average of 3,000 copies every month.

With such perennial sellers providing a cushion, the University of Chicago Press also devotes its energies to long-term low-potential projects. It invested ten years in translating and organizing the two-volume encyclopedia *Mythologies*, devoted another ten years to a translation of Satre's five-volume analysis of Gustave Flaubert, and is currently involved in a 30-year project that will ultimately produce a 37-volume edition of Verdi's scores.

First Crossword Puzzle Book
Keys Early Simon & Schuster Success

In January 1924, 23-year-old Richard Simon, a salesman for the publishing firm of Boni & Liveright, and 26-year-old Max Schuster, a trade magazine editor, pooled their worldly resources of $4,000 and rented an office at 37 West 57th Street in New York City. On the door of their new establishment was the freshly-painted firm name: Simon & Schuster, Publishers.

Crossword puzzles had started appearing in newspapers nationwide and, for their initial effort, they published the first *Crossword Puzzle Book*. It had an advance sale of 800 copies. Another 1,000 copies were sent to a news distributor on consignment. A month after publication, in May 1924, the ABA Convention was held in New York City. The partners went to the annual banquet and gave out free copies to attending booksellers.

Within a week, orders started coming in from the free sample distribution. Three months after the ABA Convention, sales had built up to 40,000 copies. By the end of their first year, two more crossword puzzle books were issued and sales for all three crossword books totaled 375,000 copies. The publishing firm of Simon & Schuster was on its way to a bright future!

A Bennett Cerf Literary Luncheon Experience

The late Bennett Cerf (1898-1971) visited England often not only as the founding president of Random House, but also to scout out promising new authors. In two of his visits to England, Cerf was invited to lunch by the well-known British literary agent, Laurence Pollinger. After each lunch at an expensive restaurant, the agent managed to be occupied when the check was presented, leaving Cerf to pay.

On a subsequent visit, Cerf decided he'd outwit the agent at his game. He invited the agent to lunch at the most expensive restaurant he could find and shortly before the check was presented he told the agent he had to excuse himself immediately; he was overdue for another appointment.

The agent said fine, but would Cerf wait just a brief minute while he went to the men's' room—he'd have something very important to tell Cerf when he got back.

Cerf, anticipating big news, waited five minutes ... ten minutes ... but no agent. So he paid the check ... again. On the way out, he encountered the agent at the door, who smilingly rendered the important message: "From now on you can call me Pollinger."

U.S. Publisher's Agony, British Publisher's Ecstasy

Fred Melcher, a U.S. book industry leader for many years prior to his death in 1963, was also editor or co-editor for over forty years of the book industry weekly, *Publishers Weekly.*

At the end of World War II, Melcher, in his role as editor of *Publishers Weekly*, was invited to speak at a dinner of British publishers in England. Melcher started his talk by telling the assembled British publishers how moved he had been earlier in the war by the bombing and burning of Paternoster Row, the great London book center where most of the leading British book publishers were located.

As Melcher was describing his anguish, many listening publishers were hard put to keep from smiling. What they knew and Melcher was unaware of was the fact that most of the books destroyed in the bombing and ensuing fires were covered by war damage insurance, and that it was the most beneficial act to English book publishing that Hitler could have contrived.

German bombardment had liquidated a wealth of out-of-date and unsaleable book inventory. The resulting insurance money enabled many of the Paternoster Row publishers to resume postwar publishing operations with profitable books and new projects.

Cabby's Gab Is Impetus for Successful Publishing Project

Good publishers are ever on the alert for possible new book ideas. Cass Canfield, for many years head of Harper & Brothers, was no exception as this example indicates. In his reminiscences, Canfield tells about an idea he got for a top Harper seller by listening to a talkative cab driver while riding along a country road.

The cabby complained to his passenger that he was exhausted having just spent some hours at home trying to keep his young children amused. "I wish," lamented the cab driver, "someone would write a book describing a thousand ways to amuse a child!"

In the year following, Harper published *838 Ways to Amuse a Child* by June Johnson. It went on to become a Harper bestseller for many years. Canfield also had Harper send the cab driver a check for $100 — the then standard Harper fee paid for any acceptable new book idea.

Coping with Racial Barriers in a 1955 Children's Book: Scribner's Solution

After World War II, school systems all over the U.S. were making substantial purchases of library books. To take advantage of this lucrative market, the children's book department of Charles Scribner's Sons initiated an intensive publishing program.

In 1955, two years after the author's death, Scribner's decided to publish Marjorie Rawlings's children's book, *The Secret River*. But Scribner's faced a quandary: Set in the South, the book told the story of a little girl whose mother was a hairdresser. But the deceased author had not made it clear whether the little girl was supposed to be black or white.

"We were troubled by this ambiguity," wrote the then Scribner president, Charles Scribner, Jr., in his 1990 memoir.[2] "Whatever our decision, we would land on the wrong side of the school boards. Then I had an inspiration. I had the entire book printed in black ink on brown paper, so there was no imputed color on the illustrations. That was one of my silent contributions to dissolving the color barrier in the 1950's."

Publisher Abuse Abounds — Sometimes from Unlikely Sources

Publishers take abuse from a variety of sources, not the least of which are irate authors who feel their work has not been given adequate treatment or promotion. In larger publishing houses that deal with bestsellers, a lawsuit per bestseller is not uncommon. In some cases publishers have faced more than one lawsuit from a single book.

But a least-expected source for problems is the publisher's own family as evidenced by the recollection of Charles Scribner, Jr., when he published Gerald Green's *The Last Angry Man* in 1959.

Scribner's mother had gotten an advance copy of the book and, while reading it, got caught up in the story of the Jewish doctor from Brooklyn. When she got to the part of the story where the doctor had a heart attack, she telephoned her son and warned him: "If anything happens to that doctor, I'll never speak to you again."

Compositor's Tale of Woe: Helps Publisher, Loses Account

Harry N. Abrams, the legendary, energetic publisher of a house specializing in oversize, colorful art books, was receiving delivery of type composition for the new edition of one of his good sellers. Called to a staff meeting, he invited his compositor, the owner of a one-person business operated out of his home, to sit with him, telling him, "I'm going to report on this book. Maybe there's a question you can help me with."

Presenting the book to his staff, Abrams discussed the number of additional illustrations, the amount of new copy being added, and the differences in the new edition. He then asked if anyone present would guess at how much bigger the new edition would be.

Getting no response, he turned and asked the compositor who promptly responded, "Fifteen percent."

"See!" said Abrams to his staff, "I pay you big money and it takes a printer to get a decent answer."

When Abrams died shortly afterward, his publishing operation continued intact without him. But the compositor never got another job from the firm.[3]

America's Largest Book Trade Fair: The ABA Convention

What started as a small annual meeting of booksellers convening to discuss mutual retail bookselling concerns, the ABA Convention has evolved into a giant book fair of national and international scope, drawing tens of thousands of participants (in which publisher attendance often outnumbers that of booksellers by more than two to one).

In addition to America's medium and large publishers, the ABA Convention also draws hundreds of small presses and scores of foreign publishers (who not only show their own cultural output and offer rights, but also seek rights to United States publications).

The largest ABA Convention ever held was the 1995 three-day event at Chicago's McCormick Place convention center, where, according to a *New York Times* report of June 5, 1995, "42,000 publishers, bookstore owners, scouts and agents gathered to inspect new book releases (from) the displays of more than 1,800 publishers and distributors."

Indicative of the ABA show's growth, the 1995 Chicago show's 1,800 exhibitors were 200 more than the previous record-breaking number at the 1994 Los Angeles convention. Further, the 1995 show's 350,000 square feet of exhibit space was also a record breaker, topping the previous record of 320,000 square feet of exhibit area at the 1994 Los Angeles show.

McCormick Place will continue as the ABA show locale through the year 2001. McCormick Place, said *Publishers Weekly* on June 12, 1995, "would be a good permanent home for the ABA show."

World's Largest Book Fair: Almost Defies Description

The sprawling, almost overwhelming Book Trade Fair in Frankfurt, Germany, is the world's largest book fair, utilizing 1.4 million square feet of exhibit space and attracting untold thousands of publishers and would-be publishers from every corner of the world.

Begun in 1947* by German publishers for the benefit of German book-sellers, the Frankfurt Book Fair now attracts well over 300,000 visitors each year. At the 1995 fair, there were about 9,000 publisher-exhibitors from over 100 countries. More than 325,000 books were displayed.

Taking place in October, the Frankfurt Book Fair serves as a world mart for the purchase and sale of translation rights, which makes it extremely valuable for the many publishers outside Germany seeking rights to books already published in other languages. At the same time, it represents a marketplace not only of the finished books, but also of the cultural achievements of the various countries through their national exhibits.

Another function of the Frankfurt Book Fair is to enhance the planning and participation by publishers from different countries in co-productions, especially of heavily illustrated coffee-table books on various subjects. Because of the substantial cost of color printing, unit costs are greatly reduced when illustrations for editions in up to a dozen languages are printed simultaneously. The various co-publishers then supply the language translations for their own particular countries.

The Frankfurt Book Fair also plays an increasing role as a world showcase for small presses, which in earlier years could not afford to participate. Recently, for example, in addition to the nearly 700 large U.S. publishers with their own exhibits, Publishers Marketing Association and COSMEP displayed the titles of nearly 200 small presses.

Summarizing the Frankfurt Book Fair, the late Fred Praeger described it as "a place where east and west, north and south, can meet ... where representatives of the long-established firms encounter the book world's newest entrants.... The atmosphere is charged with hope, camaraderie, and the sense of belonging to an international institution devoted to communication and knowledge."[4]

Black Publishing Exploding
as Interest in Black Experience Increases

One of the fastest growing areas in American book publishing is the market for books by and about black Americans. In 1992 Jim Milliot, then editor of *BP Reports*, a publishing industry newsletter, told a *New York Times* interviewer that "There's been no real accurate statistical work done to estimate the size of the black book market, but there are clear indicators that this market is growing by leaps and bounds." He had no idea how much it would grow in the next three years.

---

* According to the *New York Times* (October 14, 1995), the first official Frankfurt book fair (Büchermess) took place in Germany in 1462. By the 1750s, as a result of censorship in Frankfurt by the Archbishop of Mainz, the fair was discontinued. The 1947 start of the Frankfurt Book Fair actually was a reinstatement of the fair abandoned two centuries earlier.

Compare, for example, these numbers for publishers of books for black Americans. A 1989 *Publishers Directory* from Gale Research showed forty-two such publishers in 1988, up from about a dozen in 1980. A year later, the number of publishers of books for black Americans had increased to approximately 100 and by 1995 was close to 200.

With the advent of the 1990s, bookstores concentrating on African-American interests were springing up in and around black communities all over America. In an August 9, 1992 *New York Times* report, Clara Villarosa, owner of the Hue-Man Experience in Denver, Colorado, and a member of the governing board of the American Booksellers Association, claimed that there were then more than 300 black bookstores in the United States. By the end of 1995, according to a December 11, 1995 report in *Publishers Weekly*, the number of such stores had grown to 500, according to Haki Madhubuti, publisher of the Chicago-based Third World Press.

Ms. Villarosa's store in Denver's historic Five Points black community stocks nearly 4,000 titles about African Americans. Ms. Villarosa stated in her 1992 interview that when blacks do enter bookstores, it is usually to stores such as her own that specialize in black interests.

A Seattle-based publisher of African-American books, Anna Johnson of Open Hand Publishing confirms Ms. Villarosa's view. In an interview in *Publishing Lives*[5], she tells of soliciting sales of black-interest books in some Seattle-area bookstores and being told: "Our customers are white; they're not going to be interested in books on that subject."

Despite the claim of Ms. Villarosa and Ms. Johnson, one of the largest bookstore chains, Waldenbooks of Ann Arbor, Michigan, thinks otherwise. Waldenbooks claims that nearly 300 of its 1,150 bookstores, which are located primarily in large shopping malls, include African-American sections, and that number is continually increasing.

Terry McMillan: Rising Black Superstar Novelist

With the increase in black publishers and black-interest bookstores, as well as black-oriented departments in the large bookstore chains, there has been an accompanying increase in black superstar authors. The best evidence is that of novelist Terry McMillan, a native of Port Huron, Michigan, and holder of a tenured teaching position at the University of Arizona.

Ms. McMillan's *Waiting to Exhale*, a story about four black professional women in Phoenix, Arizona, topped the *New York Times* bestseller list for months in 1992 and became a top-grossing film in 1995. Further, the sale of paperback rights to *Waiting to Exhale* to Pocket Books was for a near-record $2,640,000. It earned Ms. McMillan the title of "the black Judith Krantz."

According to a report in *Publishers Weekly*, the $2,640,000 set a record for any guarantee for the work of an African-American writer and will be hard to top for a reprint for the rest of this century. By early 1996, the hardcover edition had sold 650,000 copies and the Pocket Books paperback had sold 1.75 million copies. A fourth Terry McMillan novel, *How Stella Got Her Groove Back*, published in May 1996, had a 1 million copy first printing and was a Book-of-the-Month Club main selection.

Landmark Advances in African-American Bookselling

Three landmark moves have highlighted the dissemination of African-American publishing information and book distribution in the United States in the first half of the 1990s.

1. The quarterly newsletter, *African-American Bookselling*, issued by the American Booksellers Association since the spring of 1991.

2. A monthly bestseller list of books written and published by black Americans. The list, called Blackboard, is compiled by the Blackboard African American Booksellers, Inc., based in Columbus, Ohio, and is distributed to black-oriented bookstores throughout the United States. The Blackboard bestseller list, since February 1992, has also been published monthly in *Publishers Weekly*.

3. The emergence of book distributors owned by African Americans that cater to the specialized tastes of their market. Some of these black-owned distributors also have their own publishing and retail divisions. One example is Kassahun Checole, whose Africa World Press and Red Sea Press publish about 80 books a year.

4. The appearance of a large body of romance novels written by black women for black women from both large and small publishing houses.

A 1920's Profile of Joyce's Publisher:
Shakespeare & Company

In 1921, when James Joyce completed his landmark work *Ulysses*, after seven years of writing and rewriting, he turned to a Paris Left Bank bookshop proprietor, Sylvia Beach, to publish his work. The Shakespeare & Company bookshop, located at 12 rue de l'Odeon, was a favorite hangout of struggling writers who were warmly welcomed and who found it easy to joke and gossip with the store's proprietor. The shop, located on a cold windswept street, was warm and cheerful, with a big stove in the center to warm the patrons in winter. There were tables and shelves of books, new books in the window, and photographs of famous writers, both living and dead, adorning the bookshop walls.

Ms. Beach, the proprietor, had a lively, sharply sculptured face, according to Ernest Hemingway, and "brown eyes that were as alive as a small animal's and as gay as a young girl's, and wavy brown hair that was brushed back from her fine forehead (and) she was kind, cheerful and interested."[6]

In addition to selling books at Shakespeare & Company, she also ran a rental library. When a patron didn't have the money to pay the deposit for the rental library, she would invite them to take the books anyway and pay the deposit when they could afford it.

Joyce and Hemingway were among the struggling young writers who frequented Sylvia Beach's book establishment, so it seemed almost logical that when Joyce's *Ulysses* was completed and promptly banned in England and America, his work should be published in Paris under the Shakespeare & Company imprint.

Americans in Paris in the 1920's were frequent visitors to Ms. Beach's bookshop, buying copies of the banned *Ulysses* to smuggle home for the U.S. equivalent of $10 a copy. Shakespeare & Company remained the primary source of copies of *Ulysses* until 1934 when Bennett Cerf's Random House published the American edition.

See also Chapter 1 — Banning and Burning Helped Popularize Joyce's *Ulysses*.

How a Publisher Nailed Down Its Most Coveted Author

In the early 1920s, the publishing firm of Henry Holt & Company underwent a serious crisis. The elderly Henry Holt, then in his eighties and reputed to be tight-fisted with authors ("Royalties exceeding 10% are immoral."), had stepped aside and elevated Edward N. Bristol to director of all departments. Immediately two department heads resigned: Alfred Harcourt, head of trade, and Donald Brace, head of production. They, together with a third partner, William Howe, formed a new company: Harcourt, Brace & Howe.

Harcourt had been encouraged to make the move by one of his authors, Sinclair Lewis, who told him, "Don't be such a damn fool as ever again to go to work for someone else. Start your own business. I'm going to write important books. You can publish them."[7]

Harcourt and Brace attempted to take with them Holt's leading authors, who included Dorothy Canfield Fisher, Robert Frost, and Louis Untermeyer. Fisher and Untermeyer joined the Harcourt, Brace & Howe roster of authors. Frost seemed ready to make the move, until he was informed by Holt that they owned the copyright for his three earlier published works of poetry and would not release them for re-publication in collected works elsewhere. Sullenly, Frost decided he must remain with Holt.

Visiting the Holt premises in November 1920, Frost met with Lincoln MacVeagh, Harcourt's replacement as trade department manager. Frost, hoping for a slightly better royalty arrangement, described his great financial difficulties since he'd resigned his position at Amherst College, where he'd been receiving a $4,000 salary. Instead of talking royalty, MacVeagh offered Frost immediate help. He appointed Frost a consulting editor of Holt at a regular salary of $100 a month; then he sealed the deal by mailing Frost his first salary check on the following day.

The Holt move had hit the mark. Frost immediately wrote back to MacVeagh: "Not so much what you did as the way you did it convinces me that I have been right all along in looking for a business relationship into which friendship could enter. I like to see the opposite of cynicism in me rewarded."

To a friend, Frost later wrote: "You know I left Amherst all so irresponsibly. You must have wondered how I could go and come as I pleased on nothing but poetry and yet seem to be taken care of as if I hadn't defied fate. I've wondered myself. (I now have) an appointment as Consulting Editor of Henry Holt and Co.... The pay will be small but large enough for a poet and the work between you and me will be nothing but seeing MacVeagh once in a while in friendship."

Holt's tiny investment was to pay handsome dividends to the publishing firm for decades to come. Frost remained with Holt and in the years to come through 1943, Holt was the publisher of all four of Frost's Pulitzer Prize winning volumes of poetry up to the 1943 winner, *A Witness Tree*.

See also Chapter 1 — Frost: Pulitzer Award Defends Old Age from the Undertakers.

Gertrude Stein's Writing: An Editor's Nightmare

Gertrude Stein's writing was an editor's nightmare. She used words for their associations and sounds rather than for their meaning, frequently employing an intricate system of repetition and variation on a single verbal theme. And what was the effect of her writing style on the editor who dealt with many of her manuscripts?

Dorothy Commins, widow of Stein's editor, Saxe Commins, was intimately familiar with many Stein manuscripts from watching her husband wrestle with them at home. She provides this unusual insight:

> To read through her entire manuscript is an experience similar to taking the drop-by-drop water torture. Repetitious sentences hammer on the brain with a monotonous thud that makes you want to scream in agony, and if you are searching for content analytically, the most that anyone can read at a time without shrieking with nervous exhaustion is ten to fifteen pages.
>
> The professional thing to do is to examine the book without prejudice and try to arrive at some fair conclusions about the contributions in thought that Gertrude Stein has to make.[8]

FDR and His Editor:
How the Great and Famous Deal With Editors

One of the more interesting aspects of book publishing is that no matter how great or famous an author—and it is often the great and famous who become authors—in matters of their literary efforts they often humble themselves in their relations with their publishers and particularly their editors and view them as close personal friends. This can happen even when the author is president of the United States.

In 1937, in his second term, President Franklin Delano Roosevelt assembled his various papers dating back to his days as governor of New York State and authorized Random House to publish them as *The Public Papers and Addresses of Franklin D. Roosevelt.* The President felt he had done much to ease the despair that had gripped the nation during the Great Depression, and now that public confidence was returning to the American public, the time seemed right for making the record public.

Bennett Cerf at Random House assigned Saxe Commins, his senior editor, to work with the president in spite of the editor's tight schedule with a number of other books. Commins worked closely with the President, shuttling back and forth to the White House for conferences and devoting every spare minute and weekend to editing and shaping the mass of Roosevelt papers into what ultimately became a five-volume work. Commins began his editing work in the spring of 1937 and by the spring of 1938 the five-volume Roosevelt work was published.

In a book of Commins memoirs, written by his wife after his death, she recalled the event: "Soon after the (Roosevelt) books came off the press, Saxe received a set from President Roosevelt with the inscription, 'To my friend Saxe Commins from Franklin Delano Roosevelt,' and a set to each of our children inscribed 'For Frances Ellen Commins,' and 'For Eugene David Commins'."[9]

Maxwell Perkins:
The Greatest American Editor of the 20th Century

In American publishing, Maxwell Perkins (1884-1947) stands alone as the most highly-regarded editor of the 20th century. Perkins, who was editor-in-chief at Charles Scribner's Sons for thirty-six years from 1914 on, was the discoverer and mentor of many of the leading writers of his day, among them F. Scott Fitzgerald, Ernest Hemingway, Marjorie Kinnan Rawlings, James Jones, William Faulkner, Ring Lardner, Thomas Wolfe, John Gunther, and Thornton Wilder.

In a 1944 *New Yorker* profile, Malcolm Crowley had these things to say about Perkins: "Many book publishers share the opinion that their colleague ... is the best editor in the trade.... Despite his refusal to do (those) things which are routine among the higher-powered editors at other publishing houses, he is known for making more literary discoveries and semi-discoveries than anybody else in the field...; there is usually a Perkins book near the top of the best-seller lists...; and it is believed that more books have been dedicated to him than any other man alive."

Of special note was Perkins' association with Thomas Wolfe, whose enormous sprawling manuscripts Perkins shaped into books by giving Wolfe considerable editorial help and advice. As Crowley's *New Yorker* profile indicates, Perkins was recipient of many book dedications, one of the most notable of which was featured in Wolfe's 1935 work *Of Time and the River*:

> To Maxwell Evarts Perkins. A great editor and a brave and honest man, who stuck to the writer of this book through times of bitter hopelessness and doubt and would not let him give in to his own despair, a work to be known as *Of Time and the River* is dedicated with the hope that all of it may in some way be worthy of the loyal devotion and patient care which dauntless and unshaken friend has given to each part of it, and without which none of it could have been written.

When Wolfe died in 1938 at the age of thirty-eight after a brief illness, he named Maxwell Perkins as his literary executor.

Despite Perkins' reputation as the consummate editor who had discovered many new talents and brought them into print, he was an extremely modest man as these excerpts from a March 1946 talk to a group of college students indicates. His topic, of course, was book editing.

> An editor does not add to a book.... He serves as a handmaiden to the author.... A writer's best work comes entirely from himself ... an editor (should not try) to inject his own point of view into a writer's work or to try to make him something other than what he is. The process is so simple. If you have a Mark Twain, don't try to make him into a Shakespeare or make a Shakespeare into a Mark Twain. Because in the end an editor can get only as much out of an author as the author has in him.

Senior Editor's View of His Job

At a cocktail party celebrating the launch of a new book, a young woman waving a highball approached the publisher's senior editor and asked, "Are you a writer?"

"No," replied the editor.

"Then just what do you do," she asked.

"I'm in the cleaning and repairing business."

The Role of the Acquiring Editor: What It Takes to Be One

How do publishers get the books they publish? In most cases, you will find, they were signed up through an **acquiring editor**. The term acquiring editor is used interchangeably in various publishing establishments to differentiate between the editor who brings the books into the house and the editor who deals with the editing of the book manuscript.

The acquiring editor may also be known as the acquisitions editor or sponsoring editor. Whatever the title, an acquiring editor is just that—the individual responsible for finding new authors, contracting books, and usually seeing the acquired works through the various stages to final publication.

In its most glamorous terms, it is the job of an acquiring editor to track down and bring in the most promising, potentially bestselling, or most illustrious writing luminaries. In trade publishing, it may be the fame or notoriety of the author; in professional and scholarly publishing, it is the author's position of prominence or leadership in a particular field or profession.

The acquiring editor must be up with the news or with the literature in his or her specialty and constantly have an antenna out for potential new publishing projects. In general fiction and nonfiction trade, a high percentage of book ideas come from agents. But in many specialized fields, it is contacts, attendance at trade and professional meetings, and familiarity with and ongoing review of the literature that produces new book leads and publishing contracts with promising authors.

Some acquiring editors, having developed great familiarity with a field or specialty, are honored for their expertise by being appointed or elected to governing boards or special committees within the field. Well connected acquiring editors are often tipped off by good contacts to potential authors who are either writing a book or have the potential to write one that may fill an ongoing need in the literature.

What does it take to be an acquiring editor? To be an acquiring editor is, in reality, to be a publisher in miniature. An acquiring editor must have maturity and imagination. He or she must be able to relate to the writer or the writer's representative. Moreover, the acquiring editor must be good at numbers, have a sense of the book's potential market, and be able to estimate what a book can bring into a particular house in relation to its cost to produce and market.

The acquiring editor must have good negotiating skills and, once a contract is concluded, be able to goad or inspire the author into delivering the promised manuscript on time, and shepherd it into production. As the job of acquiring editor varies from one publisher to another, this description is very general. However, one thing is sure, the job of acquiring editor is demanding, challenging, exciting, and probably offers a greater sense of personal fulfillment than most other jobs in book publishing.

The Role of the Copy Editor: What It Takes to Be One

The role of the **copy editor** is to edit the complete book manuscript after it has been turned over to the acquiring editor by the author. The copy editor must first of all know what style the manuscript must follow (house style). In addition, he or she must ensure consistency in capitalization, spelling, abbreviations, and every detail in the manuscript that will make it ready for turning over to the compositor to be prepared for publication.

The copy editor's job requires a set of abilities that involve being patient, objective, uninvolved, and often somewhat contemptuous, searching out errors or misstatements in the manuscript which either the author or the sponsoring editor may have overlooked.

Someone once wrote that copy editing "requires a careful and methodical mind, capable of sustained attention which must frequently be applied to the dullest of sorts of reading matter, and a memory which can recall, when the editor spots the word maneuver on page 112 of a manuscript, that the author spelled it manoeuvre on page 63."

One experienced copy editor sums up the principal attributes of a copy editor thus: "The three areas of greatest concern are numbers (whether words or figures), capitalization and compounds (proof reader, proof-reader, or proofreader)." Another thing, says this copy editor, is that copy editors keep track of personal and place names in fiction; authors are forgetful enough to make this a necessity.

Another long-experienced copy editor, who also teaches copy editing at New York University's Center for Publishing, has this to say about the past and present role of copy editing: "Once copy editors checked for spelling, grammar, punctuation, styled for consistency, and did light fact checking. Today, copy editors do all that as well as everything from minor revisions to major rewrites."[10]

Editorial Director Looking to Get Lucky

One day, the editorial director at a small technical publishing establishment was observed hanging a horseshoe over the door to his office. His colleagues, in surprise, asked the director whether he believed it would bring luck to his acquisition efforts.

"No," the editorial director replied, "I don't believe in superstitions. But I've been told that it works even if you don't believe in it."

Frequently-Banned Book Nearing 1,000 Editions

High on the American Library Association's list of books most frequently challenged in schools and libraries is Mark Twain's *Adventures of Huckleberry Finn*. As early as a month after its 1885 publication, the trustees of the Concord, Massachusetts Public Library expelled the book from its shelves, calling it "trash ... suitable only for the slums." Many other libraries fell in line, often labeling the book immoral and sacrilegious.

But for all the moral outrage this book has engendered, *The Adventures of Huckleberry Finn* has been read in 65 languages. With the issuance of a spring 1996 edition by Random House, this book has now been published in nearly 1,000 editions.

Most Honest Book Jacket Blurb Ever Written

Perhaps the most honest wording ever to appear on a book jacket was the blurb signed by Random House publisher Bennett Cerf on a 1936 Gertrude Stein book titled, *The Geographical History of America on the Relation of Human Nature to the Human Mind.* Here's what Cerf wrote:

> This space is usually reserved for a brief description of a book's contents. In this case, however, I must admit frankly that I do not know what Miss Stein is talking about. I do not even understand the title.

Chapter 3A

Book Publishing Origins, Firsts, and Curiosities in the 20th Century

---

Historical Standouts among No. 1 Authors
on the *New York Times* Bestseller Lists

For a book to win the #1 position on the *New York Times* bestseller list is an ultimate achievement for its author. The #1 spot is derived from a tally of sales records of more than 3,000 leading bookstores and from book wholesalers serving 28,000 retail outlets.

In the first fifty years the bestseller list appeared (through the end of 1992), the *Times Book Review* reported these oddities among the various authors who have been in the #1 position:

- Longest in #1 position: Norman Vincent Peale's *Power of Positive Thinking*, 98 weeks.*

- Male author with most #1 bestsellers: Stephen King, 17 books.

- Female author with most #1 bestsellers: Danielle Steel, 11 books.

- Author with most total lifetime weeks at #1: James Michener, 207

- First black author: Lillian Smith for *Strange Fruit*.

- Author with shortest pen name: "J" for *The Sensuous Woman*.

- Youngest author: Francoise Saigan for *Bonjour Tristesse* at age 19.

- Oldest author: George Burns for *Gracie: A Love Story* at age 92.

- Tallest authors: John Kenneth Galbraith and Michael Crichton, each over 6'6".

* A new record for longevity in the #1 spot on the *Times* Bestseller List was set by a hardcover fiction book on September 17, 1995. The book was *The Bridges of Madison County* by Robert James Waller, which ended a three-year-plus run at 162 weeks.

The Instant Book: What It Is, How It Came About

Every once in a while a news event captures the public fancy to such an extent that mass-market publishers capitalize on the high degree of public interest by publishing an instant book providing full details of the event. Events that merited instant books in recent years included the Iran-Contra hearings involving Lieutenant Colonel Oliver North and the U.S. ice hockey victories over the USSR team at Lake Placid, New York. In each case, instant books were on the newsstands and accessible to the public within days.

- In the case of the surprise U.S. ice hockey triumph over the USSR team, Bantam delivered a finished book 46¼ hours after completion of the manuscript. This was a new speed record for publishing an instant book.

- In the case of the Oliver North book, nearly 800,000 copies of *Taking the Stand* were printed and rushed to the newsstands and supermarket racks, of which more than half were sold.

The earliest instant book was published in 1945 to capitalize on the vast wave of American grief over the sudden death of Franklin D. Roosevelt. The president died April 12, 1945, and an instant book published by Pocket Books appeared on the newsstands six days later.

The most recent instant book was *Mad Genius: The Odyssey, Pursuit and Capture of the Suspected Unabomber.* Warner Books, in a frantic race to beat out a competing paperback from Pocket Books, was able to ship finished books on May 1, 1996, just twenty-nine days after the capture of Theodore Kaczynski, the alleged Unabomber. The Pocket Books version, *Unabomber: On the Trail of America's Most-Wanted Serial Killer,* was delayed by an FBI review because one of the co-authors was a former FBI agent.

World's Biggest Seller:
Origin and History of the *Guinness* Record Book

On September 12, 1954, Sir High Beaver, the managing director of the British brewing firm Arthur Guinness, Son and Co., Ltd., invited a pair of identical twin brothers, Norris and Ross McWhirter, to see if their fact and figure agency in London could produce a book that would help settle arguments about records. The McWhirters, sons of a prominent British journalist, had been operating an agency in London where they collected facts and trivia that would help settle arguments of others—things such as deepest lakes and highest mountains, etc.

What the brewery head had in mind for the McWhirters was to compile a book of such trivia that would tell people quickly and concisely just what was biggest, smallest, fastest, slowest, shortest, longest, hottest, coldest, and strongest in the world. Such a book as Sir Hugh Beaver had in mind could then be distributed to the many British pubs where Guinness stout was sold. It could be used in these places in settling those arguments peculiar to pubs.

Eleven months after being summoned by the head of the British brewing firm, on August 27, 1955, the first volume of the *Guinness Book of World Records* was produced. Before Christmas of that year, it was England's #1 nonfiction bestseller, and it has occupied this position on the list every year since—with the exception of 1957 and 1959 when it was not republished.

The first U.S. edition appeared in 1956 and revised, updated editions have been appearing annually in both hardcover and paperback editions. The book's sales in America duplicated the success of the English edition and some of the paperback editions have gone through as many as 17 printings.

Other successes followed as the book grew in 1996 to 182+ editions in 43 languages. It now occupies a coveted spot in *Guinness* as the topselling copyrighted book in publishing history. Global sales through February 1996 have surpassed 77 million copies.

A disclaimer in *Guinness* explains that it is not a compendium of every world record, but rather a subjective selection of those the editors have found to be the most significant and/or interesting.

The U.S. edition, about a quarter of it revised annually, is edited by Mark Young and a staff of two for the U.S. publisher, Facts on File. The U.S. edition currently lists 15,000 records.

The most impressive record in *Guinness*, according to Mr. Young, is the one set on September 6, 1981. On that date Risto Antikainen threw a fresh hen's egg 317 feet, 10 inches, nearly the length of a football field. Even more surprising, adds Young, was the feat of Jyrki Korhonen, who caught the egg without breaking it.

The Author's Bible: *The Chicago Manual of Style*

For generations of authors and editors, *The Chicago Manual of Style* has served as a bible and primary reference tool. Its main function, according to Catherine Seybold in *Distinguished Classics of Reference Publishing*[1] has been to "help them decide what to capitalize, italicize, put in quotation marks; how to abbreviate all kinds of terms, to quote from other sources, to punctuate, to form plurals of numbers, names, etc., to compile and edit tables and indexes, to deal with footnotes and bibliographies and reference lists..."

The start of *The Chicago Manual of Style* is closely tied to its publisher, the University of Chicago Press, which began in 1891 as a department of the university to carry the university's wisdom beyond its own student body.

In the early days of the Press, professors brought their handwritten manuscripts directly to the Press compositors who had to decipher them and set them in type in an acceptable form. Proofreaders then corrected typographic errors, inconsistencies in style, and errors in grammar. As the professors needed some sort of guidelines, in 1901 with the help of the university's English department, the Press set up a style sheet which it produced in pamphlet form and circulated in the university community.

When the style sheet pamphlet met with great success, the governing board of the Press approved its issuance as a regular Press publication. Consequently in 1906, the University of Chicago Press published its first formal *Manual of Style*, a 200-page book outlining the typographical rules prevailing at the Press. Nearly three-fourths of that edition dealt with type specimens and rules of composition.

By its second edition in 1910, *Manual of Style* enjoyed widespread acceptance and was used in editorial offices and proofrooms throughout the United States and Canada. The 1911 third edition called for revisions in its preface due to "the recent development of the profession of librarian, with the attendant uniformity of practice recommended by the national association of librarians, and ... daily application of these rules to a varied list of publications." The 1920 seventh edition added the article "A" to the title and *Manual of Style* became *A Manual of Style*.

Over the next 30 years, major changes included additional pages of type specimens in the ninth edition in 1927; greatly expanded Rules for Preparation of Copy and a new chapter on bibliography in the tenth edition in 1937; and a revised Hints section in the 1949 eleventh edition.

In 1969, with publication of the twelfth revised edition, *A Manual of Style* had achieved such success, that its sale of 153,501 copies matched the combined sales of the eleven earlier editions. The twelfth edition marked the change of editorial thrust toward authors and editors, and away from typographers and printers. The type specimens and hints sections were dropped and the section on bookmaking expanded.

With the introduction of the thirteenth edition in 1982, the title became *The Chicago Manual of Style*. It was 35% larger than the previous edition and substantially revised in every area. A new chapter was added on the history and current methods of composition, printing, and binding. As the sales history of the thirteenth edition closed in the summer of 1993, more than 225,000 copies had been sold.

The current fourteenth edition, introduced in August 1993, at 932 pages is 200 pages larger than the edition published eleven years earlier. Again, substantial revisions appear in every area. This fourteenth edition also includes computer technology through every state of the publishing process, from manuscript to bound books. It offers updated information on copyright and permissions. In addition, it provides revised information on quotations, names and terms, documentation, spelling, and indexing.

Origin of *Emily Post's Etiquette* — A Persistent Editor

In 1921, Richard Duffy, an editor at Funk & Wagnalls, a publisher of dictionaries and encyclopedias, decided the timing was right for Funk & Wagnalls to get into the field of etiquette and compete with the numerous other such books currently available which appeared to be popular sellers.

In his quest for an author for such a book, he turned to Emily Price Post (1872-1960). During the fourteen years since her divorce from Edwin Main Post, a member of one of New York's Vanderbilt families, Emily Post had turned to writing as a career. Having already written six novels, she was considered a minor celebrity.

Further, she was from a family that had been socially active for several generations, and she could trace her lineage back to the seventeenth century. Emily Post's father, Bruce Price, was a famous architect, who had designed the Chateau Frontenac in Quebec and most of the buildings in Tuxedo Park, New York, a high society country club estate.

When Richard Duffy called Mrs. Post to tell her, "We want you to write an encyclopedia," she immediately turned him down. The idea of writing such a work about etiquette to her meant "a lot of false and pretentious fuss over trifles." But Duffy persisted. Finally, to get rid of him, Mrs. Post agreed to look over a stack of the currently popular books on etiquette that he provided in an attempt to convince her that a new one was truly needed.

In later writing about what happened, she mentions opening one of the samples left her. She was aghast over the "shocking misinformation" she found in the book and appalled at its condescending tone. She called Duffy at his home and told him, "I will write the book for you, and at once."

Mrs. Post worked on the book for a year and a half and turned in her manuscript of 692 pages in 1921. The first edition of *Etiquette*, published in July 1922, was an immediate success. She had written a book with great wit and charm about a social world she and her family had inhabited for many years. She was the first author of such high social position to attempt such an endeavor since Mrs. Sherwood's *Manners and Social Usages* had appeared in 1884 under the Harper & Brothers banner.

Book critics of the era were enthusiastic, with laudatory reviews appearing in hundreds of newspapers all over the country. The *New York Tribune* called Mrs. Post's book "entertaining" and described Mrs. Post's efforts as "humorous, wise, witty, worldly, sympathetic, and human."

Within ten years, various editions of Mrs. Post's *Etiquette* had sold 500,000 copies. New editions appeared in 1927, 1931, 1942, 1945, 1955, and 1960. With each revision, she incorporated new situations that she had encountered in responding to mail inquiries from her books and newspaper column. With Mrs. Post's death in 1960, subsequent editions of *Etiquette* became *Emily Posts's Etiquette*. The posthumous editions have been revised and edited by Elizabeth L. Post, Emily Post's granddaughter-in-law.

Book-of-the-Month Club First Selection:
The Impartial Jury System

The Book-of-the-Month Club, which launched the book club (negative-option bookselling) revolution in America, offered its first selection to its

4,750 members on April 16, 1926. The book was *Lolly Willowes, or the Loving Huntsman*, by Sylvia Townsend Warner.

The book judges, all literary celebrities in their own right, were Henry Seidel Canby, editor of the *Saturday Review of Literature*, Heywood Braun, Dorothy Canfield, Christopher Morley, and William Allen White. For that first selection and others to follow, the judges were driven to the monthly selection meetings in the club's lower Manhattan offices in chauffeured limousines. To the judges, who were to act as an impartial selection jury, it was in recognition of their celebrity status. To the club, it was to ensure they arrived on time and did not wind up in Brooklyn—or worse.

The early BOMC selection process was very unscientific. Books were stacked on the floor and sorted into two piles—those suited for consideration and discards. The judges then made selections from the acceptable pile.

The first selection, one BOMC official later recalled, proved a blooper. Of the 4,750 mailed to charter members, a very large number came back and the club's future seemed bleak. Not until some time later when the club offered Walter Noble Burns' *Billy the Kid*, John Galsworthy's *The Silver Spoon*, and Edna Ferber's *Show Boat* did it appear that the idea of the negative option book club would catch on.

The Upton Sinclair Novel That Spurred Adoption of the U.S. Pure Food Act

Upton Sinclair (1878-1968) wrote more than eighty books during his lifetime. Many were of a documentary nature blending journalistic fact with fiction. The most famous of his novels was *The Jungle*, a landmark work published in 1906. It created a sensation by telling in shockingly graphic terms the horrors then existing in the meatpacking industry. Spurred by the book, President Theodore Roosevelt pushed through passage of the Pure Food and Drug Act of June 30, 1906.

Intended to outline the plight of Lithuanian immigrants working in the Chicago meatpacking industry, *The Jungle* aroused national and international indignation at the way meat was being processed. Sinclair's novel offered vivid details of the use of moldy meats that were often mixed with poisoned bread intended to kill rats. He also wrote of rat carcasses being incorporated into processed meat products.

The book begins with the story of a Chicago meatpacking plant worker who fell to his death from a high catwalk into a huge, boiling cauldron of meat. In seconds, the body of the worker becomes part of the day's production of sausage.

The Jungle originally appeared in serialized form in the socialist weekly newspaper, *Appeal to Reason*, for which Sinclair was paid $500. Sinclair was later to comment on his landmark novel, "I aimed at the public's heart. By accident I hit it in the stomach."

Sinclair was twenty-eight when he wrote *The Jungle*. It was turned down by at least five publishers before it reached publication as a book. However, within months after its appearance in book form, editions appeared in England and in seventeen translations.

Sixty-one years later in 1967, in recognition of Upton Sinclair's contribution to the passage of the nation's first Pure Food and Drug Act, President Lyndon Johnson included the author at the signing ceremony of the Wholesome Meat Act, an act designed to plug loopholes in earlier food laws.

In the course of writing *The Jungle* in its serialized version, Sinclair remained convinced that it would have a large sale as a book. However, readers of the series did not share that opinion. Professor G.R. Carpenter of Columbia University, after reading several installments of *The Jungle* predicted that, although Sinclair's tale was "told with great force, indeed with really terrific force at times ... (and was) an extraordinary indictment ... it is not a book that could have a wide circulation." In a published report of bestselling books through 1975, *The Jungle* was listed as having sold 2,367,600 copies.

The Book That Spurred Environmental Awareness

As Thomas Paine's *Common Sense* and Harriet Beecher Stowe's *Uncle Tom's Cabin* had earlier made a tremendous impact on public consciousness and demanded instant action so, too, did Rachel Carson's *Silent Spring* in 1962. The landmark work instantly helped create a worldwide awareness of the dangers of environmental pollution.

In a fictionalized account, she told of a small American town in a prosperous farmland with wild flowers, numerous songbirds, and well-stocked trout streams. She then described how a strange blight crept over the area and began to kill off everything and impose strange illnesses on the human inhabitants.

What *Silent Spring* did was to awaken the American conscience to the overwhelming problem of pollution of the air, water, and land, beginning with the World War II dangerous fallout from nuclear bomb explosions.

Silent Spring, an instant bestseller that remained on the *New York Times* Bestseller List for 31 weeks, sold half a million copies before the paperback version appeared. It had an immediate effect on public opinion and helped speed industrial and governmental research. One reason for the rapid acceptance and reaction for Ms. Carson's work was her fame from two earlier bestsellers, *The Sea Around Us* and *The Edge of the Sea*.

Ms. Carson built a damning and persuasive case of the destruction being wrought by pesticides, the build-up in the human body from exposure to dangerous chemicals, and their ultimate disastrous effects. A postscript to Ms. Carson's warnings: Two years after the publication of *Silent Spring*, Rachel Carson died of cancer on April 14, 1964—a month before her 57th birthday.

The 1908 Book That Predicted Japanese Attack on the U.S.

The Japanese attack on Pearl Harbor in 1941 was not the first time Americans as a nation were given to thinking about a Japanese attack on U.S. territory. The Baker & Taylor Company had published a novel based on a Japanese attack against the U.S. some 33 years earlier.[2]

It happened in 1908 with the Baker & Taylor Company, which was both a publisher and a wholesale book distributor. From its headquarters at 33-37 East 17th Street, Baker & Taylor published an American edition of a German work, *Bonzai*—an illustrated novel about an invasion of the U.S. west coast by the Japanese fleet with the cooperation of a Japanese fifth column already positioned in this country. The Baker & Taylor book had the Americans triumphing in the end.

Today, the Baker & Taylor Company, headquartered in Bridgewater, New Jersey, is America's largest library book supplier. Founded in 1828, it is the oldest book wholesaler as well. It ceased book publishing operations in 1912.

Origin of Armed Services Editions:
Sparked Growth of Paperback Industry

Armed Services Editions were cheap paperback reprints of popular hardcover books distributed to American servicemen during World War II. More than 1,300 different titles were produced under the auspices of the Council on Books in Wartime (made up of American trade book publishers, librarians, and booksellers). The books were printed in oblong shape on presses normally used to produce the popular pulp magazines of the day. They came off press magazine-size and, when sliced in half horizontally, produced two books, each approximately $4\frac{1}{2}$" high and $6\frac{1}{2}$" wide.

Readily recognizable because of their oblong shape and double-column format, they were distributed free to overseas servicemen, with explicit agreement that they not be resold, made available to civilians, or given to servicemen serving domestically.

The more than 122,500,000 copies of the World War II Armed Services Editions were said to have given the fledgling paperback reprint industry its big push toward post-war expansion. Prior to World War II, relatively few paperback reprints of bestselling hardcover books were available.

Two Publishers Who Succeeded with Fictitious Book Titles

In the 1930's, a publisher of adult books decided to test the potential market for children's books. So he created a fictitious book title with a catchy name, had a jacket designed and printed, and sent his salesmen into the field to solicit advance orders from bookstores. They turned in advance orders totaling 40,000 copies, so he made the jump into children's book publishing, eventually abandoning his line of adult fiction entirely.

In a similar vein, during the early depression years of the 1930s, when circulating libraries were in vogue, a recently-established publisher decided on a fictitious book, bearing the title *Speakeasy Girl*, about young New York City girls-about-town who spent most of their time in speakeasies. The publishing partnership produced an eye-catching jacket, advertised the nonexisting book in the publishing trade press, and sent out a thousand aluminum cocktail shakers attached to the book's jacket to bookstore buyers and chief clerks in the largest bookstores.

The response from the bookstores was substantial and motion picture companies asked for copies of the manuscript for possible movie adaptation. So the publishers found a well-known writer who produced a printable manuscript in six weeks. Though the book was poorly written, the publishers managed to avoid advance order cancellations by simultaneously releasing all copies. The book managed to sell well, but was subsequently shunned by the movie companies.

Turning History Books into Novels: Kenneth Roberts' Formula

In the early years of this century, history books did not sell as well as novels. However, one journalist-turned-historian was able to convert history into bestselling novels by weaving in a plot, giving his historical presentation a fictional title, and providing it with a happy ending. He was Kenneth Roberts.

Among his numerous notable historical works were *Northwest Passage*, *Oliver Wiswell, Rabble in Arms, Arundel,* and *Lydia Bailey*. In each, Roberts developed his stories around actual characters and historical situations, meticulously researched and authentically described. As a consequence, book reviewers were quick to recognize the historical accuracy of his various novels and to state in their reviews that the stories were indeed history.

And indeed each was history, for Roberts often spent years in researching historic archives before starting to write. His research for *Rabble in Arms* spanned three years, while for *Northwest Passage*, Roberts traveled to England and conducted searches of England's Public Record Office, War Office, Colonial Office, and other record repositories in search of authentic source material for later use in his book.

Here is a sampling of excerpts from reviews of Roberts' books that reflect how reviewers treated his novels as history:

Northwest Passage

"Northwest Passage is accurate history, graphically told." — *Brooklyn Eagle*. "In its pages an era comes to life, complete with people and things." — *Atlantic Monthly*.

Oliver Wiswell

"It is history, for all its fictional form ... a horrible civil war powerfully and dramatically brought back to life." — *New York Times.* "Gives life to people who were only names on a page of history." — *San Francisco Chronicle.*

Rabble in Arms

"Indispensable to anyone who wishes to know the true story of the War for American Independence." — *Buffalo Evening News.* "Valuable as biography, invaluable as history." — *Richmond Times Dispatch.* "Should be on the required reading list of every course in American History." — American Antiquarian Society.

Arundel

"The story of the secret expedition led by Colonel Benedict Arnold against Quebec in Revolutionary days (is) a supremely great book." — *St. Louis Globe Democrat.* "Will rank with anything ever written about that period." — *Detroit News.*

Lydia Bailey

"Here is history come to life." — *Christian Science Monitor.* "Respects history ... uses history ... spin(s) a yarn so that you despise sleep!" — *Los Angeles Times.*

The Trade Paperback: Its Evolution and Impact

One of the most interesting developments in publishing in the second half of the twentieth century has been the development of the trade paperback, i.e., a class of books identical to hardcover editions and published simultaneously with them, but issued in paper covers by the original publishers. They are usually sold through bookstores, rather than mass-market paperback outlets, and at greatly-reduced prices from their hardcover counterparts.

Trade paperbacks have vastly increased the affordability of books not normally within the range of classroom textbook use, both as texts and on recommended reading lists as supplementary texts, at colleges and universities. Trade paperbacks useful for the college classroom are sometimes called "egg head" paperbacks. They are likely to be general works on such subjects as business, history, and philosophy, or other subjects taught at colleges and universities, and stocked in depth at most college bookstores.

The advantage to the originating publisher is that the book is printed as part of the book's normal press run, thereby reducing unit costs for both editions—sometimes making possible a lower price for the hardcover edition. The advantage to the bookstore is that the books can be obtained at normal trade discounts, which are much higher than textbook discounts. The advantage to the book's author is that the author receives the full royalty, something that is not done when the book is issued as a mass-market paperback where publisher and author split reprint licensing fees.

The advantage of the trade paperback to the student is that the price is usually about half of the cost of the hardcover edition. Compare average pricing and savings from this study of U.S. book output for 1993:[3]

Subject Area	Hardcover Editions # and Ave. Price	Trade Paper Editions # and Ave. Price	Price Difference
Business	1,088 / $37.95	332 / $25.18	33.6%
Fiction	3,014 / $19.50	107 / $13.56	30.5%
History	1,962 / $40.78	338 / $21.20	48.0%
Science	2,729 / $52.71	481 / $31.79	39.7%
Technology	1,714 / $56.31	460 / $30.04	46.7%
Travel	329 / $26.22	149 / $15.90	39.4%

The trade paperback originated in April 1953 with the introduction of Anchor Books by Doubleday. Unlike its smaller-sized paper-covered counterparts which were distributed through newspaper and magazine distributors, Doubleday's Anchor Books line could be sold through traditional book wholesalers and directly to bookstores. Early Anchor Books, at a price of about one dollar, won quick acceptance. In *Between Covers*,[4] John Tebbel said, "Anchor's first four books sold 10,000 copies each within two weeks, even at what was considered high prices for those days—85¢ to $1.25."

Paperback Price Growth:
25¢ at Inception, in $6.99 Price Range Now

Mass-market paperback publishing began in the United States in 1939 when Pocket Books started distributing the little paper-covered books at 25¢ a copy. During the first ten years of mass-market paperback publishing, from 1939 to 1949, Pocket Books held firmly to the 25¢ price and sold over 135 million copies. As new publishers entered the field of mass-market paperbacks, they all matched the Pocket Books 25¢ price until Signet broke the mold by raising its paperbacks to 35¢. Signet labeled the higher priced books Signet Giants.

In the early years of mass-market paperbacks, most were light fiction and mysteries. As other types of books moved into the field and grew more substantial in size, paperback cover prices started moving up to 50¢, 75¢, and by the mid 1950's, as high as 95¢ for thicker books.

Despite the steadily rising prices, when Pocket Books celebrated its 25th anniversary in 1964, paperbacks were selling in the U.S. at the rate of a million copies a day. Other leading paperback publishers were Bantam Books, Popular Library, Meridian Books, Fawcett, Avon Books, and Dell.

In contrast with the mid-1950's prices of under $1.00 for paperbacks, by late 1979, the average cover price of a paperback was $1.95. By late 1992, ten of the 15 top paperback bestsellers were priced at $5.99—a price level that prevailed through 1993. However, by the end of 1994, the 15 top-selling paperbacks edged close to $6.25. With strong paper price increases in 1995, average prices in 1996 were $6.99 for fiction, with nonfiction much higher.

Those Record Prices for Paperback Reprint Rights: How Much Authors Get

Here are the record-breaking prices paid for paperback reprint rights to bestseller originals over the years:

Year	Price Paid	Book Title	Author
1979	$3,208,875	*Princess Daisy*	Judith Krantz
1978	2,250,000	*Love Signs*	Linda Goodman
1975	2,000,000	*Ragtime*	E.L. Docterow
1973	1,500,000	*The Joy of Cooking*	Rombauer & Baker
1971	1,000,000	*The Drifters*	James Michener
1965	700,000	*The Source*	James Michener
1960	400,000	*Rise & Fall of the Third Reich*	William L. Shirer
1954	100,000	*From Here to Eternity*	James Jones
1949	35,000	*The Naked and the Dead*	Normal Mailer

What do authors get from these paperback megadeals? According to the July 12, 1991 issue of *Publishers Weekly,* "The split between publisher and author is still 50/50 for first novels and midlist books, but it can go as high as 75/25 for major authors."

There have been fewer of these big paperback reprint buys from 1979 through 1995 because, as Jean Peters, Cahners Publishing Company librarian, advised the author in August 1995, "Paperback rights are no longer generally sold separately. Hard/soft rights are now usually acquired together for one sum by the same publisher." It seems highly unlikely, therefore, that the 1979 record set by Judith Krantz's *Princess Daisy* will ever be surpassed.

How a Disaster Led to the Invention of the Movable Page

In 1913 at New York University, a professor and his young law student collaborated on a book in business law that they decided to publish themselves with $10,000 in credit from a cooperating book printer. As a name for their new publishing venture, they chose to combine the maiden names of their mothers. The student, Richard Prentice Ettinger, took his mother's maiden name "Prentice" and Professor Charles W. Gerstenberg took his mother's maiden name "Hall." Thus was born the publishing establishment of Prentice-Hall—today a division of Simon & Schuster, one of the giants in the publishing industry.

With publication of their third book, a 4,000-copy edition, disaster struck. The law on tax regulations—one of the important chapters in the book—had just been radically changed, and there were no finances to do a reprint. Young Ettinger came up with a solution: They would strip the bindings off the printed edition, cut off the backing to reduce the book to individual pages, and then replace the obsolete pages. The book, now with the corrected sheets, would then be three-hole punched and re-issued in a ring binder.

At the same time, the publishing duo made a decision to offer a loose-leaf subscription service so that the book would never be out-of-date. The publisher would simply send a new chapter whenever changes in the law were made. Thus was born the modern aspect of book publishing known as loose leaf publishing.

By October 1981, this branch of book publishing had become so large that, "in recognition of the unique nature of publishing loose-leaf services and its growth as an important segment of book publishing," the Association of American Publishers established the Professional and Scholarly Publishing Loose Leaf Committee, with Ted Caris of Aspen Systems Corporation as its first chairman.

Kenneth T. Hurst, President of Prentice-Hall International, who supplied the historic data for this entry, also made this noteworthy comment: "Gutenberg claimed to have invented movable type; Ettinger claimed to have invented the movable page."

John Steinbeck:
Writing under Pressure between Pills and Bedpans

Although written a number of years earlier, John Steinbeck's *The Long Valley* was not published until 1938, when it rode the popularity of his *Tortilla Flat*, *Of Mice and Men*, and *In Dubious Battle*. *The Long Valley* consisted of sixteen short stories Steinbeck wrote between the fall of 1933 and the summer of 1934. Most were written during the months when Steinbeck was living in the family home in Salinas, California, and helping his mother to die. Steinbeck's writing table, says Wallace Stegner,[5] "was set up outside his mother's room; he wrote in the odd half hours between pills and bedpans, and it is little wonder that he wrote short."

Salinas is the county seat of Monterey County south/southwest of San Francisco. It was originally settled by migratory farm workers. Steinbeck's greatest novel, *The Grapes of Wrath*, was about the Depression decade and the plight of migratory farm workers. Steinbeck won the Nobel Prize for Literature in 1962. The accompanying citation praised the social perception and humor of Steinbeck's "realistic and imaginative writings."

The Making of IDMB:
The Century's Leading Scientific Dictionary

The *International Dictionary of Medicine and Biology* (IDMB) is the largest medical dictionary ever published in the English language and one of the largest of its kind ever published in any language. Its 160,000 definitions occupy 3,300 pages in three volumes, drawn from a database of 27.5 million keystrokes, and covering 70 different subject areas from anatomy to zoology.

This is the inside story of how it was conceived and created by John Wiley & Sons over a ten-year period starting in 1975. That year, Wiley contracted to translate a four-volume French dictionary of medicine and biology into English. Utilizing the services of a medical doctor and one or two consultants, it was estimated the project would take two to three years.

In 1977, with virtually no progress on the translation, Wiley engaged the services of the former editor-in-chief of Funk & Wagnalls dictionaries, Sidney Landau, to assume responsibility for the project. Landau quickly realized the proposed translation would provide fewer terms than leading American medical dictionaries and, moreover, that many of the French terms were obsolete or based on outdated concepts. He also found that there was no unanimity between the English and the French on many medical conditions.

Landau then undertook to create an entirely new dictionary independent of the French dictionary. Editors in eighty-one subject areas were selected and each was commissioned to provide an independent word list for a particular subject. By the end of 1978, a year after Landau had entered the project, the list had grown to 220,000 terms. Landau subsequently appointed an in-house managing editor, who was also a trained lexicographer, and half a dozen medical specialist editors to refine the enormous word list.

By June 1979, the 220,000-term list had been trimmed to 185,000 through elimination of duplications and trivial variations of the same term. Simultaneously, all current medical publications were screened for inclusion of new terminology.

By November 1979, the 185,000 defining terms were sent to 81 subject editors—all research scientists and clinicians selected by an editorial board of five distinguished scientists. Over the next six years, from 1980 to 1985, each prepared definitions for the 81 subjects.

By 1985, after all of the definitions had been submitted to Landau by the subject editors, they were edited by an in-house staff editor and restricted to the number of definitions warranted by the complexity of the subject. Many definitions were cleared by one or more specialist staff editors before being cleared for inclusion in the dictionary.

Following review and clearance of each definition, the original subject editor was sent the list of his or her assigned terms as edited for last minute corrections and final review. A final tape of all definitions was merged with an etymology tape and, finally, The *International Dictionary of Medicine and Biology* was published in January 1985.

The ten-year Wiley project was well received by scientific and professional library publications and is now the established standard reference in hospital and medical libraries worldwide. Project director Landau is currently editorial director at Cambridge University Press.

Most Prolific Author of the Twentieth Century

In all likelihood, the most prolific author of the 20th century was the Russian-born American author and scientist, Isaac Asimov (1920-1992). Asimov wrote 470 books on every subject, from robots to Shakespeare. He is recognized as the most important science fiction writer of this century as well as the acknowledged father of modern popular science writing. During most of his writing career, Asimov was a professor of biochemistry at Boston University.

Largest Single-Book Print Order of this Century

The largest print order in publishing history for a single book was for the book about Elvis Presley titled, *Elvis: What Happened?* The order, placed by Ballantine Books on August 20, 1977 (four days after Presley's death), was for over two million copies. The paperback dealt with Presley's drug addiction, violent outbursts, and obsession with death. The book is still in print.

First Novel Ever Set Directly from Author's Computer-Written Manuscript

In his 1983 novel, *Run Before the Wind*, author Stuart Woods noted that this was the first novel ever transmitted electronically directly from the author's computer to a typesetting machine. Woods wrote the book on a PolyMorphic 8813 microcomputer using a basic word-processing program. Then, after being manually copy edited and spelling corrected with a special computer program, the final manuscript was transmitted over telephone lines by the author direct to ComCom, which then typeset the book for the New York City publisher, W.W. Norton.

Unhappy with Book as Published, Author Took His Life; Novel Went on to Become a Classic

Larry Lockridge wrote the 1996 book, *Shade of the Raintree: The Life and Death of Ross Lockridge, Jr.*, to help him disentangle his childhood image of his father singing while doing dishes with the conflicting image created by his father's suicide in 1948—just weeks after his classic novel, *Raintree County*, was published.

What caused his father to end it all when he was apparently at the threshold of a major success? The answer: Ross Lockridge, genetically predisposed to bouts of depression, felt let down after the publication of his book. Not happy with some of the editorial cuts made to his 1,066-page book, Ross had come to think that *Raintree County* was not the masterpiece he had originally felt it was. Even with shock treatments, his depression did not lift. Born too soon to have access to today's new antidepressant drugs, Ross never overcame his depression.

On March 6, 1948, he told his wife he was going to the post office. Instead, he headed for the garage, turned on the ignition to his car, and let the carbon monoxide do its work. He left behind a wife, four children, and a bestselling novel that is still a solid seller nearly half a century later.

Largest Novel in English Ever Published in a Single Volume

The record for the largest English-language novel in a single volume was set in 1965* by the 1,198-page novel, *Miss MacIntosh, My Darling*, published by Charles Scribner's Sons. It was the work of Marguerite Young (1908-1995), an Indiana-born writer, longtime respected literary critic in New York's Greenwich Village, and teacher of writing at The New School.

The book contained some 750,000 words and took eighteen years to write. A *New York Times* writer[6] wrote of Ms. Young's lengthy opus: "Anyone who has not read her magnum opus need not feel ashamed. Surely one of the most widely unread books ever acclaimed, it has actually been read by comparatively few; by few still all the way through." Ms. Young died on November 16, 1995, at the age of 87.

Author Book Signings Big Business as Century Nears End

As the 20th century nears its end, in-store author book signings have evolved into a major bookselling vehicle. How do author signings affect sales? When Colin Powell's book, *My American Journey*, was published in 1995, Random House required a 2,000-copy minimum order guarantee from a bookstore before arranging for a Powell signing at that store.

How big have book signings gotten? In 1996, the Elliott Bay Book Co. in Seattle has scheduled at least one signing every day and, on some days, two such events, most of them on its own premises. The chains have gotten into these events in such a big way that one chain, Borders Books & Music, employs a publicity person in every one of its 110-plus stores to handle and publicize such events. Each Borders store averages thirty events a month.

---

* This record was surpassed in 1992 by Norman Mailer's *Harlot's Ghost*, which has 1,310 numbered pages. For additional details on *Harlot's Ghost*, see the Chapter 11 entry on How American Book Pricing Has Grown Since 1990.

Chapter 3B

Book Publishing Origins, Firsts, and Curiosities in the 19th Century

Jules Verne: Author, Visionary, and Inspiration for a World of the Future

Jules Verne (1828-1905) enjoys a unique place in the world of literary achievement. Long before a future world existed, he allowed his mind to roam and described a world of the future for the children of his time. Along the way, he instilled in their young minds the vision that such things could happen. In time, his young readers grew up and made them happen.

Verne, with no formal scientific training—he'd been trained to be an attorney—wrote about a future that went beyond the wildest dreams of his contemporaries. Until his first novel was published when he was thirty-five, he considered himself a failure as a writer. Yet, he lived to see fifty-seven of his works published, with eight more to follow after his death in 1905.

Verne described swift airplanes and helicopters at a time when people were still experimenting with hot air balloons. In 1865, after Verne's heroes had crossed unknown Africa in a balloon, discovered the North Pole, and penetrated the interior of the earth, he wrote about man's first trip to the moon in *From the Earth to the Moon*. He wrote so convincingly about the moon trip that hundreds of people volunteered to ride in the space ship he'd invented. One hundred and four years later, on July 20, 1969, Verne's 1865 vision became a reality when Apollo 11 astronauts Neal Armstrong and Edwin Aldrin took a two-hour walk on the fine, powdery surface of the moon.

Verne is referred to as the founder of modern science fiction. But for many, he was also the inspiration for many twentieth-century scientists, inventors, and engineers. For it was Verne's ideas and stories that planted the seeds that his youthful readers later converted into reality.

Verne wrote about a future where men could control the weather by flicking a switch and turning a dial, about deserts that would be transformed into gardens, about cities of the future with skyscrapers a thousand feet tall (the U.S.'s tallest office building is the Sears Tower in Chicago at 1,454 feet), about boulevards a hundred yards wide, and moving sidewalks for pedestrians. He envisioned and wrote about homes throughout the world linked by TV-telephones, about the sun's rays supplying energy for mechanical power, about trains speeding through pneumatic tubes, giant airliners that would fly nonstop to any point on earth, and spaceships that would circle distant suns.

Interviews with many of the great achievers indicated they'd been influenced by Verne's works as young children. Simon Lake, the pioneer submarine builder, once told of having his imagination fired at the age of eleven by reading Verne's *Twenty Thousand Leagues Under the Sea*. Arctic explorer Richard Byrd, before he took off on the first airplane flight over the North Pole in 1926, said, "It was Jules Verne who launched me on this trip." Werner von Braun, who helped design the Saturn super rocket, admitted his dream of space travel was first stirred by Verne's *From the Earth to the Moon*. And scores of others—engineers, scientists, and explorers—have attested to early influence by Verne's works that later inspired their careers of invention, exploration, and discovery.

Many of Verne's stories continue to have lasting appeal, not only because some of his many prophesies have yet to be realized, but also because he was a superb storyteller.

Robert Louis Stevenson:
Literary Great, Considered a Chief by Samoans

Robert Louis Stevenson (1850-1894), born in Edinburgh, Scotland, is best remembered for such romantic adventure stories as *Treasure Island* (1881), *Kidnapped* (1886), and *The Master of Ballantrae* (1889). But in remote Samoa, where the British novelist, poet, and essayist spent the last four years of his life, he was regarded by the Samoan natives as their chief.

Handicapped from youth by his delicate health, Stevenson struggled all his life against tuberculosis. His fragile health forced many changes in his life and literary development, though he enjoyed a long period of health and vigor after settling on Samoa in 1890.

Stevenson was the son and grandson of engineers, but because of his fragile health, took up law at the University of Edinburgh. He never practiced; instead, he turned to writing, an activity in which he had found great delight since he was first published at the age of fifteen.

Stevenson married an American woman, Mrs. Fannie Osbourne, in 1880, and traveled widely in the United States during the 1880's before leaving for the South Pacific in 1889. He first visited Samoa on Christmas Day in 1889 and, after travels throughout the area, settled in Samoa in 1890 at Vailima.

Taking up residence in a wood frame house 500 feet above the Pacific, he developed a keen understanding of the land and the native people. In 1892, he wrote a book, *A Footnote to History: Eight Years of Trouble in Samoa*, designed to win British sympathy for his native friends.

Stevenson was given by the Samoan natives the name Tusitala, which in their language translated to "teller of tales." When he died in 1894, sixty Samoan natives carried his body to the summit of the precipitous peak of Vaea, where he was buried "under the wide and starry sky" he had described in his famous "Requiem," with the Pacific Ocean at his feet below.

Toward the end of the 19th century, the collected works of Robert Louis Stevenson were published in twenty-eight volumes as the Edinburgh Collection. Two Stevenson classics, *Treasure Island* and *A Child's Garden of Verses*, are both included in Hackett and Burke's *Eighty Years of Best Sellers* (1977) as books published in America before 1895 that sold over a million copies.

Noah Webster:
The Man Behind the Original Webster Dictionaries

Although more than one hundred dictionaries of various types call themselves "Webster's" or "Webster," the original Webster dictionaries were all the creation of one man—Noah Webster (1758-1843).

Webster, son of a Connecticut Colony farmer near Hartford, compiled his first word-oriented book—a speller—while employed as a $10 a month high school teacher in Goshen, New York. He was twenty-four at the time.

After showing his speller manuscript to various college professors for suggestions, he had it published in 1783. Having graduated from Yale, he used the title for it suggested by the Yale president: *A Grammatical Institute for the English Language* (with an 18-word long subtitle). This title lasted only through the early editions, after which it was retitled *The American Spelling Book*.

The speller sold for about 30¢ in a blue cover and eventually became known as the *Blue-Backed Speller*. Webster's average royalty was about half a cent on each copy sold. The book went on to become a school standard; in the century after initial publication, sales reached 60 million copies. *A Grammar*, published separately in 1784, a year after the *Speller*, was combined with the *Speller* in later editions so that the two were published as a single volume.

Some years later when he was nearing the age of fifty and after numerous additional books which Webster published at his own expense, he published his *Compendious Dictionary of the English Language* in 1806. Webster's *Compendious Dictionary* was built on the various dictionaries that had been published earlier and in other countries. But for his dictionary, Webster wrestled with every word until he could define it in the American language.

Webster's *Compendious Dictionary* was only a beginning; his most famous dictionary was yet to come. Approaching the age of seventy in 1828, after nearly 20 years of preparation, Webster published his *American Dictionary of the English Language* in two volumes. It quickly became the recognized American standard for word meanings.

Webster had conducted part of his research for his monumental dictionary in 1824 at the royal library in Paris, the Bibliotheque de Roi. He'd traveled there on borrowed funds in order to look up scientific terms that had no American equivalents. He then traveled to the library of Cambridge University in England where he continued his research and completed his dictionary early in 1825. He later wrote, as follows, about the day his dictionary was completed:

> When I had come to the last word I was seized with a trembling which made it difficult to proceed. However, I summoned up strength to finish the last word, and then, walking about the room a few minutes, I recovered.

Rechecking his manuscript for mistakes required three assistants and took a year and a half. When finally completed, the printing began on May 8, 1827, as Webster neared his sixty-ninth birthday.

Financing for the 70,000 word dictionary had not come easily. After a six month search, Webster had found a man in New York, Samuel Converse, who had agreed to put up the money required for the monumental task of checking the manuscript and producing 2,500 sets of the two-volume work. Once the 2,500 sets of Webster's *American Dictionary* were sold, no additional copies were available for many years. The original publisher had gone bankrupt and ceased operations.

Finally, in 1840, Webster himself sponsored the next edition by mortgaging his home in New Haven to pay for it. The venture eventually paid for itself and Webster was able to continue living in that home until 1843 where he died peacefully just five months short of his eighty-fifth birthday. Subsequent editions of his dictionary went on to sell 300,000 copies annually.

Henry Holt:
First American Publisher Not Tied to Printer or Bookseller

As with many old-line American publishing establishments, Henry Holt & Company has had many changes of both name, ownership, and management since it was founded in 1866—a little over six months after the end of the Civil War—by a 26-year-old Yale graduate, Henry Holt. It was his $11,000 that provided the entire capital for the fledgling publishing establishment though he took on a partner for a time who provided, in lieu of cash, practical experience in book publishing and bookselling.

What made the founding of the New York City book publishing company (initially called Leypoldt & Holt to pacify his German immigrant partner

Frederick Leypoldt, from Stuttgart) special was that it changed the face of American book publishing for the first time since books were first printed in this country. Until the end of the Civil War, printing, publishing, and book-selling were intertwined. Prior to January 1, 1866—the date the Holt publishing firm was established—every publishing enterprise in America was affiliated either with a printer, a bookseller, or a combination of both.

Henry Holt, the founder (1840-1926), endeavored to conduct his business as though it was a profession up until his retirement in 1915 at the age of seventy-five. Even after his retirement he maintained a firm grip on the company's affairs until his death at the age of eighty-six in 1926.

In the second half of this century, Holt was merged with Rinehart & Company and the John C. Winston Co. in 1959 to become Holt, Rinehart and Winston. Subsequently, it became affiliated with CBS publishing operations until 1985 when it was sold to a German publisher (Verlagsgruppe Georg von Holtzbrinck) and the operation was again allowed to resume its former name, Henry Holt and Company, under which it continues to operate.

Washington and the Cherry Tree — The Truth at Last!

One of the earliest biographers of George Washington was Mason Locke Weems, a book-peddling parson who traded his preaching duties in various Episcopal parishes in his native Maryland to become a traveling book salesman, writer, editor, and publisher.

When Washington died in 1799 at the age of 67, Weems contacted his printing/publishing associate, Mathew Carey in Philadelphia, and offered him what turned out to be a piece of historical fiction: *A History of the Life, Death, Virtues and Exploits of General George Washington*. The widely-accepted book, mixing historic fact with fiction, was published in 1800 and went through numerous editions and reprintings, some of them long after Weems's death in 1825.

"This is the biography," said John Winterich in *Early American Books and Printing*, "which gave to the world the whole-cloth fiction of the cherry tree episode; it is significant to note that this incident did not appear until the fifth (1910) edition."

See also Chapter 8 — First Use of a Publisher's Blurb in an American Book.

The Inventing and Selling of Sherlock Holmes

As a young doctor, Arthur Conan Doyle (1859-1930) set up practice in an eight-room brick house on a busy street in Bush Villas, Elm Grove, Southsea, in England. His yearly rent, including taxes, was 50 pounds a year. As his income from his practice grew to 300 pounds a year, Doyle also began to enjoy some income from his writing. Soon, writing stories for magazines became more important to him than his medical practice.

His first Sherlock Holmes effort was based on two fictional characters he'd invented. Holmes was modeled after a doctor whose outpatient clerk he had been in medical school. He recalled how the doctor's sharp eyes and acute observation took in telling details at a glance that enabled him to make startlingly accurate deductions from what he'd seen. His Watson was taken from a Doctor James Watson that Doyle knew.

Doyle sent his first Holmes adventure, *A Study in Scarlet*, to one of the magazines he had sold to earlier, *The Cornbill*. It was returned after a month, probably because the story was too long for a short story and too short to be a book. When Doyle sent *A Study In Scarlet* to another publisher, it again came back unread. A third publisher finally said that while the story was not publishable immediately, if Doyle would accept 25 pounds for the complete rights, he would hold it for a year and then publish it as one of a collection of stories. Doyle agreed, and the public met Sherlock Holmes for the first time in *Beeton's Christmas Annual* for 1887.

In 1900, thirteen years after Arthur Conan Doyle's detective character first appeared in print, Sherlock Holmes made his first appearance in a film. Since that time, more than 100 actors have portrayed Holmes, more than for any other fictional character.

Origin of the Detective Mystery Novel

The first detective mystery novel was *Murders in the Rue Morgue* by Edgar Allen Poe, a Boston-born literary genius who died of alcoholism. While Poe is recognized as the father of the detective mystery, a 26-year-old British physician by the name of Conan Doyle is credited with doing the most to further the concept.

In 1878, forty-six years after the appearance of *Rue Morgue*, Doyle wrote *A Study in Scarlet*, his first Sherlock Holmes novel. It was Doyle's Sherlock Holmes works that undoubtedly made the largest contribution to the growth of and interest in detective mysteries.

The results of a worldwide poll, announced in the November 21, 1986, issue of *Publishers Weekly*, indicated that 62% of those sampled worldwide said they had read a detective mystery.

Birth of *Grimms' Fairy Tales* and the Science of Folklore

The brothers Grimm, Jacob Ludwig (1785-1863) and Wilhelm Carl (1786-1859), were sons of a distinguished German lawyer in the city of Hanau, Germany. They, at first, collected folk songs and tales, mainly oral, for their friends. In 1812-14, they had them published as *Kinder und Haus-Märchen*, which is customarily translated as *Grimms' Fairy Tales*.

The two hundred stories in the collection gained wide popularity, first in Germany and then worldwide, ultimately undergoing translations in seventy languages. *Grimms' Fairy Tales* became a model for the collecting of folk tales everywhere and are credited in the *Encyclopedia Britannica* with "initiating the science of folklore."

The Advent of the Dime Novel

The birth of the dime novel began on June 7, 1860, when this historic advertisement appeared in the *New York Tribune*:

BOOKS FOR THE MILLION!

A Dollar Book for a Dime ! !

128 pages complete, only Ten Cents ! !

BEADLE'S DIME NOVELS NO. 1

MALAESKA:

Indian Wife of the White Hunter

by Mrs. Ann S. Stephens

128 pages, 12 mo. Ready Saturday Morning, June 9

The publishers of the dime novel were three men who roomed together in Brooklyn. Their firm was advertised as Irwin P. Beadle & Co., and their publications were known as Beadle's Dime Novels. Such was the popularity of the dime novel, that by 1861 they were also being sold in the London bookshops under the heading Beadle's American Library.

The first dime novel was a reprint from a magazine, but soon the publishers were buying original manuscripts. Authors were paid $75 to $150 per manuscript. Books were heavily into Western U.S. expansion with such heroes as Buffalo Bill and Kit Carson as well as such fictional heroes as Deadwood Dick, Gospel George, and Darky Dan (the colored detective).

Dime novels were 4½" x 6½" and usually ran 96 pages, with orange colored paper covers of approximately the same paper weight as the text.

The dime novel attracted many imitators and with the outbreak of the Civil War, they became extremely popular with the men in uniform. As one magazine put it, they were "the soldier's solace and comfort ... contributed in a wonderful degree, to ameliorate the trials and sufferings of army life."

By the end of the Civil War, more than four million dime novels had been published. The dime novel continued to be published into the 20th century, disappearing finally in 1937, doomed by the emergence of the smaller, cheaper Little Blue Books series.

Historic Novel That Sparked U.S. Anti-Slavery Movement

An historic novel that was instrumental in awakening national resistance to slavery was published in 1852. It was Harriet Beecher Stowe's *Uncle Tom's Cabin*, the first American novel to sell over one million copies.

Stowe's highly popular anti-slavery novel showed great understanding of both slaves and slaveholders, both Yankee and Southern, and revealed the denigrating effects of slavery on both. Slaveholders were quick to condemn Stowe's book as unfair since the story centers on a noble-minded Christian slave, Uncle Tom, who is sold to the degenerate planter, Simon Lagree.

Uncle Tom's Cabin sold 300,000 copies in its first year of publication in the United States and well over a million copies with succeeding years. In England, the book was quickly reprinted and sold one million copies in its first year of publication.

According to a sales poster for the book, issued in the 1850's and currently in the possession of the New York Historical Society, the book sold for 37.5¢ in a popular one-volume edition, 50¢ in a one-volume German edition, $1.50 in a two-volume cloth edition, and $2.50 to $5.00 for the one-volume illustrated edition with 153 engravings.

Stowe (1811-1896), a native of Litchfield, Connecticut, moved to and settled in Cincinnati, Ohio, a town torn with strong abolitionist conflicts. Stowe, herself, had helped a runaway slave before writing her book and worked vigorously for the anti-slavery effort. She married Professor Calvin Ellis Stowe when she was twenty-four and had seven children. To augment her husband's modest salary, she wrote numerous other novels.

Origin and Historic Development of Bartlett's Quotations

In 1836, a 16-year-old public school graduate obtained a job at the University Bookstore just around the corner from Harvard College in Cambridge, Massachusetts. By 1849, the bookstore employee had read virtually every book in the store, so he decided to use his life savings to become the store's proprietor. His name was John Bartlett.

Bartlett maintained a reading room at the back of his book shop, which was frequented mainly by Harvard students and professors. When they needed the source of a familiar phrase or quotation, they turned to Bartlett, who was usually able to provide the desired information.

In 1855, Bartlett assembled and published a volume of familiar quotations. A 258-page paperback which contained quotations from 169 different sources, the 1,000-copy first edition bore the title *Familiar Quotations*.

The work, which Bartlett lived to edit through its ninth edition in 1891, continues to be a worldwide perennial bestseller. The 15th edition, the 125th Anniversary Edition, was published in 1980 with 1,540 pages and 2,500 author sources—400 more than the earlier edition. In contrast to the original 1849 edition's 258 pages with 36 pages of index, the current edition consists of 936 text pages containing 22,500 quotes as well as 604 index pages (nearly 40% of the total pages).

In 1836, when Bartlett published his first thin little book of familiar quotations, one third of the entries were from the Bible and the balance from

English poetry. In the current edition, one of the 2,500 new quotes is from astronaut Neal Armstrong while standing on the moon: "That's one small step for mankind and one giant leap for mankind."

Who's Who: Its Origin and Growth as an International Reference Format

Directories providing information about famous people have been published on a continuing basis since the mid-eighteenth century. However, the world's foremost, best-known, and longest-established directory of the famous is England's *Who's Who*, first published by Alfred Head Baily in 1849.

The original 1849 *Who's Who* was a small book that contained a group of lists that included members of the Houses of Parliament, bishops, and so forth. For members of Parliament, the listing also included age, political affiliation, and constituency. For all other listees, no biographical information was provided.

This simple list format remained unchanged in 48 editions through 1896. In that year, the directory was sold by the Baily Brothers to the publishing firm of A. and C. Black. The new owners of *Who's Who* had also owned the *Encyclopedia Britannica* since 1827 and had published the seventh, eighth, and ninth editions of that work. Black also published scholarly works and fiction, including the novels of Sir Walter Scott.

When *Who's Who* was taken over by its new owners, Adam Black decided to change the scope and format of the book. Where previously *Who's Who* had been a handbook of the titled and official classes, henceforth it would include all the most prominent persons in the kingdom.

Black further decided that those who were to be featured in the directory, selected for their reference merit, would themselves supply the information for the entries by filling out a specially-worded questionnaire which would accompany each invitation. The first new edition in revised and expanded format was *Who's Who 1897*. A. and C. Black described the new edition in its fall 1896 catalog thus: "Entirely remodelled ... Contains a complete list of all who have the right to bear any British title; also biographies, mostly autobiographies, of all the prominent persons in the United Kingdom."

The remodelled edition appeared in the forty-ninth year of issue and contained 4,000 biographies. This British work has been continuously expanded over the years. It currently also includes many American and foreign personalities of particular interest to the British public.

Origin of the First American Who's Who

In 1899, two years after the appearance of the remodelled *Who's Who* in England, Albert Nelson Marquis published the first *Who's Who in America*, which Marquis admitted he copied and modeled after the British edition. Just as the British *Who's Who* became and continues to remain the reference book of choice about famous British subjects, so, too, the U.S. version, *Who's Who in America*, has done an equally competent job in presenting a collection of the most famous Americans. Neither the British nor the American versions has ever had any serious competition.

Today, *Books In Print*, which contains every American book in print, lists about 250 titles of various types that start with "Who's Who." There are numerous other regional and local Who's Whos that are not included, nor are the numerous foreign language Who's Whos such as *Wer Ist Wer?* in Germany and *Qui è?* in Italy.

Who's Who in America continues to be published by Marquis Who's Who, now a division of Reed Reference Publishing of New Providence, New Jersey. The three-volume 50th edition (1996) lists over 100,000 biographies in 5,258 pages, contrasted with the 8,602 Americans featured in the first 1899 edition.

How Mark Twain Typed His Way to an Historical Publishing First

In 1875, when Mark Twain (Samuel Langhorne Clemens) turned to his Remington typewriter to type the manuscript for *The Adventures of Tom Sawyer*, he inaugurated a new era in book publishing history. His was the first book manuscript ever prepared on a typewriter. Twain's achievement was duplicated later that same year when he also used his Remington to type the manuscript of *Life on the Mississippi*.

The Remington keyboard apparently posed little difficulty for the 40-year-old author of *Tom Sawyer*. At the age of thirteen, he left school and became a full-time apprentice of a Hannibal, Missouri, printer. By the age of eighteen, he was employed as a journeyman printer in St. Louis and at various times in succeeding years earned a living as a typesetter.

The "qwerty" keyboard now used on most typewriters and computers was introduced on the Remington typewriter on September 12, 1873. Even with the advent of the computer age, Remington's "qwerty" keyboard remains the originating manuscript medium for virtually every book published.

Sarah Josepha Hale: A 19th Century Author Who Shaped Her Time

Among the earliest nineteenth-century American woman authors was Sarah Josepha Hale. Widowed at the age of thirty-two with five children to support, she made a living as an author and editor. Harper published her *Keeping House and Housekeeping* in 1845 and *Boarding Out; or, Domestic Life*, a companion volume, in 1846. In addition, she edited various ladies magazines for over forty years.

Among her other accomplishment was a poem she wrote for the pleasure of her children about a girl named Mary, whose pet lamb followed her to school one day. That poem, "Mary Had a Little Lamb," was published in her book, *Poems for Our Children*, in 1830. She also persuaded President Lincoln to make Thanksgiving Day a national holiday. In addition, she helped to establish Vassar College. She died in 1879 at the age of ninety.

Early Feminist Author Also the First Book Review Editor

Sarah Margaret Fuller (1810-1850), one of America's earliest feminist authors, was also America's first newspaper book review editor. An ardent feminist, her *Women in the Nineteenth Century*, published in 1845, treated feminism in its economic, intellectual, political, and sexual contexts. In 1844, the very outspoken Cambridge, Massachusetts, native was summoned to New York by the founding editor of *The New York Tribune*, Horace Greeley, who admired her outspokenness and earlier literary efforts.

She became *The New York Tribune*'s (and nation's) first book review editor—a position she held for two years. So strong was her personality and impact on her times that she appeared as a recognizable character in at least two books, Lowell's *Fable for Critics*, and Hawthorne's *Blithdale Romance*. She drowned in a tragic boating accident off the south shore of Long Island, New York, at the age of forty.

The Dictionary That Took 117 Years to Complete

Perhaps the book that took the longest to produce was a German dictionary started in 1854 by the brothers Jacob and Wilhelm Grimm (of *Grimm's Fairy Tales*). When finally completed in 1971, the *Deutsches Wörtebuch* consisted of 34,519 pages in thirty-three volumes.

This greatest work of the Grimm brothers was designed to present all the German words found in the literature over a 300-year period, together with their historical variants, their etymology, their semantic development, and their use in specialized and everyday language, illustrated by quotations of idioms and proverbs.

The Grimm brothers lived only to complete four volumes. Their labor of scholarship was continued for more than another century by other German philologists until its completion.

"Civil Disobedience": Night in Jail Sparked Famous Essay

Henry Thoreau's most famous essay "Civil Disobedience," which in his collected works was to win him international fame and inspire world leaders, was sparked by his refusal to pay a small poll tax.

It was the summer of 1846. Thoreau was living in a shack he'd built at Walden Pond, and he came into nearby Concord one afternoon to pick up a pair of shoes he had left to be repaired. He was promptly arrested by the local constable, an old friend, for his refusal to pay his overdue poll taxes.

The U.S. war against Mexico was then in progress, and Thoreau had argued his refusal to pay the tax was on moral grounds—that he refused to support a government that aided slavery and waged war.

Thoreau was released after spending one night in jail (his aunt had paid the tax). But the episode is said to have been the departure point for what was to become his greatest work—his manifesto on civil disobedience, that was to inspire nationalist leaders the world over.

The famed essay was originally published in a periodical under the title, "Resistance to Civil Government," but was later reissued in 1849 as "Civil Disobedience" in Thoreau's collected works. The two main themes of the essay were contempt for the existing government and the supreme importance of the individual's own moral values.

First Comprehensive Encyclopedia in America:
A Retitled *Britannica*

The first comprehensive encyclopedia produced in the United States was an 18-volume work titled, *Encyclopaedia; or a Dictionary of Arts, Sciences, and Miscellaneous Literature*. It was produced and published a volume at a time beginning in 1790 with completion in 1798 by the Philadelphia printer Thomas Dobson. The encyclopedia was a reproduction of the third edition of the *Encyclopedia Britannica*, originally published in Edinburgh between 1788 and 1797.

First Noteworthy American Encyclopedia:
The *Encyclopaedia Americana*

The first noteworthy encyclopedia of American origin was the *Encyclopaedia Americana*, a 13-volume work published in Philadelphia between the years 1829 and 1833.

It was edited by Francis Lieber (1800-1872), who had immigrated to the United States from Germany in 1827 and became a U.S. citizen shortly thereafter. Lieber, who settled in Boston, spent five years editing the encyclopedia. He later became a professor of history and political economy at South Carolina College in Columbia, South Carolina.

During the Civil War, at the request of President Lincoln, Lieber prepared the important *Code of War for the Government of the Armies of the United States in the Field*. As a youth, Lieber had fought in the Battle of Waterloo and in the Greek War of Independence against the Turks.

Melville, Author of Greatest American Novel, Died in Near Obscurity

Herman Melville's masterpiece, *Moby Dick*, is now widely recognized as one of America's greatest novels. It has been required reading for generations of students. Yet, when published in 1851, *Moby Dick: or the Whale*, was widely misunderstood, sold slowly, and attracted poor to devastating reviews, as the following excerpts indicate:

"...contains some wild descriptions of a dreariness such as we do not remember in marine literature." — *The Athanaeum*

"...raving and rhapsodizing in chapter after chapter ... sheer moonstruck lunacy. " — *London Morning Chronicle*

"...sad stuff, dull and dreary, or ridiculous." — *Southern Quarterly Review*

"The Judgement Day will hold him liable for not turning his talents to better account." — *The Independent* (New York City)

Melville portrayed seafaring life and character with vigor, based on personal experiences as cabin boy and crew member on a number of sailing vessels. Yet readers were confused by the book's symbolism and failed to grasp Melville's complex vision of man's struggle against the metaphysical incongruities of life and his inevitable defeat.

Over his lifetime, Melville's income from *Moby Dick* was only $1,260.00. Although the author of half a dozen other books, he was dependent on handouts and an inheritance from his wife's family for support. In 1866, at the age of forty-seven, Melville took a job as a customs inspector on the New York City docks and lived in the city in near obscurity for the last twenty-five years of his life until his death on September 28, 1891.

The year 1866 was also notable as the year Melville had a book of poetry published. The collection of poems about the Civil War sold fewer than 500 copies. In 1995, DeCapo Press reissued a facsimile edition of this book.

Rediscovered in the 1920's, Melville now ranks as one of America's greatest writers. An up-to-date biography of Melville, reflecting new information from a find of Melville letters in the mid-1980's, is due in December 1996 from Johns Hopkins University Press. The biography is by Hershel Parker, an English professor at the University of Delaware.

First Nursing Textbook in America

In 1878, eighteen years before the formation of the American Nursing Association, J.B. Lippincott of Philadelphia published the first nursing textbook in America, *A Handbook of Nursing*. Assembled under the direction of the Connecticut Training School for Nurses, it was continued through many editions and firmly established Lippincott as the pre-eminent publisher in the nursing field.

Lippincott followed in 1900 by founding the first journal in America devoted exclusively to the interests of nurses, the *American Journal of Nursing*. It continues today, in other hands, to serve 275,000 nurses every month.

Irving's Sketch Book:
America's First Great Book of Comic Literature

Considered the first great book of comic literature by an American, *A History of New York from the Beginning of the World to the End of the Dutch Dynasty*, a satire by Diedrich Knickerbocker, was actually written by 26-year-old Washington Irving in 1809. Originally intended as a parody on a pretentious guidebook of New York City written by Dr. Samuel Mitchell, the idea was expanded as Irving wrote. The parody evolved into a great book of comic literature, eventually to be known as *Diedrich Knickerbocker's History of New York*.

Irving (1783-1859) was the father of many literary firsts. He was considered "the first American man of letters," "inventor of the short story," and "father of American comic literature."

His 1819-20 work *The Sketch Book of Geoffrey Crayon, Gent*, is considered Irving's most successful book. It included the short story, "Rip Van Winkle, Legend of Sleepy Hollow," and other sketches, mostly of English life. Dealing with both English and American themes, *The Sketch Book* achieved great success on both sides of the Atlantic. It is included in the 1977 reference *Eighty Years of Best Sellers* as one of the early American books that sold a million or more copies.

Washington Irving:
America's First Great Man of Literature

Washington Irving was born in New York City on April 3, 1783, just five days before the signing of the treaty that ended the American revolution and seven years of war with England. Irving's mother, Sarah, named her infant son after the victorious general.

Six years later in 1889, when Washington became the first president and was in New York, the new nation's first capital, he was spied in a shop by Irving's Scottish nurse while walking six-year-old Irving down Broadway. She dashed into the shop and managed to tell the president that the child with her was named after him. Washington patted young Irving and gave him his blessing. By coincidence, in the last five years of Washington Irving's life, he had published *The Life of George Washington*, a project on which he had devoted some thirty years.

Few American writers lived more colorful lives than Washington Irving. The son of a New York City merchant and the youngest of eight living children, he was on intimate terms with virtually every famous person of his time including Sir Walter Scott, Charles Dickens, Henry Wadsworth Longfellow, Edgar Allan Poe, and William Makepeace Thackeray. As an American diplomat in Europe, Irving moved freely in the court circles of England, Germany, and Spain. He was on good terms with six United States presidents and a dozen kings and queens.

He is best remembered for his contributions to American folklore, including the stories of Diedrich Knickerbocker, Ichabod Crane, and Rip Van Winkle. From Diedrich Knickerbocker, the fictitious author of one of Irving's works, came the dictionary word "Knickerbocker" as either a native of New York or a descendent of the Dutch settlers of New York.

Vidal's *Burr*:
Early American History Authenticated, Then Told as Novel

Gore Vidal's 1973 novel, *Burr*, deals with the life of Aaron Burr, third vice president of the United States under Thomas Jefferson (1801-1805), and the early years of the American republic. Burr is frequently recalled in history books for his 1804 duel in which he killed his political rival, Alexander Hamilton.

Vidal chose Burr as the subject for his historical novel for an unusual reason: Vidal's stepfather was a descendent of the Burr family. So keen was Vidal's interest in Burr, that when an Aaron Burr collection came on the market some years before the book, Vidal purchased several hundred items from it and used them for his research. Subsequently, he devoted time and research to Burr and his time at the New York Historical Society Library. Then, even though Vidal's work was a novel, his publisher engaged two historical researchers to recheck the facts in the Vidal manuscript.

The effect of the *Burr* novel, Vidal wrote in a Book-of-the-Month Club newsletter in 1973, was that "readers (could) learn in a few hours just about everything it took me twenty years to discover about the first half century of the American republic."

Told that history was the least popular of fifty subjects tested in a national high school poll, Vidal was asked why he wrote about things most Americans are not interested in. Vidal replied, "I write to try to make these things interesting...I wish that at twenty I had *Burr* to read. Instead I had to write it. That was the hardest work I have ever done."

Evolution of University Press Publishing in America

While the first press in North America was housed at Harvard College in the seventeenth century, the university press as an institution did not emerge in the United States until 1869, nearly four centuries after the founding of the world's first university press at Oxford in 1478. America's first university presses were established at Cornell in 1869, John Hopkins in 1878, and Chicago in 1891. In their early years, the mission of the university press was to fill the printing needs of the parent university. Today, there are some more than eighty university presses in America, the largest being at the University of California, with the University of Chicago second, and Harvard third.

Over time, the university press has evolved into a modern, widely diversified publishing operation in which it will sometimes compete with a commercial press for books on non-academic subjects. Similarly, the first college press at Harvard did not turn inward for its publishing effort but, rather, devoted itself to such regional needs as psalm books, Latin broadsides, catalogs, almanacs, and a Bible.

Most Prominent Literary Figure of the 19th Century

Abraham Lincoln (1809-1865), the 16th president of the United States, figures more frequently in literature than any other individual who lived in the 19th century. No one knows how many books have been written about Lincoln but, according to an article in the October 22, 1995, *New York Times*, one prominent book collector estimates that there have been more than 7,000 such books.

Most Widely-Used Text in the 19th Century

It is believed that 60 million copies[2] of the 1879 edition of *The McGuffey Reader* were distributed to public schools in the United States. Published by Van Antwerp Bragg and Company, the *McGuffey* book originated with educator William Holmes McGuffey (1800-1873), who combined reading lessons with moralistic teachings to create the most widely-used textbook in the 19th century.

Chapter 3C

Book Publishing Origins, Firsts, and Curiosities in the 18th Century

---

First Novel Printed in America Bore B. Franklin Imprint

In 1740, Samuel Richardson (1689-1761), the well-known British author and writer, wrote a novel, *Pamela, or Virtue Rewarded*. The long story, told in letters, described how a virtuous English servant girl repelled the dishonorable advances of her master, reformed him, and ultimately married him. This first novel was extremely popular and thus gave rise to a number of satirical parodies.

In 1744, the Philadelphia printer and publisher—considered the most prominent printer in the colonies and the official printer of Pennsylvania, New Jersey, and Delaware—published the first American edition of Richardson's *Pamela* under the B. Franklin imprint at a price of six shillings. Not only was this the first American printing of a novel, but the British edition is usually regarded as the first real English novel, forging a path for the many others to follow.

First American Novel, Scandal-Tinged, Is Suppressed After Short Life

The first novel of American origin published in the United States was William Hill Brown's *The Power of Sympathy or the Triumph of Nature, Founded in Truth*. For the Boston publisher, Isaiah Thomas & Co., the 1789 novel was a highly profitable, though short-lived work. The reason: an episode in the book reflected a scandal involving Perez Morton and his sister-in-law, Frances Theodora Apthorp.

The story has been authenticated that *The Power of Sympathy* actually was written by Sarah Wentworth Morton, a neighbor of William Hill Brown, and that the two families involved—the Mortons and the Apthorps—with the author's consent, bought up all the copies from the publisher and suppressed the book.

Origin of America's First Bestseller: The Call to Freedom

Under the sponsorship of Benjamin Franklin, Thomas Paine (1737-1809) emigrated from England to America in 1774. Shortly after his arrival, he took a job as editor of Robert Aitken's periodical, *The Pennsylvania Magazine: or, American Monthly Museum.*

Paine was known to write his best when inspired by several glasses of brandy. Under this inspiration Paine wrote with such a poetic fervor that his impassioned words were long remembered and quoted.

In January 1776, while still editing Aitken's magazine, Paine had published under the imprint of Robert Bell, his work *Common Sense*, which presented a persuasive argument for colonial America's independence from England. With the publication of *Common Sense*, often attributed to Benjamin Franklin, Paine established his reputation as a cogent penman of the American Revolution.

Paine's *Common Sense* was undoubtedly the first American bestseller. In all, about 400,000 copies were sold, mostly in editions of about 2,000 each. More than 100,000 copies were sold in the first two months.

Common Sense was reprinted with such zeal that virtually every literate inhabitant of the Colonies read it and most illiterates at least knew it. *Common Sense* enjoyed wide distribution in England as well and was quickly translated into several foreign languages, thus winning sympathizers for the Revolution and, ultimately, complete freedom for the United States.

History recognizes Paine as an American patriot and an important crusader for democratic rights, yet he died in poverty, denounced as a radical, a drunkard, and an atheist. Denied burial in consecrated ground, Paine's remains were lost while being taken to England for reburial.

Origin of First Complete Bible
in English Printed in North America

A patriot of the American Revolution, Robert Aitken was born in Scotland in 1734, later settled in Philadelphia, and in 1771 established a business in Philadelphia as a bookseller and bookbinder. In 1773, the year of the Boston Tea Party, he added book and magazine publishing to his business activities and quickly established a reputation as a pioneer among early American printers and publishers.

When the Continental Congress moved to import 20,000 Bibles, Aitken was stirred into action. In 1777, the year the Continental Congress adopted a flag with stars and stripes, Aitken published a *New Testament*, which went into four editions in four years.

In 1782, with his completion of an *Old Testament*, he published America's first complete Bible, containing both Testaments in English. The Aitken Bible consisted of 353 pages without pagination and was approximately 7¾ inches tall. Referred to as "the Bible of the American Revolution," the Aitken Bible was also described as chunky, unlovely, and too nearly cubic to fit into the pocket of any piece of clothing.

Aitken died in 1802 but his press was continued for many years by his daughter, Jane.

Origin of First Encyclopedia in English

The first alphabetical encyclopedia in the English language was published in 1704 as *Lexicon Technicum, or an Universal English Dictionary of Arts and Sciences*. Its pages were not numbered.

A second printing was made in 1706. In 1710, a second volume was added in which the major portion consisted of mathematical and astronomical tables. It included an entry on acids by Sir Isaac Newton. A fifth and final edition was published in 1736.

Origin of the *Encyclopedia Britannica*

The *Encyclopedia Britannica* is the oldest and largest continuously published English language general encyclopedia in existence. Its founders were three Scotsman from Edinburgh, Andrew Bell (1726-1809), Colin Macfarquhar (1745-1793), and William Smellie (1740-1795).

The original work was published in three volumes at the printing establishment of Macfarquhar on Nicolson Street in Edinburgh, two volumes being made available in 1768, and the third in 1771. All three volumes were placed on sale at the premises of the printing establishment.

The first edition consisted of 2,670 pages, along with 160 copperplates engraved by Bell. The title page of the original edition bore this imprint:

Encyclopedia Britannica: or a
Dictionary of the Arts and Sciences
Compiled Upon a New Plan in Which
The Different Sciences and Arts are digested
into distinct Treatises and Systems and
The Various Technical Terms, etc., are explained
as they occur in the order of the alphabet

The founding trio's design called for an encyclopedia covering about forty-five principal subjects, supported by another thirty lengthy articles. The whole was to be in one alphabetical sequence, interspersed with numerous brief entries and enhanced by references. Principal articles, such as medical subjects, ran over a hundred pages and included highly practical topics such as beekeeping, horsemanship, brewing, curing baldness, and midwifery.

While the first edition title page referred to the three founders only as "a Society of Gentlemen in Scotland," their capabilities were quite varied. Smellie was a distinguished natural historian and a master printer. Macfarquhar was a printer and owner of the print shop where the encyclopedia was printed. Bell was a highly-regarded engraver who did all 160 copper-plate engravings for the first edition. He lived forty-one years beyond the publication of the first edition and engraved the plates for the second and third editions as well.

Bell and Macfarquhar were equal partners in the encyclopedia. Upon Macfarquhar's death in 1793, Bell became the sole proprietor. Bell's arrangement with Smellie was never known, but Smellie never participated in the encyclopedia's ownership.

Over the next 200 years, the encyclopedia went through many changes of hands and underwent many innovations. A highlight of the *Britannica*'s history was a 225th anniversary celebration held in Chicago in early 1993 at which *Encyclopedia Britannica* president Peter Norton said *Britannica* has "shaped Western thought unlike any other institution."

The *Britannica*, now in thirty-two volumes, is updated and revised approximately 10% every year, and, since 1993, has offered an electronic index on CD-ROM with ready access to 16 million references to the current edition. It has also undergone an extensive translation program and been reworked into Chinese, Russian, Greek, Italian, and other languages.

In early 1996, the ownership of Encyclopedia Britannica, Inc. passed to an investment group led by Jacob E. Safra, a Switzerland-based financier. It had been sold by the not-for-profit Benton Foundation, which had acquired control of the encyclopedia in 1980 from Sears Roebuck & Co, whose founder, Julius Rosenwald, had acquired the *Britannica* in 1920.[1]

Origin of First Bible Printed
in European Language in North America

After the printing of the Scriptures in an Indian dialect in 1661 and 1663, no other Bible was printed in pre-Colonial America until eighty years later. In 1743, Christopher Sauer (also spelled Sower) of Germantown, Pennsylvania, printed and published a Bible in German, using the highly popular Martin Luther translation. Luther's was the first complete translation from the original Hebrew and Greek into a modern European language.

Sauer (1693-1758) was born in Ladenburg, Germany, and migrated to Germantown, Pennsylvania in 1724 with his wife and son. Shortly after trying his hand as a farmer, he established a business in 1731 dealing with imported theological treatises. He established his own printing business in 1735 and soon was operating a large and prolific press.

The German language Bible followed eight years later and remained popular with many early Americans of German extraction or familiar with the German language until the appearance of the first Bible in English issued by Robert Aitken in 1782.

An interesting sidelight to Sauer's German Bible took place in 1778. Sauer's outspoken pacifist views during the Revolution resulted in his being arrested on suspicion of treason and all of his property being confiscated. The sheets of his German Bible that he had printed in 1776, after confiscation, were converted into gun wadding by the colonial American troops and that edition became known as the "Gun-Wad Bible."

See also Chapter 6 — Origin and Growth of Papermaking in Colonial America.

The First Dictionary Printed in the U.S. and the Dynamic Printer Behind It

The first dictionary printed in the United States appeared on September 13, 1790, in Worcester, Massachusetts. It was *The Royal Standard English Dictionary; The First American Dictionary Carefully Researched and Corrected, from the Fourth British Edition.*

The dictionary was published by 41-year-old Isaiah Thomas, an American printer, publisher, and bookseller, born and raised in Boston. The American patriot had moved his printing establishment from Boston to Worcester fifteen years prior to printing the dictionary—on April 15, 1775—just three days before the Battle of Concord, (the beginning of the American Revolution), in which Thomas took part.

A multifaceted person, Thomas had been apprenticed as a printer in Boston at the age of seven. When he settled in Worcester at the age of twenty-six, he was a printer, publisher, and bookseller and owned paper-making and book-binding operations as well. Prior to leaving Boston in 1775, Thomas published *The Royal Magazine*, which contained many of the engravings of another American patriot, Paul Revere.

Origin of *Gray's Anatomy*: Bible of Medical Students

The medical publishing establishment of Lea & Febiger in Philadelphia traces its roots back to Mathew Carey, an Irish emigrant who opened his print shop at the age of twenty-four in 1785. The company, over two centuries later, is still run by Carey's descendants.

In the 1850's, with heavy competition in the literary publishing field, the printing establishment—now called Lea & Febiger—turned exclusively to medical publishing, an area in which it continues to specialize. One of its earliest medical titles was *Gray's Anatomy of the Human Body*, by Harry Gray, a 34-year-old highly-regarded English doctor whose work was simultaneously published in an English edition.

Dr. Gray (1825-1861), whose father had served King George IV from 1820 on as the King's private messenger, had lived with his family in Buckingham Palace. On leaving the King's service, the Gray family settled at 8 Wilton Street in the shadow of Buckingham Palace. It was near here, at St. George's Hospital in London, that Harry Gray completed his medical studies and practiced medicine. At the young age of twenty-five, Dr. Gray was made a fellow of the Royal Society for his already distinguished medical record.

Gray's Anatomy, when originally published in 1859, was titled *Anatomy, Descriptive and Surgical*. After its appearance, Gray prepared a second edition which he completed shortly before he died in June 1861. The second edition was published in the U.S. in 1862.

When in 1984, Lea & Febiger published the 30th American edition of *Gray's Anatomy*, it was still a top-selling reference work, with U.S. sales of over a million copies. The 30th (and current) edition has 1,676 pages and 1,367 mostly color illustrations—up from 1,466 pages for the 29th edition published in 1973. By contrast, the first edition of *Gray's Anatomy* contained 754 pages with 363 figures drawn by Dr. H. Van Dyke Carter, demonstrator of anatomy at St. George's Hospital in London. Interestingly, over 200 drawings in the current American edition are still based on Dr. Carter's original illustrations, while only 25 of Dr. Carter's illustrations have been retained by the current British edition.

Origins of Mother Goose Nursery Rhymes

In various books of nursery rhymes published in the United States, Mother Goose is pictured as a beak-nosed, sharp-chinned granny riding on the back of a flying gander. Whether a real Mother Goose ever actually existed is a matter of question as these two versions of her origin from different published sources indicate.

Mother Goose was first associated with nursery rhymes in an old collection of "the most celebrated songs and lullabies of old British nurses," titled *Mother Goose's Melody; or Sonnets for the Cradle*, of which a 1791 printed version still exists. This version was published by the successors to John Newbury (1713-1767), British publisher and bookseller, one of the first publishers of children's books.

The name Mother Goose is believed to have been derived from the subtitle of Charles Perrault's 1697 French-language book of fairy tales, *Tales of Mother Goose*, the term "Mother Goose" being a French folk expression approximating "old wives' tale."

Despite the strong historic background of the Newbury version, the legend persists in the United States that Mother Goose was an actual Boston woman, Elizabeth Goose. The wife of Isaac Goose and mother of six children and ten stepchildren, Elizabeth is reported to have made up rhymes, songs, and tales to keep her children occupied.

Because she repeated them endlessly, her son-in-law, a printer, is reported to have collected them and printed the stories under the title, *Songs for the Nursery, or Mother Goose's Melodies for Children*, in 1719. Although no copy of this 1719 book has ever been found and although the fifteenth edition of *Encyclopedia Britannica* labels the Boston Mother Goose legend as false, there is a grave of Mother Goose in Boston's Old Granary Burying Ground which continues to be a popular tourist attraction.

Book Title That Became a Medical Specialty

In 1741, Nicholas André (1658-1742), a professor of medicine at the University of Paris, wrote a book on the prevention and correction of musculoskeletal deformities of children. For the title of his book, *L'orthopédie ou l'art de prevenir et de corriger dans les enfans, les difformités du corps*, André coined the word "orthopedic" from the Greek roots *orthos* (straight) and *paedia* (rearing of children). Today that word has come to define orthopedics, the branch of medicine dealing with the preservation and restoration of function in the musculoskeletal system, particularly the joints and bones.

18th Century Book That Launched
Modern Industrial Medicine

The first book ever on industrial medicine and hygiene was *De Morbis Artificum Diatriba*, written in 1700 by Bernardino Ramazzini (1633-1717), a professor of theoretical medicine at the University of Modena in Italy. In his landmark book, Professor Ramazzini examined diseases prevalent in various occupations and provided the first synthesis of all knowledge available on occupational health. Translated into English in 1705, the book served as the basic reference on public health for more than a century.

Book Piracy: A Flourishing 18th Century Custom

Book piracy—that is, the reprinting and distribution of a book without permission of or payment to the originator or copyright owner—was a flourishing custom in the 18th century. Because competition was strong among U.S. publishers to be the first to publish important new books, publishers would often send someone to the dockside to obtain any incoming new books from England. Once a copy was obtained, they would swiftly turn out a pirated edition for American readers.

In the absence of international copyright agreements, the English authors usually received no payment from American sales of their books. A notable exception was the U.S. publisher Harper & Brothers, which paid considerable royalties to Charles Dickens and Thomas Macaulay, among others.

The 18th century's greatest example of piracy in reverse involved Harriet Beecher Stowe's *Uncle Tom's Cabin*. After its 1852 publication in the United States, 1.5 million copies rapidly appeared in England, from various publishers and at extremely modest prices.

Chapter 3D

Book Publishing Origins, Firsts, and Curiosities in the 17th Century and Earlier

First English Publisher: Introduced King Arthur Stories

William Caxton (1422-1492), the man who introduced printing to England in 1476, was also England's first book publisher. During his printing career, he produced about one hundred volumes from his shop on the grounds of Westminster Abbey in London (which was opened on September 29, 1476). Prior to setting up shop in England, Caxton had learned the art of printing in Cologne, Germany. He began his professional practice in a printing partnership in the North Sea town of Bruges, Belgium, where he turned out three books.

Paxton's London print shop was also a bookstore, where he actively sold not only his own publications, but also low-priced books in Latin and French that he imported from the Continent. As a publisher, he brought many literary masterpieces into print, including Chaucer's *Canterbury Tales*. He also personally translated into English twenty-four classic French works.

As a bookseller, Caxton catered to the tastes of the British upper classes who were able to read. He regularly published tales of chivalry and, thus, in large part, is responsible for the enduring popularity of the legend of King Arthur (which dates back to the ninth century and later appeared in medieval French literature as well as stories popular in eleventh century Wales).

In his quest for such works, Caxton came upon a manuscript left behind five years earlier by Sir Thomas Malory when he died in Newgate Prison in March, 1471. The compendious manuscript described the rise and fall of King Arthur and the fellowship of the Round Table. Since Caxton found the manuscript overlong and rambling, he edited it by tightening up Malory's language and making the manuscript more readable.

Caxton divided the lengthy work into eight tales of romance, which he published in 1485 as a continuous narrative of twenty-one books collectively known as *Le Morte D'Arthur*. Such was the popularity of Caxton's King Arthur series, that it was reissued again in 1493 by Wynkyn de Worde, another publisher. Such, also, was the fame of the Caxton edition that Thomas Malory has often been hailed as the greatest writer of the fifteenth century.

Origin of First Dictionary in the English Language

The first dictionary in the English language was created by the British lexicographer Robert Cawdrey. Published in 1604 under a lengthy title, it was generally referred to as *A Table Alphabeticall*. The 3,000 words in the dictionary were defined by Cawdrey, a schoolmaster from Oakham, England, in collaboration with his son, Thomas, a schoolmaster in London.

Most of the content in Cawdrey's work was taken from Edmund Coote's *English School-Master*, a grammar prayer book and lexicon with brief definitions that was published in 1596, and from a 1588 Latin-English dictionary by Thomas Thomas, *Dictionarium Linguae et Anglicanae*.[1]

The Cawdrey dictionary listed difficult English words and then gave their meaning and language of origin. It lacked, however, such things as an etymology, part of speech, and illustrative quotations—features developed in later dictionaries.

The 1604 edition was followed by a second in 1609, a third in 1613, and a fourth in 1617. The full title of the first dictionary in the English language was: *A Table Alphabeticall, conteyning and teaching the true writing and understanding of hard usuall English wordes, borrowed from the Hebrew, Greeke, Latine, and French &c.*

Origin of the Word and Concept of Dictionary

The word "dictionarius" was used as early as the year 1225 for a list of Latin words. However, the word was not applied to anything identifiable as a dictionary until the 16th century, when a 1538 Latin-English work by Sir Thomas Elyot was originally called *Dictionary*, but later called *Bibliotheca Eliotae*. In 1553, there was also published a small English-Latin manual with the title of *A Shorte Dictionarie for Yong Begynners*.

Origin of the Earliest Latin Dictionary

The earliest Latin dictionary was compiled sometime during the lifetime of the most learned of early Romans, Marcus Terentius Varro, who served in the Roman military with Pompey. His dictionary, titled *De lingua Latina*, was published in twenty-five volumes of which six still exist. The title in English reads: *On the Latin Language*.

Varro, one of the most learned of Romans, is known to have written about 620 books on a wide range of subjects during his ninety years of life. Writing with a great love of learning as well as a regard for Rome's history, he intended his written works to further Rome's greatness.

First Indian-English Dictionary
Created by Founder of Rhode Island

Roger Williams (1603-1683), the founder and first president of Rhode Island, is also famous for an Indian-English dictionary that he compiled to aid people's understanding of the Indians.

Williams, a pioneer of religious tolerance, arrived from England in 1631 and settled in Salem. But in 1636, he was expelled by the Massachusetts Bay Colony for his unorthodox religious views and his defense of the Indians. So, with a small band of followers, he founded the town of Providence on land purchased from the Narragansett Indians. In Providence, Williams worked at making and keeping peace with the local Indians. He learned their language and customs and, thus, earned their trust.

In 1643, Rogers took a ship to England to seek a parliamentary patent to unite the four settlements he had founded in and around Providence into a single colony, the Providence Plantations. Aboard ship en route to Southampton, England, Williams compiled the first Indian-English dictionary, for which he arranged publication later in 1643 in England.

Williams' dictionary was titled: *A Key into the Language of America or an help to the language of the natives in that part of America called New England; together with briefe observations of the customes, manners and worships, etc., of the aforesaid natives.*

Origin of the Second Most Popular Book: The Cookbook

For over 500 years, the cookbook has ranked second only to the Bible in sales and popularity.* In a single recent year, *Subject Guide to Books in Print* showed 833 new cookbook titles!

The world's first printed cookbook made its appearance just twenty-four years after the invention of printing in 1450. The book bore the title *De honesta voluptate et valetudine*, which roughly translates as *Of Honest Indulgence and Good Health.* The author was an Italian by the name of Bartolomeo Sacchi. Published in Rome in 1474, the book went through fifty-three editions in four languages during the next hundred years.[2]

---

* The Bible has always been the world's top-selling book. According to an Associated Press report (*Publishers Weekly*, October 9, 1995) 20 to 23 million Bibles are sold annually in the United States alone.

Origin of First Printed Book in the New World

Less than 50 years after the discovery of America, the craft of printing, which had yet to spread through Europe, was already being practiced in the New World. The earliest print shop in the New World opened in Mexico City in 1539 so the Spanish archbishop in Mexico could have books printed in the native languages for the use of his priests and missionaries.

The first printing office in Mexico was established by Juan Cromberger, the leading printer of Seville, Spain. Operating it as a branch of his Seville operation, he appointed as his manager and partner Juan Pablos, an Italian native of Seville skilled in the printing craft. When Cromberger died about 1540, Pablos took over and continued the printing and publishing operation under his own name.

The first book printed in the New World, according to Latin-American historians, was accomplished on a printing press operated by Pablos. The book, believed to have been titled *Escala spiritual*, was written by San Juan Climaco and translated from the Latin into Spanish.

Origin of First North American College Press and Library

At his death in September 1638, John Harvard, a bachelor Puritan minister, bequeathed his personal library of 260 books and half his estate (780 British pounds) to a seminary college "in the wilderness at Newetowne" in Massachusetts. Established two years before, the seminary was as yet unorganized. Harvard's bequest marked the founding of the first public library in America.*

The general court of the Colony Society of Massachusetts, mindful of John Harvard's generosity, ordered the just-organizing college to change its name to Harvard. It also ordered the name of the college's locale to be changed from Newtowne to Cambridge to reflect the fact that most of the Colony's leaders had been educated at Cambridge University in England.

John Harvard's death coincided with the arrival of a ship from London bearing the first printing press to reach British North America. The press had been bought in London by Reverend Jose Glover, who died en route while accompanying the press to Massachusetts. A locksmith, Stephen Daye, who had accompanied the press for the purpose of assembling it, subsequently placed the press in operation. It came under the supervision of Harvard College when its first president, Henry Dunster, married the Widow Glover.

* The Harvard Library, at the present time, ranks among the five largest libraries in the world and the largest university library in North America. Its current holdings are 12.2 million volumes, of which 5% are unduplicated anywhere else in America. They include a Gutenberg Bible, a 1623 Shakespeare first folio, a 1520 treatise by Martin Luther, and Benedict Arnold's journal of the 1775 expedition against Quebec. The Harvard Library holdings also include the papers of Louisa May Alcott, Emily Dickinson, Henry Wadsworth Longfellow, Herman Melville, Leon Trotsky, and John Updike.

The first printing press to begin publishing operations in British North America thus also became the first college press in North America. From 1638 to 1692, the press issued more than two hundred books, pamphlets, and broadsides. Known as the Glover press, it was operated by Stephen Daye with his two sons, Stephen Jr. and Matthew. Their first printed publication was a broadside, *The Freeman's Oath*; the second was Peirce's *Almanack* (noted below). Their third publication, which some histories claim to be the first book produced in British North America, was the famed *Bay Psalm Book* of 1640, of which numerous copies still exist.

Origin of the First American Almanac

The first almanac printed in British North America was produced in 1638 by Cambridge Press at Cambridge, Massachusetts, under the supervision of Harvard College. It was a triple first for the almanac: (1) It was the first book ever published in British North America; (2) It was the first college press title in North America; and (3) It was the first almanac published in North America.

Titled *An Almanack for the Year of Our Lord, 1639, Calculated for New England*, it was produced late in 1638, although the months in the almanac started with March 1639. The almanac's author was William Peirce, a noted mariner and acknowledged leader among New England's sailmasters. In the year in which Peirce was preparing his almanac, he found time to transport a company of captive Pequot Indians to the West Indies and to bring back a shipload of Negro slaves, the first slaves to reach New England. Peirce died a violent sailor's death in 1641 in the Bahamas. No copy of Peirce's almanac is known to survive.

See also Chapter 11 — Almanacs in America Since the Colonial Era.

First Bible Printed in British North America:
Eliot's Indian Bible

The first Bible printed in British North America was for a specialized audience—Algonquin Indians. *The New Testament of Our Lord and Savior Jesus Christ* was printed in 1661 in the Massachusetts dialect of the Algonquin Indian language.

The translation had been carried out by John Eliot (1604-1690), who had arrived in Boston from England thirty years earlier in the autumn of 1631 on the ship "Lyon." Eliot had been affiliated with the church in Roxbury, Massachusetts, as a teacher for most of his adult life and had mastered the native Indian dialect in the hope of using it to convert Indians to Christianity.

The paper for the 130-page Indian New Testament was imported from England. The printing, funded by an act of Parliament through the New England Company, was done in Cambridge, Massachusetts, by Samuel Green and Marmaduke Johnson. 1,500 copies were printed, of which 1,000 were reserved to be combined two years later with the printing of an Old Testament in the same Indian dialect.

With the printing of the Old Testament in 1663, the Commissioners of New England, the governing body, authorized John Ratliffe to bind Eliot's *Indian Bible* and to "take care of the binding of 200 of them strongly and as speedily as may bee with leather, or as may bee most serviceable for the Indians." With this binding assignment, Ratliffe became the first bookbinder of record in British North America. An *Eliot Indian Bible* in its original calf binding by John Ratcliff sold for $43,000 at public auction in 1966.[3]

World's Oldest Publishers in Continuous Operation

Twenty-four years after Johannes Gutenberg perfected the movable type printing press, Oxford University Press was founded in 1478. It is the world's oldest publisher in continuous operation. A close rival for the oldest publisher honor is Cambridge University Press, started in 1534.

It took Oxford University Press 418 years to "discover" America. Its American branch was launched in 1896 at 91-93 Fifth Avenue in New York City. Initially the U.S. branch sold bibles and religious tracts produced in England. Eventually, with an experienced American manager, it began manufacturing operations in the U.S. and eventually expanded its program to include non-religious works as well.

First Printed Hebrew Book: A Story of Failed Censorship

The first printed Hebrew book, a code of Jewish law, was printed in Italy in 1470, just 15 years after the appearance of the Gutenberg Bible. As was the practice at that time, the book was submitted to a censor who carefully inked out all the complimentary references to Judaism.

A copy of that first printed Hebrew book has been in the possession of the Jewish Theological Seminary in New York City for many years. During a recent check of the Seminary's rare book holdings—according to a November 1995 published report—the librarians there discovered a remarkable occurrence: The ink used by the censor in Italy in 1470 had completely faded away, and the original Hebrew text was as clear as ever.

World's Oldest Printed Book

The world's oldest printed dated book is believed to be the Chinese *Diamond Sutra*. The book was discovered in 1906 by Sir Marc Aurel Stein (1862-1943), the British archaeologist and Asiatic scholar, in a cave while traveling through the deserts of Gansu Province in China.

The *Diamond Sutra*, a Buddhist work written in Sanskrit, contains one of the sermons of Buddha. It was printed from a series of woodblocks, each reproducing an unalterable image of an entire page. The sheets were glued side-to-side and rolled into a scroll sixteen feet long. The title block shows a serene Buddha on a lotus throne guarded by angels and lions.

Origin of Science Fiction: A 160 A.D. Book

The father of science fiction writing is the Greek writer and lyricist Lucien of Samasata. The first genuine science fiction story is believed to be his *True History (Vera Historia)* written about 160 A.D. In his *True History*, author Lucien tells of being carried in his sailing ship by a whirlwind to the "great country in the air" where he encountered moonmen who differed from earthmen only in their culture.

In a later story by Lucien he made another moon visit wearing bird wings. His later story became even more interplanetary because in it he went on to Heaven where he met and displeased the inimical immortals who order Hermes to fly him home.

Lucien's *True History* is believed to have inspired Rabelais's *Voyage of Pantagruel*, Swift's *Gulliver's Travels*, and Cyrano de Bergerac's *Journey to the Moon*. Lucien's works are also said to have influenced Voltaire.

World's Highest-Priced Single Manuscript Page

Perhaps the highest price ever paid for a single page of manuscript was the $1.19 million paid in April 1996 by an anonymous American collector for a richly decorated page from *The Shahnama of Shah Tahmasp*, a 16th century Persian manuscript. The page, lavishly gilded with gold, was described in an Associated Press report as "a classic work of art [that] shows a scene from the legend of Rustam, the Persian equivalent of the Greek hero Hercules, who as famed for his strength and courage." The page was sold by Sotheby's London gallery for the British Rail Pension Fund, which bought it in the late 1970s.

The page is from a work attributed to Aqâ Mîrak, a Persian painter and manuscript illustrator who was a companion to Shah Tahmasp from 1525 to 1530. An excellent colorist, he painted in a sumptuous style. Working in the city of Herât, then part of Iran, Mîrak was a pupil of Behzad, the greatest of the Persian painters. Mîrak, in turn, was the teacher of the painter Sultan Muhammad and of Shah Qoli, a Persian painter who later worked at the court of the Ottoman sultan Süleyman. Only a small number of Mîrak's drawings and paintings have survived, which most likely accounted for the high price paid for the single manuscript page.

The *Shahnama* manuscript in its original 759 richly decorated pages included 258 miniatures that illustrated the history and legends of Persia from prehistoric times to the end of the 7th century. In 1568, Shah Tahmasp presented the manuscript to Sultan Selim II of Turkey. It remained in the Ottoman royal library until the end of the 19th century when it became part of the collection of Baron Edmond de Rothschild. The majority of the work is now divided between the Metropolitan Museum of Art in New York City and the Iranian National Collection in Tehran.

Legendary Authors and Historic Works
That Suffered Banning and Censorship

Throughout recorded history, censorship and banning have plagued some of the greatest writers and written works of history. The long list of banned works and writers include the following:*

American Heritage Dictionary
Francis Bacon
Roger Bacon
The Bible
Giovanni Boccaccio — *Decameron*
Edgar Rice Burroughs — *Tarzan*
John Calvin
Lewis Carroll — *Alice's Adventures in Wonderland*
Miguel de Cervantes
Confucius (K'ung-Fu-tzu)
Dante — *The Divine Comedy*
Desiderius Erasmus
The Brothers Grimm — *Grimm's Fairy Tales*
Homer
James Joyce — *Ulysses*
Martin Luther
Michaelangelo
Mother Goose
William Shakespeare — *The Merchant of Venus*, and others
Socrates
The Talmud
Virgil
Voltaire — *Candide*

* The last week in September is devoted to celebrating banned books, since so many of the world's finest authors and books have at one time or another been banned or censored. For more information on the Banned Books Week celebration, contact the Office for Intellectual Freedom at the American Library Association, 50 E. Huron Street, Chicago, IL 60611; 312-944-6780; 800-545-2433; Fax: 312-944-8520.

Chapter 4

Landmark Advances & Events in Bookselling

Behind the Scenes at the
World's Largest and Most Unusual Bookstore

A bookstore so big that it is in the *Guinness Book of World Records* is W. & G. Foyle Ltd. of London. *Guinness* has verified that Foyles carries the most titles (though no one is sure of how many), the longest shelving (more than 30 miles of it), and an overflowing inventory that is spread over a floor area of nearly 76,000 square feet.*

Foyles is located in an impressive-looking landmark building in the heart of London's bookstore district on 119-125 Charing Cross Road at the corner of Manette Street. The store is almost impossible to miss. Any visitor is immediately stopped by its fifteen display windows—five facing Charing Cross Road and ten more facing the Manette Street side of the building. These fifteen show windows have been purchased by various English publishers who maintain them on an ongoing basis with their latest offerings. Foyles calls them their Publishers Display Windows.

Inside, Foyles's book inventory occupies five huge floors, with high stock levels of virtually every book in every general, scientific, technical, and medical area—and often not only in the current edition, but also in many or all of the previous editions.

Book lovers and browsers find Foyles a great place for book bargains because all of the inventory is priced at time of purchase from the publishers. As prices increase annually, and new higher-priced editions are issued, all of the earlier purchases retain their original prices and become bigger and bigger bargains with the passage of years.

---

* In terms of square feet, the largest bookstore in the world is the Barnes & Noble bookstore at 105 Fifth Avenue in New York City. It totals 154,250 square feet.

The five floors of book inventory in Foyles includes a basement level and four additional floors at ground level on up. The basement store, according to one London publisher of medical books, carries a larger stock of medical books than any other specialist store in the entire United Kingdom.

Established in 1904, Foyles enjoys an international reputation and attracts scientists, scholars, and book collectors from all over the world, who make Foyles a primary stop on any visit to or through London.

Publishers like selling to Foyles because all sales to Foyles are final. Foyles never returns a book to a publisher, keeps no individual title records, and conducts no annual stock checks. Truly, the world's largest bookstore is also the world's most unusual bookstore and well worth a visit from anyone visiting London.

History's Earliest Record of Trade in Books

History's earliest reference to bookselling occurs in ancient Egyptian and Hebrew literature. Here is a partial summary of what is known:

Egyptian: Among the earliest known Egyptian books was the Egyptian *Book of the Dead*, copies of which were required at every funeral. The *Book* contained a collection of mortuary texts made up of spells and magic formulas which, when placed in tombs, was believed to protect and aid the deceased in the hereafter. *Coffin Texts* date from 2000 BC while *Pyramid Texts* date from about 2400 B.C. Both were probably compiled and re-edited about 16th century B.C.

Hebrew: In the *Book of Jeremiah*, one of the major prophetical writings on the *Old Testament*, the prophet Jeremiah (born about 650 B.C.) is represented as dictating to Baruch the scribe who, when questioned, described the mode in which his book was written. These scribes, says the 14th Edition of the *Encyclopedia Britannica* (1942), "were, in fact, the earliest booksellers and supplied copies as they were demanded."

European: Bookselling as a trade in Europe can be traced back to Athens, Greece, in the 5th Century BC. The bookseller's stock was scrolls (volumes) hand copied by educated slaves from an original.

History's First Recorded Great Bookseller—And His Fate

The first great bookseller in recorded history was Titus Pomponius Atticus (109-32 B.C.), a close friend of Cicero, a patron of letters, and author of numerous works including a history in Greek, a Roman history (54 B.C.), and genealogical works. As a publisher, Atticus engaged a staff of educated slaves to make copies of valuable works which he then sold. His bookselling business was mainly in Rome with branches in the provinces. Believing himself to be suffering from an incurable disease, Atticus starved himself to death at the age of seventy-seven.

America's Earliest Book Fairs

The first book fair in New York City, held in June of 1802, was sponsored by twenty-four New York booksellers. A year earlier, these Literary Fair sponsors had banded with booksellers from Philadelphia and Boston to form The American Company of Booksellers for the purpose of promoting the sale of books by means of fairs.

America's first book fair took place in the long room of the old Coffee House on Beaver Street near the tip of Manhattan. The fair sponsors invited other booksellers "accessible to water" to attend and bring samples of such books as they desired to sell or exchange. The fair was considered a success, although attendance is not known. It concluded with a grand banquet.

The next American fairs, also sponsored by the American Company of Booksellers, took place in Philadelphia, Pennsylvania (1803) and Newark, New Jersey (1805). Because of dissension among the members, the Company dissolved after the book fair in Newark.

When Books Were Banned in Boston:
Causes and Consequences

In the 1920's, a number of groups, acting as self-appointed censors, brought pressure on book retailers and distributors as well as official bodies to prohibit the distribution or sale of books they considered to contain material objectionable for reasons of politics, obscenity, or blasphemy. In the Boston area, the censoring body was the Watch and Ward Society, which had as a New York City counterpart the New York Society for the Prevention of Vice.

Between the two groups, attempts were made to suppress the sale of thousands of books during the early years of this century. But book censorship began in earnest in the early 1920's under the eyes of Boston's Watch and Ward group. Its method was to warn the book trade when it found a book it considered in violation of the Massachusetts obscenity statutes. If the bookseller did not remove the offending book, he was taken to court.

By 1927, the district attorney of Boston's Suffolk County was listing one book after another, thus threatening booksellers with legal action. In desperation, the Boston booksellers made up a list of books that they feared might be offensive and submitted it to the district attorney's office for clearance. This had the counterproductive effort of adding numerous new books to the disapproved list.

While being "Banned in Boston" was of serious concern to the Boston book trade and led to numerous cases of "booklegging" by those wishing to cash in on the book bannings, the publicity of a "Banned in Boston" book made it a big seller in other parts of the country, thus helping publisher sales and boosting author royalties.

Banned in Boston Books: Literary Greats Dominant

The Authors League of America, a professional organization of authors founded in 1912, has as one of its principle concerns "guarding freedom of expression." At one time, it included in its *Bulletin* this sampling of books that were banned in Boston in 1927:

The Allinghams, by May Sinclair
The American Caravan and *Move Over*, by E. Pettit
An American Tragedy, by Theodore Dreiser
The Ancient Hunger, by Edwin Granberry
Antennae, by Herbert Footner
As It Was, by Helen Thomas
Ariane, by Claude Anet
The Beadle, by Pauline Smith
Black April, by Julia Peterkin
Blinded Kings, by J. Kessel and Helene Iswolsky
The Butcher Shop, by Jean Devanny
The Captive, by Edouard Bourdet
Circus Parade, by Jim Tully
Cleopatra's Diary, by Henry Thomas
Count Bruga, by Ben Hecht
Crazy Pavements, by Beverly Nichols
Dark Laughter, by Sherwood Anderson
Doomsday, by Warwick Deeping
Dream's End, by Thorne Smith
Elmer Gantry, by Sinclair Lewis
Evelyn Grainger, by George Frederick Hummel
From Man to Man, by Olive Schreiner
The Hard Boiled Virgin, by Francis Newman
High Winds, by Arthur Train
Horizon, by Robert Carse
In Such a Night, by Babette Deutsch
The Irishman, by St. John Ervine
Little Pitchers, by Isa Glenn
The Madonna of the Sleeping Cars, by Maurice Dekobra
The Marriage Bed, by Ernest Pascal
Master of the Microbe, by Robert W. Service
Mosquitoes, by William Faulkner
Nigger Heaven, by Carl Van Vechten
Pilgrims, by Edith Mannin

The Plastic Age, by Percy Marks
Power, by Lion Feuchtwanger
Pretty Creatures, by William Gerhardi
The Rebel Bird, by Diana Patrick
The Revolt of Modern Youth, by Judge Ben Lindsey
The Sun Also Rises, by Ernest Hemingway
The Sorrows of Elsie, by Andre Savignon
The Starling, by Doris Leslie
Spread Circles, by F.J. Ward
Tomek the Sculptor, by Adelaide Eden Philpotts
Twilight, by Keyserling
The Wayward Man, by St. John Ervine
What I Believe, by Bertrand Russell
Wine, Women and War and *Manhattan Transfer*, by John Dos Passos
The World of William Clissold, by H.G. Wells
Young Men in Love, by Michael Arlen

Bookselling Success Story

One of the bookselling success stories of this century is that of the Readers Digest Condensed Book Club. The club, which offered new selections every three months, went from zero to four million members in a short span of years. Its first offer was a free book if the respondent (a *Readers Digest* subscriber) agreed to buy three more books within a year. Its second offer, the same free book but with no subsequent buying requirement, ultimately produced just as many copies sold. Its third offer sent the first book for only 10¢. This 10¢ book offer produced double the response of the free book offers and, as they used this offer more and more, the Readers Digest Condensed Book Club was on its way to record-breaking success.

Famous People Who Sold Books for Subscription Publishers

In centuries past, book salesmen or agents have traveled the countryside selling books by subscription that might otherwise never have been published. They performed the useful function of bringing books to people who were unaccustomed to buying or reading books. Through the volume sales generated by these agents, subscription book publishers were able to produce works of literature that otherwise never would have appeared.

Among history's subscription agents was Napoleon Bonaparte, who as an unemployed lieutenant, served as a sales agent for a work titled, *L'Historie de la révolution*[1]. Then there was George Washington, who as surveyor for Fairfax County in Virginia, also sold 200 copies Rydell's *The London of*

Stok-on Trent Square in and around Alexandria, Virginia. Another general, Ulysses S. Grant, sold Washington Irving's *Columbus* for Putnam after he resigned from the army but before he became president. Then, too, there was a young lad who traveled through southern Ohio selling subscriptions for Baxter's *Lives of the Saints*; that lad later became America's 19th president —Rutherford B. Hayes.

Other notable sellers of subscription books were Mark Twain, Henry Wadsworth Longfellow, Daniel Webster, and Bret Harte. Many of the leading book publishers of the 19th century also started their careers as book canvassers.

Publishers as Retail Booksellers in the Latter 19th Century

Retail bookselling in the United States developed slowly during the latter years of the 19th century. A majority of the important publishers, particularly those clustered in lower Manhattan, maintained store-front departments for the retail sale of their own publications and those of fellow publishers located nearby.

In a 1950's recollection about one such retail operation in a publishing establishment, an aging bookman recalled his first job as a young boy on roller skates racing up and down the book storage aisles picking books from stock and speeding them up to the store front to meet the needs of waiting customers.

These publisher-run retail bookstores were weakened by inventories of stationery, various other paper goods, and other non-book matter which, combined with liberal discounts to various types of customers, kept most such operations unprofitable. By the turn of the century, around the founding of the American Booksellers Association in 1900, most publisher-operated retail operations had been phased out.

Two remained well past mid-20th century, of which only one exists today. The landmark Scribner's Bookstore in the Scribner Building at 597 Fifth Avenue in New York City lasted well past mid-century, even though it was a substantial and continuous money-loser for the company.[2] Still open, and apparently thriving, is the McGraw-Hill Bookstore in the McGraw-Hill Building at 1221 Avenue of the Americas in Rockefeller Center.

Booksellers Rejected FDR's Books During His Second Term

In the earlier entry in this book, FDR and His Editor, details were given on the publication of *The Public Papers and Addresses of Franklin D. Roosevelt*, published in the second year of Roosevelt's second term in office. Because Random House was heavily dependent on bookstores for the sale of this five-volume work, they had purposely priced the books at a low $3.00 per volume to ensure a speedy sale.

What the publisher hadn't counted on was Roosevelt's vast unpopularity in the early years of his second term. As a result, many booksellers refused to order the books. One famous old Boston bookstore wrote the publisher, "We'll buy as many sets of the Roosevelt papers as you can deliver bound in his own skin." Bookseller reluctance resulted in the sale of slightly less than half the 15,000 set printing. Eventually the publisher was forced to remainder the unsold copies at about $1.00 each.

Mason Locke Weems:
The Book Peddling Parson of Early America

Mason Locke Weems (1759-1825), the earliest biographer of George Washington in 1800, was better known as "The Book Peddling Parson." Despite his authorship of Washington's biography and numerous moral tracts, Weems spent the better part of his adult life out on the road, year after year, selling books.

Weems arrival in a book-starved community was an event in itself. Potential book buyers thronged to examine his offerings, and he was a welcome guest wherever he went.

"I have ever glowed with book vending enthusiasm," he confided to his principal book supplier, the printer/publisher Mathew Carey of Philadelphia. "Do send me books that will sell and at the right price. Let me have useful books on the care of horses, the cultivation of kitchen gardens, books on quilting and preserving, and simple medical books with recipes for anti-bilious pills, worm lozenges, ague drops, itch ointments and 'the far wors worms of envy & vice.'"[3]

Weems had been ordained a clergyman in 1784 at the age of twenty-five. He got his first taste of bookselling, however, by offering subscriptions to an imported two-volume set of sermons produced in Edinburgh. When sales went slowly, he augmented his income by printing and selling "the first American edition" of *An Estimate of Religion of the Fashionable World* for 12¢ a copy.

Churchless for several years, Weems took to roaming the countryside on foot, by horseback, or sometimes in a sulky—going from one settlement to another selling books and seeking subscriptions to others that he would later supply. He had, he wrote, adopted "a peddling way of life."

In his travels, he learned many valuable lessons about book publishing and bookselling that others would not learn until later generations. Among other things that he and his publisher, Mathew Carey, learned were the following: Small books sell better than large books. Sometimes a single chapter lifted from a larger book can become a very saleable item when published by itself. And price books low enough so they are affordable to the masses.

Weems died on May 23, 1825. While he authored numerous works to aid his sales, he is not listed among the literary greats. But Weems, in traveling up and down the coastal states of the struggling republic, probably came to know more people in more places than any other person of his generation and was probably better attuned to the cultural pulse of America than any other American of his century.

In Weems obituary, which appeared in the July 23, 1825 issue of the Raleigh, North Carolina *Register*, he was described as "the author of the *Life of Washington* and various other popular works ... a man of very considerable attainments." It went on to say, "In the course of his life, he has been instrumental in circulating nearly a million copies of the scriptures and other valuable works." Truly, the Book Peddling Parson left an indelible mark on early America.

Sherlock Holmes, Bookseller

Like so many of his admirers, Sherlock Holmes was obviously a browser in the back-street shops, an Autolycus* of the bookstalls, a man instinctively drawn to those wistful-foolish members of the human race called by the directories Booksellers. Old inhabitants will remember that once he assumed the disguise of an old bookseller— what is the disguise of an old bookseller?—for good and sufficient reasons. That was in the spring of the year 1894, when the murder of the Hon. Ronald Adair was filling London with fearful joy and poor Watson with despair. At the time, indeed, Holmes had a little shop of his own—"at the corner of Church Street," he told Watson; a vague enough address, since it is not clear just where at the moment the doctor was living.[4]

First U.S. Book Traveler, Also Father of *Publishers Weekly*

In 1852, the year Harriet Beecher Stowe's *Uncle Tom's Cabin* was published, America's first book traveler of record made his first road trip. A *traveler* was the term used in earlier years to identify publisher sales representatives who traveled from city to city to call on bookstores, representing one or more publishers, usually on commission.

The first traveler, Charles B. Norton, made the two-month road trip, covering 4,000 miles by railroad, stagecoach, and river steamer for Harper & Brothers of No. 8 Cliff Street in New York City. Along the way, he called on bookstores from Elmira, New York, to New Orleans. Other cities covered were Rochester, Buffalo, Cleveland, Columbus, Cincinnati, Louisville, and New Orleans. On his return trip, he stopped off at Philadelphia in time to attend Harper's annual spring trade sales meeting.

* From Greek mythology: Autolycus, a son of the god Hermes, was famous as a thief and swindler.

Norton, during this historic trip, also took subscriptions for a new periodical he was starting, *Norton's Literary Gazette and Publishers Circular*, in which he reported details of his trip. Subsequently, his publication evolved into *Publishers Weekly*, the American book trade weekly, making him the father of that publication as well. Norton's periodical, also known as *Norton's Literary Advisor*, was published through various changes in style, title, and ownership until January 1872 when it became *The Weekly Trade Circular*. In 1873, it assumed the name of *The Publisher's Weekly*. Under this name, it has grown and thrived to serve a national and international book publishing and bookselling community under the 1990's title: *Publishers Weekly: The International News Magazine of Book Publishing*.

British Reaction to a Book Bargain

In a published collection of reminiscences,[5] noted British publisher Sir Stanley Unwin relates how his firm, Allen & Unwin, overcame bookseller and book buyer price resistance to a two-volume set of art books they had published. The work had been priced at the equivalent of $10.50 to booksellers and $15.75 for the set to the book-buying public, but it was not selling.

Unwin recalls, "We changed the price to $31.50 per set; told the booksellers that they could sell it at 'half price' and pay us $10.50. The stock just melted away. There was no change in the price either to the booksellers or to the Public."

Origin and Principle of Negative Option Bookselling: The Book Club

Millions of Americans belong to a wide array of book clubs today that operate under the negative-option principle. So popular has the term become, that in the publishing industry negative-option publishing is a synonymous term for book clubs.

Just what are negative-option clubs? They are mail order bookselling operations that send books to club members, usually at about the same time as they are offered in bookstores, but at a reduction off the established list price. The idea of the negative-option book club was a brainstorm of Harry Scherman who translated his idea into reality with the start of the Book-of-the-Month Club in April 1926.

Here is how the negative-option principle works: The club sends members a bulletin at stated intervals of about once a month. Each bulletin offers a new book as a main selection and, often, several other books as alternate selections. If a club member does not wish the main selection, the member sends back a notice to the club indicating rejection of the main selection offering (or, perhaps, making another choice offered in the club bulletin). If the notice is not returned, the member automatically gets the book.

The strong appeal of the negative-option club to book lovers was that it could assure its members the book offerings made to them would be selected by an independent board of expert judges, untainted by commercialism and moved only by their interest in good books.

Nearly half a century after the start of BOMC operations, the Federal Trade Commission in the 1970's undertook an examination of negative-option bookselling and threatened to ban the negative option principle. But, with liberalization of customer terms, club members wound up with buying options even more generous than FTC requirements so the ban was dropped.

Scherman's invention of negative-option bookselling was not his first brainstorm for moving masses of popular books. Prior to starting Book-of-the-Month Club, Scherman hit on and pursued the idea of selling books with candy. Since, Scherman assumed, people generally ate candy when they read a book, why not tie the two together? He convinced the people at the Whitman candy company to take copies of Herman Melville's *Moby Dick* and distribute them with Whitman's Samplers. A January 28, 1983 *Publishers Weekly* article, which described the plan, noted that "it proved an overwhelming success."

See also Chapter 3A — Book-of-the-Month Club First Selection.

Bookseller Sidelines: A Lot Has Changed Since 1712

Booksellers were originally printers and publishers as well. They printed and sold books from the same premises. In modern times, booksellers are more likely to be merchants offering a wide variety of sidelines in addition to books to help pay the rent. These sidelines may include such items as note cards, post cards, greeting cards, gift wraps, party goods, announcements, invitations, and stationery.

A comprehensive business analysis by *Publishers Weekly* of the largest and most popular bookstore in the Midwest in the early 1960's, Kroch's and Brentano's in Chicago, produced the surprising revelation that the leading bookseller's greatest source of revenue came from a sideline—party goods.

But there was a time, before the American Revolution, when booksellers in New England pursued a most unusual sideline. John Tebbel, in *Bookselling in America and the World*,[6] tells about it this way:

> Only in the context of the times can one understand how a printer-publisher-bookseller like Thomas Fleet, an educated and otherwise compassionate man, could advertise from the Boston bookshop he opened...in 1712...a very valuable Negro woman about thirty years ...with a fine healthy boy two years old.

> Fleet, primarily a publisher of children's books...saw nothing reprehensible in selling a two-year-old child and his mother.

The Bookseller Who Won International Honors for Her Services to Literature

American booksellers are rarely honored for the services they perform for their patrons. But a notable exception was Miss Sylvia Beach, who elected to open her "American bookshop" on the left bank of Paris in 1922. A few years later, she received international notoriety when she published a book for one of her customers that had been banned in every country in the English-speaking world. It was James Joyce's *Ulysses*.

Once opened, Miss Beach's shop—Shakespeare and Company—quickly became the meeting place for many American expatriates prominent in the literary world. Her customers included Ernest Hemingway, Ezra Pound, Gertrude Stein, F. Scott Fitzgerald, and numerous others. Her shop also attracted many French writers of note, who were interested in American literature.

Her bookshop, which featured a mix of new and used books, sold some books but enjoyed most of its activity from its lending library. Members of her lending library could take out one or two volumes at a time for which they paid a subscription price plus a deposit which was refunded on return of the books. Miss Beach once recalled that James Joyce took out dozens of books and sometimes kept them for years.

Miss Beach's bookshop, which received wide publicity in the United States because of its famous literary customers, was one of the first places that American travelers looked up when visiting Paris. Some would give Shakespeare and Company as their Paris address, and Miss Beach was happy to hold and distribute their mail.

For her services to literature, Miss Beach was awarded the French Legion of Honor in 1936 and the degree of Doctor of Literature by the University of Buffalo in 1959. She died in 1962 at the age of seventy-five.

Origin of the American Booksellers Association

Organized and incorporated in New York City in May 1900, the original intent of the American Booksellers Association (ABA) was to protect booksellers from price-cutting through the maintenance of a net price system. Under this system, the retail prices for all books intended for general sale were fixed by the publisher, with penalties for those who failed to do so.

Early in ABA's life, the principle of price maintenance was challenged in the courts by the R.H. Macy department store, which claimed that price fixing of books was illegal under the Sherman Antitrust Act of 1890 and that, whatever its worthy aims, it constituted a restraint of trade. After a lengthy court battle that went all the way to the Supreme Court, the department store won. But, by the time the suit was settled, the booksellers were well organized and the ABA had broadened its goals to "working toward establishment, improvement and maintenance of favorable trade conditions."

Over the years, the ABA has continued to prosper and to offer increasing benefits to its 6,000 bookseller members. The annual ABA Convention has evolved into a major international media event with extensive press and television coverage, international participation, and the appearance of scores of celebrity authors touting recently-written or forthcoming books.

Changing Patterns in Bookselling: Chains Outselling Independents

Despite the electronic revolution, Americans continue to buy books in record-breaking numbers. A *Consumer Research Study on Book Purchasing* found that Americans bought 1.54 billion books in 1994. What has changed as this century comes to an end is where these books are being bought.

Chain bookstores are the major outlet for book sales, outselling the far more numerous independently-owned stores. According to the *Consumer Research Study*, 25% of 1994 book sales were through chain bookstores. Sales through independent bookstores was 21%. Another 18% were sold through book clubs, 8% through discount stores, and 4% each through used bookstores, food/drug stores, and mail order. All other sources accounted for the remaining 10%.

The three largest bookstore chains at the end of 1995 were Barnes & Noble with 305 superstores, Borders Group with 116, and Crown Books with 84. In its fiscal year ending on January 28, 1997, Borders planned forty additional superstore openings.

Superstores Killing Off Independents: One Recent Example

With the rapid growth of the superstore chains, many long-established independent bookstores across the country have been driven out of business as they watched their customers turn to the discounted prices and larger selections of nearby superstores.

So great has been the impact of superstores on independents that in spring 1996, the 23-year-old Adventure Bookstore in Lawrence, Kansas, faced with the impending arrival of both a Barnes & Noble and a Borders Books & Music, announced to its customers that it would shut its doors on April 15, in advance of the two superstore openings. In an open letter to their customers, the owners, Walter and Mary Michener, wrote in part: "On the day a chain superstore opens in Lawrence, our sales will fall dramatically (and) we would be getting poorer every day. When independent bookstores with supporters as devoted as our own and with much deeper resources have failed, we can find no reason to believe that Adventure would survive."

Chapter 5

Book Reviews and Reviewers

The Different Kinds of Reviewers—And How They Operate

The book review editor of a newspaper or magazine usually works with a stable of reviewers who prepare reviews on request for specific books sent to them for that purpose. There are two potential problems with such reviewers. If the reviewer is a specialist in the field of the book or even a competitive author with a similar book, he or she may not be able to write an objective review. On the other hand, if the reviewer is a professional writer, he or she may find it difficult to be impersonal about a contemporary artist, or may be overly critical, or may overcompensate and praise too lavishly. Perhaps the best reviewers are college faculty. As a rule, academics will render a judgment of a book in their field on its merits and objectivity.

Book review sections in trade magazines take on a different light. These magazines often see new books as new products in their field; hence, book reviews become new product news. Those responsible for preparing the "book reviews" make little or no effort to read and interpret the book's content, but rather build reviews around the publisher-supplied blurb.

The author recalls including specially worded phrases into publisher blurbs to trade magazines in the early 1960's that would look good in review quotes. Then, when the so-called reviews appeared in the trade magazines bearing these phrases, they were lifted out and attributed to the publications in which they appeared.

The Inside Facts Behind Book Reviews

You open your local Sunday book review supplement and you see a full page of rave testimonials for a book that is about to be published. How did it happen so fast, and is this true in all of book publishing? The answer is that it happens only for popular fiction and nonfiction trade books. The reason it happens so fast is that galley proofs are sent to known professional reviewers and review media months in advance of publication.

For publishers of books in the sciences, the review picture is vastly different. Scientific books are not sent for review until after publication and often do not show up in the specialized review journals of their interest area until months later under the heading, New Books Received. Only later do the reviews happen. As a rule, the reviewer is an unpaid peer of the author — someone not only in the same field, but often in the same narrow specialty, and on some occasions, an author of a competing book. Many reviews are voluntary; that is, the author requested an opportunity to review the book after seeing it listed under New Books Received. The payment to the reviewer is to keep the copy of the reviewed book.

So reviews for scientific books are slow. One study of 3,500 reviews in more than fifty scientific journals showed that it took from two months to nine years after publication for reviews to appear. Occasionally a rave review will appear long after the book has ceased to be offered for sale since some scientific publishers remove a book from its list when sales fall below a certain annual level.

Reviews in Major Newspapers: What Influences the Reviewers?

Do those striking, colorful book jackets that catch your eye in store windows or on book display racks influence the book review editors of major newspapers? Not in the slightest. Here's why: Reviewers usually receive the book prior to publication in galley proof form and write their reviews after reading the rough page proofs. Most book review editors, as a rule, have a pretty good idea of where a book is going after reading ten or twelve pages.

Factors that may sway book review editors or cause them to pay special attention to a book include the author's previous books, the author's special qualifications for writing the book, the importance of the publisher, and books with big cash advances or with movie rights deals tied to them.

Anatomy of a Good Book Review

A good book review should answer the following questions: What did the author try to do? How well did the author succeed? Was it worth doing? Basically, a review should offer sufficient information to convince the reader that the book is worth reading (or not worth reading). All too often, though, a reviewer may fulfill all of these functions and still write a dull review. Hence, one final criterion of a good book review is that it be interesting, well-written, and a delight to read on its own.

Noted Author's Offbeat Response to Wealth of Bad Reviews

Novelist Normal Mailer was determined that *Deer Park*, which followed his wildly successful *Naked and the Dead*, should also become a "powerful best-seller" and make him the first serious writer of his generation to produce two bestsellers in a row. Instead *Deer Park* attracted a host of bad reviews and failed to score with the book buying public. So a month after publication a frustrated Mailer assembled about a dozen excerpts from the worst reviews and placed them in an advertisement for the book which he placed in New York's *Village Voice* in November 1955. It was his hope that such a powerful assortment of put-downs "might excite some people to buy the book." It didn't.

The following are some of the review quotes Mailer assembled for his advertisement:

"Sordid and Crummy" — *Chicago Sun-Times*

"Disgusting" — *Houston Post*

"The Year's Worst Snake Pit in Fiction" — *Cleveland Press*

"Unfair" — *Los Angeles Herald Express*

"Embarrassing" — *Hartford Times*

"Junk" — *Little Rock Gazette*

"A Bunch of Bums" — *Los Angeles Mirror News*

"Golden Garbage Heap" — *New York Herald Tribune*

Want to Review My Book?
Publisher Says: Buy Your Own Review Copy

Publishers are known to go to almost any extreme to get their books reviewed in major newspapers and periodicals. This desire is even more acute when it comes to news weeklies like *Time* or *Newsweek* since these magazines review only two or three books per issue.

This anecdote about New York publisher Lyle Stuart is noteworthy because he has a reputation for launching books with pizzazz and, long after it happened, is still legendary among book publicists. Terry Garrity,* the publicist for Lyle Stuart, once sent a book to *Time*, which they did not initially review. But, as Ms. Garrity later told it,[1] "With insistent prodding from me (*Time*) finally relented and decided to review the book after all. The original *Time* magazine review copy had long since disappeared, so they asked Lyle for another review copy. He refused! He told them to go out and buy a copy if they wanted one. *Time* said 'Forget it,' and the book never got reviewed."

---

* Apparently undaunted by this earlier experience, Ms. Garrity, writing under the nom de plume "J," later went on to write *The Sensuous Woman* which, in selling nearly nine million copies, became one of the biggest selling books ever by a woman author. Published in 1970 by Lyle Stuart, the book drew a $1,500 advance for the author, paid in five installments.

University Press Experiences Power of a Good Book Review

University presses generally are devoted to publishing the fruits of scholarly research so reviews come slowly, as often do sales—sometimes one copy at a time over a protracted period. But one university press tried something different and got a surprising response. Johns Hopkins University Press published a book on a medical subject that would appeal to general readers: *Staying Dry: A Practical Guide To Bladder Control.*

One of the copies got into the hands of Ann Landers, the syndicated newspaper advice columnist, who reviewed and recommended the book to her readers. The result: On one morning following the review, the press received 18,000 orders. The book went on to sell over 100,000 copies.

Times Reviewer Learns Value of Checking Sources

A *New York Times* book editor, Shirley Horner, was interviewing a much-published author and highly regarded scholar at his university. Responding to her questions with great authority, he added emphasis to one of his responses with an "as Shakespeare said" quotation. While writing up the interview, Ms. Horner came to the Shakespeare quote and decided to follow a *Times* guideline to its writers: "Always check your sources."

She discovered that the Shakespeare quote was actually from Thomas Gray. When she informed the author that she was changing the source of his quotation, she later recalled that "he sounded so grateful."

How Publisher Made Book Reviews Evidence
in Landmark Obscenity Trial

James Joyce's *Ulysses* was still banned in the United States when Random House contracted with Joyce for permission to publish his controversial work in the United States. Publisher Bennett Cerf feared that once he undertook publication, there would be a long and costly court battle before the published work could win court clearance for public sale. So he hit on the ruse of importing just one copy of *Ulysses* and having an agent on hand to ensure that it was seized by U.S. Customs when it arrived. Thus, Cerf reasoned, if the government refused entry of the single volume and the government's claim was later sustained by the courts, Random House would be the loser only by the cost of the single copy, plus legal fees.

"The copy itself," Cerf wrote in a letter to Columbia University in 1935, "was a rather special one since inside its blue paper cover were pasted critical essays on the book by leading authors and critics of both England and France. By having these reviews pasted inside the copy, we were able to quote from them when the case actually came before the court."

In due course, the juryless two-day trial was held before Judge Woolsey, the reviews were read, and the book was cleared. *Ulysses* was published in the United States by Random House in January 1934.

Reviewers Vary in Opinions on Book Writing Quality: Result of 15-Year Study

Book reviewers frequently give opinions of a book's writing quality in their written reviews. In a study of some 25,000 reviews that appeared in newspapers and periodicals over a fifteen-year period from 1980 through mid-1995, here are 150 variations of book writing quality that reviewers have described:[2]

accessibly written
adeptly written
admirably written
adroitly written
amateurishly written
appealingly written
archaically written
archly written
artfully written
artlessly written
articulately written
awkwardly written
beautifully written
best written
blandly written
boldly written
breezily written
brightly written
brilliantly written
briskly written
carefully written
casually written
clearly written
cleverly written
closely written
clumsily written
cogently written
collabortively written
colorfully written
cooly written
compassionately written
compellingly written
competently written

concisely written
convincingly written
courageously written
crisply written
dazzingly written
deftly written
delightfully written
densely written
dexterously written
diligently written
directly written
dramatically written
drolly written
dryly written / drily written
ebulliently written
economically written
effectively written
elegantly written
eloquently written
engagingly written
entertainingly written
evocatively written
excellently written
expertly written
exquisitely written
extremely well written
felicitously written
fervently written
finely written
flawlessly written
floridly written
fluently written
fluidly written

gracefully written
handsomely written
horribly written
idiosynchratically written
ill written
imaginatively written
immaculately written
ineptly written
informally written
insightfully written
intelligently written
intelligibly written
intensely written
inventively written
knowledgeably written
laboriously written
limpidly written
loosely written
lovingly written
lucidly written
lushly written
lyrically written
magnificently written
marvelously written
masterfully written
meticulously written
movingly written
nicely written
opaquely written
painstakingly written
passionately written
penetratingly written
perceptively written
perfectly written
philosophically written
pleasantly written
ploddingly written
poetically written
poorly written
popularly written
powerfully written
precisely written

pretentiously written
prodigiously written
provocatively written
pungently written
sensibly written
sensitively written
serviceably written
sharply written
sincerely written
sloppily written
smartly written
smoothly written
snappily written
solidly written
sophisticatedly written
soundly written
spectacularly written
splendidly written
startlingly written
stodgily written
straightforwardly written
strongly written
stunningly written
stylishly written
superbly written
sweetly written
sympathetically written
tastefully written
tautly written
tersely written
tightly written
thoughtfully written
trenchantly written
turgidly written
unaffectedly written
unflinchingly written
untidily written
vividly written
well written
wittily written
wretchedly written
wryly written

Chapter 6

The Evolution of Bookmaking

Domestic Type Foundry Stimulated
Early American Book Publishing

Two years after Great Britain formally recognized the existence of the thirteen colonies and fixed the boundaries of the new nation (Treaty of Paris, 1783), book publishing in America began in earnest. In August 1785, a 73-year-old type founder, his grandson, and his type founding machinery arrived in Philadelphia from Edinburgh, Scotland. Shortly thereafter, John Baine (1712-1789) and his grandson, also named John, established the firm of John Baine & Grandson, Letter Founders, and began selling type to printers. When, after four years, the elder Baine died at the age of seventy-seven, his grandson continued to cast and sell type to various book printers until 1796, when he sold the type foundry to Binny & Ronaldson.

Two noteworthy American publications were produced from Baine types in 1790. The first was Mathew Carey's *Bible*. Carey, in advertising his *Bible*, made it a point to indicate that it was printed with type cast expressly for it by the Baines. The second noteworthy publication was one of the most impressive American publications of that period, the first ten volumes of Thomas Dobson's *Encyclopedia* (the type source for the remaining eight volumes is not known).[1]

Origin of Paper in Europe
Aided Gutenberg's Invention of Printing

Like inventors who preceded him, Johannes Gutenberg could not have invented printing were it not for inventors who preceded him. Printing would not have been practical without paper, and paper was not manufactured in Germany until about half a century before Gutenberg's invention.

The original inventor of paper made from vegetable substances was a Chinese named Ts'ai Lun in 105 A.D. In the 8th century, the Arabs learned from Chinese prisoners how to make paper. The Arabs carried their knowledge of papermaking to Morocco where the Moors progressed in the papermaking art. In their occupation of Spain in the 11th century, they brought the craft to Europe. Papermaking knowledge eventually traveled north from Spain, and in 1390 a mill was set up near Nuremberg, Germany, less than 200 miles from Gutenberg's home city. It probably didn't take too many years before the knowledge spread from Nuremberg to Mainz, most likely in Gutenberg's own century.

Following the introduction of papermaking in Germany, it was to take yet another century, 1494, for papermaking to come to England, and two centuries before it reached the North American continent in Philadelphia in 1690.

Use of Parchment in Printing Before Paper

Consider the problems of printers before the introduction of paper. Early printing, dating back to the second century B.C., was done on parchment, which gradually became a substitute for papyrus.

Parchment consisted of the processed skin of sheep, goats, and calves, prepared in such a way as to render it capable of receiving writing on both sides. Before a sheet of parchment could be created to receive writing, the skin had to be soaked in water, treated with lime to loosen the hair, scraped, cleaned, washed, stretched, dried, and rubbed with chalk and pumice stone. Parchment made from the more delicate skins of calf or kid (or from stillborn or newly born calf or lamb) came to be called *vellum*. Ultimately the term *vellum* was broadened to include any specially fine parchment.

Parchment became the favored replacement for papyrus because it was more durable and capable of being folded into book form. In the early years of printing in Europe, paper was widely distributed but important documents continued to be written on vellum up until the nineteenth century. Gutenberg's printed works were done on both vellum and paper.

The Book With the Most Firsts in the History of Printing

There is no book that recorded more firsts in the history of printing than the *Psalter* of 1457, the second book ever printed. The so-called Gutenberg Bible, printed in 1456, was the first book. Both books are believed to have been in the last stages of completion by Johannes Gutenberg, the inventor of printing. However, Johan Fust, a prominent goldsmith of Mainz, Germany, acquired Gutenberg's premises and equipment when Gutenberg defaulted on a loan in 1455. Then Fust (1400-1466), together with a partner, Peter Schoffer (1425-1502) set up their own printing business and completed both the Gutenberg Bible and the famed *Psalter*.

The *Psalter* was the first book ever printed in color. The capitals were all floriated initials of lacy design posted in three colors. On the ten existing copies of the *Psalter*, the color register is so perfect that typographic experts remain puzzled in their efforts to discover the method by which it was accomplished. The large type is printed in red and black ink throughout, and printing experts have described the entire effect as magnificent.

The *Psalter* was also the first book ever printed that was both dated and signed. On the last page appears history's first colophon in Latin. Translated into English, it reads as follows:

> The present copy of the Psalms, adorned with beauty of capital letters and sufficiently marked out with rubrics, has been thus fashioned by an ingenious invention of printing and stamping without any driving of the pen, and to the worship of God has been diligently brought to completion by Johann Fust, a citizen of Mainz, and Peter Schoeffer of Gernsheim, in the year of the Lord 1457, on the vigil of the Feast of the Assumption.

Origin and Growth of Papermaking in Colonial America

America's first papermaker was William Rittenhouse. The 44-year-old immigrant, a papermaker from Mulheim, Prussia, settled in Germantown, Pennsylvania in 1688. He soon formed a business partnership with Philadelphia's first printer, William Bradford (1663-1752), an English-born Quaker colonist, who up until then had struggled to maintain paper inventory with imports from England. The partnership resulted in the construction of America's first paper mill on the banks of Wissahickon Creek near Germantown—a log cabin with a waterwheel. Papermaking began in 1690 using linen and cotton rags as the basic raw material.

As the demand for paper grew and paper shipments from England continued to be slow, additional paper mills were built in the colonies in the first half of the 18th century. Two more paper-making facilities were built in Pennsylvania—one in 1710 and one in 1729. Also, in 1728, paper mills began operations at Elizabethtown, New Jersey, and at Milton, Massachusetts.

When the American Revolution began in 1776, England completely stopped all exports of paper to the colonies, thus causing a terrible shortage of paper for General Washington's armies. Paper was a critical commodity since soldiers needed paper to wrap up the powder and bullets for their muskets. So desperate was the situation that General Washington authorized the discharge from the army of any soldier knowledgeable in the making of paper, so that he could help alleviate the paper shortage.

See also Chapter 3C — Origin of First Bible Printed in European Language in North America.

After 437 Years, First Book Set in Non-Movable Type

Johannes Gutenberg is credited with printing the first book with movable type in 1450. But it took another 437 years before the first book was printed with non-movable type. The book, *The Tribune Book of Open Air Sports*, was edited by Henry Hall and published in 1887 by the Tribune Association in New York City. The Foreword to Hall's book stated, "This book is printed without type being the first product in book form of the Mergenthaler machine which wholly supersedes the use of movable type."

The Mergenthaler Linotype was the invention of a German immigrant machine shop worker, Ottmar Mergenthaler (1854-1899) of Baltimore, Maryland. In 1885, he took out a patent for his new invention—a slug casting machine that would cast a one piece line or *slug*. First tested in 1886, the machine made book publishing history in 1887 by creating the first book ever set by non-movable type.

Origin of Bookbinding

Bookbinding began at about the time of the start of the A.D. calendar, with the change from continuous scroll or volume to the book made up of separate sheets of vellum (and, later, paper). Early books consisted of single sheets folded once and collected into sections of convenient size. The leaves were held together in the section by sewing through the central fold. The sections then were held together in correct order by sewing them on to flexible bands at right angles to the backs. Subsequent books differ only in that the section is usually a large single sheet folded several times so that the outer folds require cutting.

To keep the leaves flat and uninjured, early books (usually of large size) were placed between thin wooden boards. Soon it became convenient and easy to join book and boards together by fixing the ends of the bands holding the sections together to the boards. Ultimately, a leather covering was stretched over the wooden boards to hide and protect the back of the book's sections, overlapping or completely covering the boards. Since the boards were about a quarter of an inch thick, binders tried to conceal the thickness of the boards covering smaller books by sharply beveling the board edges.

Although in modern binding, cloth and other materials have been substituted for leather and boards have been replaced by either binder's board, chipboard, or pasted board, the early principles of book binding still prevail.

Origin and Purpose of the Title Page: An Italian Innovation

The eminent British scholar and bibliographer, Ronald B. McKerrow, defined a title page as "a separate page setting forth in a conspicuous manner the title of the book which followed it and not containing any part of the text of the book itself." History records that credit for the original book title page belongs to the Italian scribes who penned and illuminated Europe's earliest books in the centuries that preceded the invention of printing. The first title page of record was discovered in a handwritten Italian work of about 800 A.D.—a general title page to the four gospels in the manuscript Bible known as *Codex Aureaus*.

This phenomenon was not to repeat itself until the 15th century when title pages were introduced in a few handsomely-written Italian manuscripts. In these manuscripts the title was engrossed on the first leaf in a centrally-positioned space, surrounded with elaborate ornament in the illuminator's most effective style. Sometimes, the penman would put the title page on the reverse side of the first leaf to protect it from wear. The main function of these early hand-penned title pages seemed to be the embellishment of the books in which they appeared. Nevertheless, they fulfilled the definition of what a title page should be.

Fifteenth century development of the printed title page is said to have begun with *Bulla cruciatae contra turcos...* printed by Fust and Schöffer in 1463. This very first printed title page provided the title and author's name only on an otherwise blank protecting leaf at the beginning of the book. The first decorated title page proper was in the *Calendar of Regiomontanus* by Johannes Müller, which was printed in Venice in 1476 by Ratdolt, Löslein and Maler. The first title page in English was printed by Machlinia for *Treatise of the Pestilence* in 1489.

Purpose, Origin, and Current Usage of Book Indexing

A book index is an alphabetical listing, usually at the end of a book, containing names, subjects, places, catch or key words and phrases—according to the requirements of the work in question—that guides the user to specific page numbers (and sometimes to locations within the page) on which the information being sought appears. An index may also be in a separate volume associated with a set of books. The origin of book indexing varies as the following research indicates:

- The *Oxford University Dictionary*, Third Edition, 1955, shows the first usage of the word "Index" as 1580.
- The first book ever on indexing was by Henry Wheatley, secretary of The Index Society, formed in London in 1878. The book, *What Is An Index?*, issued in 1878, cites these as the earliest known examples of Indexing:

    1) *Concordance of the Bible*, 1247.

    2) *First English Concordance of the New Testament*, 1536. This was the first index in English mentioned in Wheatley's book.

    3) An index to Boccaccio in *La Ricchezze della Lingua volgare*, compiled by Francis Alunno, 1545.

    4) *English Concordance of the Entire Bible*, by John Marbeck, 1550.

- In the July 1965 *The Library Quarterly* (University of Chicago Press), Francis J. Witty wrote that alphabetical indexing appeared no earlier than the 14th century and cited the following examples:

  1) Egidio Colonna's *Commentarius in primum senteniarum.*

  2) Pedanius Dioscorrides' *De material medica.*

  3) An incunabulum, *Liber cronicarum of Schedel*, printed by Anton Koberger in 1493.

  Witty also cited these two 16th century indexed works: Erasmus' edition of *St. Augustine* printed by Foben in 1529 and *Bude's De asse et partibus* printed by Vascosanus, Stephanus, and Roigny in 1451.

  By the end of the 18th century, the practice of book indexing was well established, and today is the mainstay of all information-bearing books. A classic example of the value of indexing as a contribution to book content is the 371-page *Oxford Dictionary of Modern Quotations* (Oxford University Press, 1991) in which a page of index is provided for every 1.8 pages of text.

Book Endpapers: Purpose, Usage, and Differences

Every hardbound book has *endpapers*, the heavier-weight protective sheets that attach the first and last pages of a book to the boards around which the cloth or other covering material of the book is wrapped. A leaf of each folded endpaper is pasted to the board to conceal the edges of the covering material. The fold in the endpaper also forms a hinge for the cover.

Endpapers are usually supplied by the binder and left blank. These papers have distinctive and significant strength requirements. Books with many pages and heavy coated paper, for example, will require a much stronger endpaper than another book of the same trim size but printed on a lighter-weight paper. Reference books also require endpapers with special qualities of folding and tensile strength as they must serve through many usings.

Endpapers can also have a utilitarian value. *Worldmark Encyclopedia of the Nations*, a classic school library reference since 1960, has specially-drawn maps in each of the five volumes—on both front and back endpapers. Similarly, endpapers of some engineering books often have important tables or equations for ready reference by their users. So, in general, the type of paper used in a book's endpapers is often dictated by the book's special characteristics and its intended end use.

History of Book Illustrations

In the early years of the 15th century, woodcuts of religious subjects were printed and inserted in manuscript books for the first time. While the practice of printing illustrations from engraved wooden blocks dates back to the eighth century in Japan, the use of printed illustrations in books did not come about until about the time of the invention of printing

The earliest illustrations appearing in printed books were tooled out of wood blocks that were carved by hand, leaving raised surfaces for printing. The earliest known book using a woodcut illustration was printed by Albrecht Pfister in Bamberg, Germany, about 1460.

The use of copperplate engravings for book illustrations began in 1570. These engravings were metal plates in which a design had been incised with a special tool. As the use of these engravings increased, woodcut book illustrations lost their popularity and were used less and less frequently until about 1770. At that time, a revival of woodblock illustrations took place in book publishing when the Englishman Thomas Beewick developed a special engraving tool for cutting wood across the grain instead of with the grain, making the accomplishment of wood illustrations faster and less difficult.

Thumb Index Over 100 Years Old

The thumb index, those rounded notched indentations cut into the edges of pages to facilitate quick reference, have been around for over a century. The process was invented in 1884 by Alfred A. Butler of Bay City, Michigan. In thumb indexing, markers are first placed in the book indicating the places to cut. Then the thumb grooves are clipped out, and finally half-round labels are pasted into place.

Origin and Evolution of the Book Jacket

The book jacket was introduced in 1833 by the English publisher Longmans & Company. Commonly called dust covers or dust wrappers because their original purpose was to keep books clean until they were sold, the jackets usually consisted of plain kraft paper in shades of brown, gray, or blue.

Soon thereafter, for convenience in identifying individual books, the author's name and book title were printed on the spine or front cover and, ultimately, on both. Later, some descriptive matter was also added. By the middle of the 19th century, illustrations were added to the jackets. And, by the turn of the century, with the development of multi-color printing, the book jacket gradually evolved into an advertising poster, especially for books intended for display in bookstores.

Artists found book jacket designing a new lucrative field and, thus, helped speed the process of making jackets selling vehicles—once the book was exposed to a prospective buyer in a bookshop. So established had the field of book jacket design become in the years prior to World War II that, in 1947, a group of the leading U.S. jacket artists established an organization, the Book Jacket Designers Guild, mainly to pressure publishers into paying higher prices for jacket art.

Today, jackets are common on every type of book, whether professional, scholarly, consumer, or children's book. According to Betsy Groban, publisher of children's books at Little, Brown, "A book's cover is absolutely the single most important thing about the physical object that is a book."

In the same *Publishers Weekly* article,[2] Barbara Marcus, publisher of the Scholastic Book Group, described the most important current function of a book jacket, "We look at the jacket as advertising."

In modern book publishing, the jacket is viewed with such importance that in some publishing houses, "jacket committees" consisting of key executives from editorial, marketing, advertising, and trade sales meet regularly with artists to iron out decisions on jacket design.

See also Chapter 9 — Introduction of Publisher Jacket Blurbs Sparks Wodehouse Book Sales.

Origin of Plastic Book Jacket Cover: Birth of an Industry

The plastic book jacket cover, now a standard protective wrapping for jacketed books in virtually all public libraries, had its origin in Newark, New Jersey. In 1939, Arthur Brody, son of a neighborhood pharmacist and a former stock clerk in Bamberger's downtown Newark department store, invented the plastic book jacket cover.

Since his father ran a profitable book lending library out of his drugstore on Bergen Street, young Brody looked for ways to protect the thin paper book jackets, which frayed and tore easily, so that the books would have a longer lending life. He experimented with rigid sheets of clear plastic which he cut to book jacket size, folded between the rubber wring rollers of his grandmother's washing machine, and wrapped around the lending library book jackets.

Thus was born the plastic book jacket industry. Virtually all of the early patents involving plastic jacket covers were held by Brody's fledgling, but fast-growing company, BroDart Industries. The company, currently operating as the Brodart Company of Williamsport, Pennsylvania, is a major wholesale bookseller and seller/manufacturer of library supplies and equipment.

Behind the Scenes in Book Jacket Design and Approval

As you browse for books in a bookstore or scan a book club offering, the first thing you look at is the book jacket. Unless the jacket design makes a promise that this particular book is something that is good or fun or useful or shocking or something you should be reading, the book will fail to attract.

So what do publishers do with popular books to create a design that will get you hooked on a book's jacket?

It starts with the publisher's art director. If it's considered an important book, the art director is likely to read the manuscript, consult with the sponsoring editor, and even sit in on any meetings where the book is likely to be discussed or analyzed. Only then will the art director assign the jacket to a free-lance designer who is believed to be appropriate for the assignment. The designer will be carefully instructed on what the book is about and what the jacket is expected to accomplish visually so the cover will reflect the true spirit of the book.

When the art director is ultimately given a sketch by the free-lancer that is considered acceptable, the sketch will be shown to the book's sponsoring editor. It may then also be presented at the next jacket committee meeting which will be attended by various company officials, most likely including the publisher and editor-in-chief. The more important the book, the greater the involvement of others in the publishing establishment.

When the free-lance designer's sketch has won the acceptance of the various concerned individuals, advance sketches are prepared that are fairly close to the final printed jacket. These will be shown to the sales representatives who call on the bookstores and also to selected bookstore ordering people to help build advance or pre-publication sales for the book.

In some publishing houses, jacket sketches that have gone through many stages of internal approval will be shot down by the sales reps as unacceptable. In such instances, however rare, it's back to the drawing board for a different design that will find acceptance with the reps.

18th Century Type Designs:
Key Influence on Modern Bookmaking

The 18th century saw many great advances in bookmaking as publishing evolved into a trade supported by the reading public (rather than by a single patron) and writing, for the first time, began to pay a living wage. Some of the greatest advances were in type design. A number of pre-eminent 18th century designers of type gave book printing a distinctness, elegance, and flexibility previously unknown in the history of book making.

Among the 18th century type creators that advanced the art of printing were two Englishmen—William Caslon, who produced a new roman typeface in 1720, and John Baskerville, who introduced a typeface bearing his name in the early 1760s. The Baskerville typeface is still a favorite among many modern printers for its clarity and balance.

Baskerville set up his printing business from profits earned earlier in a varnishing business in Birmingham, England. His experience in experimenting with colors led to his invention of a truly black ink that enabled printing of superior quality. He used this ink to print the *Cambridge Bible* of 1763, considered a masterpiece, when he was the printer to Cambridge University.

In France, Pierre-Simon Fournier led in the design of handsome new typestyles that were favored by printers for many years. In Italy, Giambattista Bodoni of Parma created typefaces of finely-graduated weights and sizes that helped speed the growth of modern typography. Bodoni typefaces are still widely used.

Early Book Publishing in 15th Century Europe

While the birth of the book as it is presently known began with the appearance of the *Gutenberg Bible* in 1455, by the end of the 15th century printing had taken place in over two hundred European communities. As a result, more than 30,000 different editions of printed books were produced during those forty-five years.

More than half of these books were church or religion related, consisting of sermons, commentaries, polemics, lives of the saints, church histories, brevaries, psalters, and Bibles. Of the remainder, publishing was done on such subjects as astrology, astronomy, alchemy, chemistry, and the art and practice of healing. There were also an abundance of textbooks of grammatical and philological content made necessary by the rapid spread of the printed word.

With the spread of printing and the printed book in Europe, the main type of books published for reading by the educated public were the Greek and Latin classics. For the man in the street, there were treatises on such topics as household economics, farming, cookery, and home remedies—almost always in the language of their country of origin (mostly French, German, Italian, and English).

The spread of printing and book publishing throughout Europe was largely a result of traveling German craftsmen, who carried the printing art with them. The first printers in Italy were two Germans named Sweynheym and Pannartz, who started a press in Subiaco near Rome in 1464. By the end of the 15th century, there were forty printers in Italy of whom thirty were German. The first printing in France was also by three German craftsmen named Freiberger, Gering, and Krantz, who were brought to Paris in 1470 for a press at the Sorbonne. In 1473, they started their own press in Paris.

Chapter 7

Book Titling Tidbits and Trivia

Sex Movie Copies Mystery Novel's Title;
Book's Author Wins Disclaimer

A book's title cannot be copyrighted. A 1960 legal work, *Rights and Writers*, discussing duplicate use of book titles, stated, "Sometimes a title that has been used previously is made safe for subsequent use by the fact that it has been used, not once, but many times before." And, in fact, in the fall of 1980, five books were published with *Great Expectations* as their main title. However, the courts have ruled that under Federal law, use of an existing book title can be cause for suit if such use is found to cause confusion with the public.

Such a title duplication conflict occurred early in 1993. It involved the novel *Body of Evidence* by Patricia Cornwell, originally published in 1990 by Scribner's and a bestselling paperback when reissued by Avon Books in 1992. *Body of Evidence* was part of author Cornwell's widely acclaimed mystery series featuring coroner Kay Scarpetta.

When the MGM film studio announced that its 1993 schedule of movie releases included a sexually explicit film titled *Body of Evidence*, author Cornwell engaged an entertainment law attorney to demand that MGM change the forthcoming film's title. MGM refused, citing that *Body of Evidence* had already been used in several television movies. Eventually, though, the filmmaker relented and in all of its trailers and advertisements it ran disclaimers stating: "Not based on the novel by Patricia Cornwell."

A subsequent novelization of the MGM movie by Harper carried a changed title, *Deadly Evidence*. At the time of the settlement, author Cornwell was negotiating with another film studio to produce a movie based on her book which would retain her book's title, *Body of Evidence*.

Heroine in 1913 Novel Now Dictionary Word for Optimist

In 1913, the Grand Central Terminal opened in New York and a new dance, the fox trot, was introduced to the American public. It was also the year *Pollyanna* was published.

Pollyanna was about a girl who played a "glad game" in which she found something to be glad about no matter what happened. The book was an instant success selling over a million copies. It made such a mark on the era, that *Pollyanna* quickly moved into everyday language and, ultimately, into all dictionaries as the standard term for anyone who was foolishly and blindly optimistic.

Pollyanna was the fourth novel of author Eleanor Hodgman Porter, born in Littleton, New Hampshire in 1868. While she wrote a sequel, *Pollyanna Grows Up*, in 1915, several other *Pollyanna* sequels published in later years were written by others. Mrs. Porter died in 1920 at the age of fifty-two.

What All-Time Bestseller
Was Best Known by Its Title's Initials?

What all-time bestseller, at the height of its popularity, was more often referred to by its title's initials than by its full name?

Answer: Margaret Mitchell's *Gone with the Wind*. During the lengthy period it remained on the bestseller lists, this modern fiction classic was more often refered to as *GWTW* than by its full title.

When *Scarlett: Sequel to Margaret Mitchell's Gone with the Wind* was published, it picked up the *GWTW* cue and was promptly dubbed *GWTW II*.

The title *Gone with the Wind* is taken from a phrase used by Scarlett O'Hara in the book: "Was Tara still standing? Or was Tara also gone with the wind which had swept through Georgia?" Earlier title considerations by the author and her publisher, the Macmillan Company, had included *Pansy, Tote the Weary Load*, and *Tomorrow Is Another Day*.

Kenneth Roberts Diary Reveals
Title Search for *Rabble in Arms*

How much agonizing do famous authors do over titles for their books? And where do their ideas come from? There is solid information on one such title in the diary of Kenneth Roberts,[2] author of numerous authentically historic novels dealing with American colonial and revolutionary history.

In his November 24, 1931, diary entry, Roberts reports searching for an appropriate title for a work to which he had already devoted three years of research and a year of writing—and which was still six months from completion. Roberts's diary entry showed he had considered these possibilities:

It doesn't take/A man of giant mold to make/A giant shadow on the wall

The Giant Shadow	Freedom's Fetters
The Scarlet Shadow	Webs in the Wilderness
The Dreadful Wedge	The Ragged Rabble
The Scarlet Web	Shackles of Ignorance
The Sublime Rabble	The Webs of Ignorance
Rabble Rivers	The Splendid Rabble
The River of the Free	Rabble, A Chronicle of Arundel

None of these title possibilities apparently seemed right because Roberts's diary does not mention his search for a title until about five weeks later when the January 2, 1932, diary entry reads: "Struck the right title at last...*Rabble in Arms.* That was what Burgoyne, writing on Lord Rochfort, called the volunteers who fought at Bunker Hill.... It describes the volunteers who fought at Bunker Hill perfectly. They were undisciplined, rough, ragged, insubordinate—just a rabble in arms."

Inside Story on John Gunther's *Inside* Book Titles

John Gunther had been a journalist stationed in Europe for the *Chicago Daily News.* His assignment was to provide midwestern readers of the *Daily News* with news of what was happening in Central Europe. Home on leave in 1934, Gunther met Cass Canfield of Harper & Brothers who asked if he would do a book on Europe. Gunther was offered an advance of $5,000— "the largest sum I had ever heard of"—and he accepted.

Working out of London, Gunther finished the book in seven months. While updating the material, prior to submitting it for publication, he still lacked a title. One day, riding a train bound for London, Gunther recalls, "I kept saying to myself, 'I must find a title, I must find a title.' I sought to reason the matter out. What was my book about—it was about Europe. What kind of view did it give—well it tried to tell the story from a particular point of view—an intimate view, an inside view."

"Suddenly," Gunther recalled,[3] "I had it. An Insider's Europe...Looking at Europe from the inside...*Inside Europe*!...I scribbled the title in the margin of a copy of the *London Times*...and later called my publisher and tried *Inside Europe* on him. He like it instantly...so our book had a title at last."

Gunther's first *Inside* book, *Inside Europe*, was published in February 1936 and was an instant hit. It was followed by *Inside Asia* (1939), *Inside Latin America* (1941), *Inside U.S.A.* (1947), *Inside Africa* (1955), and *Inside Russia Today* (1958).

The American reading public readily took to Gunther's *Inside* books over the quarter of a century they were published. Gunther had developed a successful formula for blending his journalistic expertise with careful research and colorful writing to produce in-depth analyses of various parts of the world—each of which instantly made the bestseller lists.

Gunther was amazed not only at how well his *Inside* books caught on, but at the wealth of imitators they attracted. Gunther wrote in *A Fragment of Biography*[3] that after he started with his *Inside* titles, he saw at least twenty books using "Inside" as part of their title, and in one year, 1952, he came across no fewer than seventy-two uses of titles containing "Inside" in newspaper and magazine articles.

See also Chapter 1 — The Author Who Lived to See Himself in Lower Case.

A Squash by Any Other Name Can Become a Bestseller

In 1974, Paula Simmons wrote her *Squash Cookbook*. It sold about 1,500 copies. When consumer tests showed that zucchini was in and squash was out, the book was reissued as the *Zucchini Cookbook*. By 1987, an Association of American Publishers report indicated, the retitled book had sold over 300,000 copies. The 1983 third revised edition of the 132-page paperback is still a brisk seller.[4]

Publisher's Monkeyshines with Title Fools Author

When mass-market paperback publishing started in the late 1930's, virtually all of the early books were reprints of formerly popular hardcover editions. In those years, it was not uncommon for a paperback publisher to issue a reprint with lurid cover art and a more sensational-sounding title.

Thomas Bonn, in *Under Cover*, the story of the paperback industry, tells of an author who, browsing through a paperback display, saw a book on the rack that had an author with the same name as his. When he opened the book, he found that it was his. The publisher had changed the title of his hardcover book from *Deadlines and Monkeyshines* to *Chicago—City of Sin*.

Title That Horrifies Reprinted by Victims

In 1923 and 1924, while in a Bavarian prison, Adolph Hitler wrote *Mein Kampf**—a work that foretold his later attempted extermination of the Jewish people. Nearly seven decades later, the sinister work was published in the language and in the country of the people he tried to exterminate.

In 1992, a version of *Mein Kampf* was quietly published in Israel from a German-to-Hebrew translation accomplished by a survivor of the Nazis whose parents died in the Nazi-run death camps. The limited-edition printing, in a plain black and white cover, was produced, according to a professor of German history at Hebrew University in Jerusalem, "for people interested in learning about National Socialism in the course of study."

* According to one *Time* magazine report, *Mein Kampf* was not Hitler's first choice for a title. It was *Four-and-a-Half Years of Struggle Against Lies, Stupidity, and Cowardice.*

Translator Dan Yaron told *New York Times* writer Clyde Haberman in August 1992 that it took him three years and a dozen rejections to find an Israeli publisher willing to take on the clouded publishing project.

Book Title Eases Trump Down from the Top

In April 1991, when Donald Trump was facing personal bankruptcy, he agreed to give some of his properties to his creditors in exchange for being released from hundreds of millions of dollars in loans that he had personally guaranteed.[5] In July of 1991, Warner Books was about to release Trump's second book, *Surviving at the Top*. But, in reviewing Trump's slight-of-hand maneuver in evading personal bankruptcy, Warner decided to release the new Trump book under the somewhat downgraded title, *The Art of Survival*.[6]

Note: Several years earlier, Trump's first book, *The Art of the Deal*, had been a huge bestseller.

Mailer's *Advertisements for Myself*: Origin

In 1959, when Norman Mailer was dismissed by many in the literary community as a one-book author for his early success at age twenty-five for *The Naked and the Dead*, followed by tepid reception for his successor works, *Barbary Shore* (1951), *Deer Park* (1955), and *The White Negro* (1957), Mailer came back into the limelight with his 1959 book *Advertisements for Myself*, a collection of stories, essays, parts of novels, and articles.

The idea for the book's title came from one of the Harvard-educated author's actions in the early months after he helped found *The Village Voice* in April 1955. Shortly after the founding of the Greenwich Village weekly, in which Mailer owned a share, he had a falling out with his partners over editorial policy and direction. As a consequence, he continued to write his weekly *Voice* column, but ran it as a paid advertisement in the *Voice*. These were, he once admitted, "advertisements for myself."

Why the Author's Name
Must Sometimes Be the Book's Title

Academic textbook publishers often use as a book's title the course name for which the book is intended. At any given time there could be up to a dozen or more texts bearing the same course name. In algebra, for example, there are fifteen texts bearing the title *Basic Algebra*. In such instances, both publishers and users of the book always refer to it by the author's name. For *Basic Algebra*, it might be *Barker* or *Kinger and Wright* or *Carman and Carman*. At McGraw-Hill, one of their basic physics texts was known by generations of students only as *Weber, White and Manning*, the names of the work's three joint authors.

Titling a Textbook to Sell: One International Approach

In college textbook publishing, it is common knowledge that the title of a textbook is often the name of the course for which it is intended. The title also serves to identify the level of the text's presentation—elementary, introductory, intermediate, advanced, or whatever.

In the light of this understanding, a former acquisitions editor at one of the largest technical publishing houses in New York recalls an annual editorial meeting at which he was called on to describe a major new textbook project for which he was about to offer the authors a publishing contract. He explained to those assembled that the proposed book would be titled *Elementary Particle Theory*. The vice president of the publisher's International Division interrupted the presentation to ask the acquisitions editor if he could suggest a slight title change to the authors that he felt would help him sell another thousand copies in the international market: Would they remove the word "Elementary" from the title?

Proposed Book *Getting Along With People* Strikes Gold

In 1934, Leon Shimken, the 27-year-old business manager of a small New York City publishing firm, wrote up an enthusiastic publishing proposal to the company's editors. He told them he had just completed attending a 14-week lecture course at the Hommock Country Club in Larchmont, New York. He felt the lectures were good enough for the company to publish as a book. He even proposed a title: *The Art of Getting Along with People*.

When the editors indicated an interest, the Brooklyn-born business manager made a proposal to the lecturer. After some arm twisting and a promise to provide a stenographer to sit in on the lectures and transcribe them, a publishing contract was signed.

The book was published two years later under the title *How to Win Friends and Influence People*. It was one of the top sellers of the 1930s and, starting with an initial royalty check of $90,000, made the author/lecturer, Dale Carnegie, a wealthy man.

The young man with the idea, Leon Shimken, advanced up the company's ranks and in 1966 at the age of fifty-nine assumed control of the company, Simon and Schuster, and became its president. His brain child is still a substantial seller over half a century later.

Cabby Tosses Question at Passenger— Presto, He's an Author!

As was his custom, a New York cabby was in the habit of asking his nighttime passengers, "Heard any good jokes lately?" When he heard a good one, he would write it down on paper while waiting at stoplights.

One night a female passenger who traded jokes asked the cabby what he did with his jokes. When he told her that he saved them, Patti Breitman, then an acquiring editor at Warner Books, suggested he put them in a book and gave the driver her business card. When the cabby followed the editor's suggestion, his jokes were published in 1986 as a successful Warner paperback that went through many printings. Can you guess the title? *The New York City Cab Driver's Joke Book* by Jim Pietsch.

Errol Flynn's *Wicked Ways* —
How Childhood Reproof Became Bestselling Title

In the mid-1950's, G.P. Putnam contracted with Errol Flynn, the swashbuckling movie idol of the 1940s and 1950s, to publish his autobiography. They had previously agreed to a demand by Flynn's movie agent for an advance of $6,500.

Howard Cady, editor-in-chief at Putnam, recalls that as the work neared completion, it still lacked a title. Cady remembered that during one of his many conversations with Errol Flynn, the movie star had reminisced about his early years and how his mother had once said to him: "You're a wicked, wicked boy!"

Cady reflected that the remark of the actor's mother seemed to fit Flynn's account of his life, so "that's where we got our title."

My Wicked, Wicked Ways, Flynn's autobiographical work, was published in 1959 and became an overnight and much-talked-about bestseller. Two versions of Flynn's book are still in print.

Different Titles from Four Publishers Yet Content Identical

Four books from four different publishers with four different titles—yet, the content of all four was identical. How was it possible?

It started when the Honolulu Zoo issued a book bearing the title, *Zoo Snakes of Hawaii*. One reviewer praised the book as being "completely devoid of zoological, gramatical, and typographical errors."

Similarly, some years ago, a European publisher issued a book titled *The Memoirs of an Amnesiac* that contained only blank pages.

When a New York publisher subsequently issued *The Nothing Book* containing only blank pages, he was sued by the European blank-page publisher, who accused him of plagiarism. The accusation was promptly rejected; the judge ruled blankness is in the public domain. Since that time the publisher has brought out numerous cover variations on *The Nothing Book.*

Finally, years later, a self-publishing couple brought out a book titled *Everything Men Know about Women*. It, too, was blank. Yet the book went on to sell over half a million copies.

Shortest Book Titles Ever

While short two-letter and two-numeral titles have made the bestseller lists, books such as Stephen King's *It* and Avery Korman's *50* about a sportswriter facing his 50th birthday, they are by no means the shortest book titles to appear in this century. Here is a rundown of the eleven titles known to be the shortest:

A, a 1978 book by Louis Zukofsky

C, a 1984 book by Peter Reading

G, a 1960 novel by John Berger

I, a 1985 Yale University Press book by Norman Holland

J, a 1971 book by Robert Durand

K, an undated book by Kathleen Norris

K, a 1996 book by Vassilis Vassilikos

M, an undated paperback by Fritz Lang (Lorrimer Classic Screenplay)

S, a 1976 book by Cid Corman

V, a 1968 paperback by Thomas Pynchon

Z, a 1960s book by Vassilis Vassilikos
(from which a 1969 movie of the same name was also made)

Reminiscent of the one-letter book titles of earlier decades, in 1995, author Wendy McElroy used the repetitious one-letter title *XXX* for her book dealing with pornography and feminist attitudes toward it.

Who's Who Books Prove Costly to Imitator

Marquis Who's Who has been publishing *Who's Who in America* and other *Who's Who* biographical reference works for decades. When a Lake Success, New York, company attempted to publish closely-related *Who's Who* titled directories, a Federal magistrate found in the fall of 1995 that the copycat operation had infringed on the federally registered trademarks of Marquis Who's Who and awarded Marquis $1,649,000 in damages. The *Who's Who* imitator immediately filed for bankruptcy in an effort to avoid paying the damages.

Book Titles with "Beyond" Strong 1990s Favorites

A mid-1990s study of academic book titling reveals that in the six years through the end of 1995, 554 academic book titles started with *Beyond* something—many of them the same things. For example, there were multiple cases of books titled *Beyond Blame, Beyond Borders, Beyond Words, Beyond Conflict, Beyond Death*, and so on down the alphabet to *Beyond Survival* and *Beyond Winning*.

Recurring Themes in 20th Century Book Titles

One of the more interesting phenomena in publishing in the 20th century was the evolution of book titling themes—often patterned after a single successful book or series of books. Some of the more popular book titling themes dealt with numbers, minutes, days, nights, seasons, colors, landscapes, and even the earth, sun and moon.

Some Numbers in Book Titles

Some numbered book titles included: *The Taking of Pelham One Two Three* ... *Four Horsemen of the Apocalypse* ... *Five Against the Sea* ... *Six Degrees of Separation* ... *House of Seven Gables* ... *Eight Strokes of the Clock* ... *Nine Giants* ... *Ten Little Indians* ... *Eleven Harrowhouse* ... *Twelve Days of Christmas* ... *Cheaper by the Dozen* ... *Thirteen Days to Glory* ... *Thirty Degrees North* ... *One Sixty-Five East.*

Advent of Minutes in Book Titles

"Minutes" became a much-used title word in the early 1980s after Kenneth Blanchard and Spencer Johnson converted their business expertise into *The One Minute Manager*, a runaway bestseller for over a year. There soon followed more than fifty other books with *One Minute* in the title (including *The One Minute Lover*). By the mid-1990's, the *One Minute* phenomenon had mushroomed to hundreds of minute variations from *The Five-Minute Interview* ... *Six-Minute Soufflé* ... *Thirty-Minute Panorama of the Bible* ... *The Sixty-Minute Flower Gardener* ... *The One-Hour Negotiator.*

Days of the Week as Book Titles

Days of the week have been used in hundreds of book titles from *Monday to Friday Cookbook* to *Saturday Night and Sunday Morning*. But it took Harry Kemelman's beloved *Rabbi Small* mystery series to bring the word "day" to a fine art. Kemelman used a different day of the week in each of seven mysteries thus: *Monday the Rabbi Took Off* ... *Tuesday the Rabbi Saw Red* ... *Wednesday the Rabbi Got Wet* ... *Thursday the Rabbi Walked Out* ... *Friday the Rabbi Slept Late* ... *Saturday the Rabbi Went Hungry* ... *Sunday the Rabbi Stayed Home*. And, having exhausted the seven days of the week for titles, Kemelman added: *Someday the Rabbi Will Leave, The Day the Rabbi Resigned,* and in March 1996, *That Day the Rabbi Left Town.*

Night as Popular Title Favorite

As days of the week have been popular with authors, so, too, has the word "night" been a heavy titling favorite. Over one thousand book titles include the word "night" in them, more than half having "Night" as the title's starting word. A selection of night examples included *Night Before Christmas* and *Night After Christmas* to *Nighttime* ... *Night to Remember* ... *Night Vision* ... *Night Voyage* ... *Night Walker* ... *Night Without Stars* ... and F. Scott Fitzgerald's *Tender Is the Night.*

Using Seasons in Book Titles

While lacking the popularity of days of the week, seasons have been incorporated into numerous successful book titles as these examples show: *Torrents of Spring ... Summer's Lease ... Autumn Encore ... Fall ... Indian Summer ... The Winter of Our Discontent.*

Many Uses of Color in Titles

Scores of top-selling titles in the 20th century used color in the title—sometimes as an unintentional word, sometimes as an intentional book identifier. Some color-dominated titles included *Black Like Me ... The Color Purple ... A Clockwork Orange ... Dress Gray ... Forever Amber ... Indigo Blue ... Red Storm Rising ... The Scarlet Pimpernel ... White Fang ... Yellow Dog Contract ...* and even Ross Macdonald's *Zebra-Striped Hearse.*

One author in particular, John D. MacDonald, in what many consider the greatest mystery series ever written, used color in the titles of every Travis McGee book so that mystery addicts wouldn't buy the same book twice. Here are MacDonald's color-coded titles: *The Deep Blue Goodbye ... Nightmare in Pink ... A Purple Place for Dying ... The Quick Red Fox ... A Deadly Shade of Gold ... Bright Orange for the Shroud ... Darker Than Amber ... One Fearful Yellow Eye ... Pale Gray for Guilt ... The Girl in the Plain Brown Wrapper ... Dress Her in Indigo ... The Long Lavender Look ... A Tan and Sandy Silence ... The Scarlet Ruse ... The Turquoise Lament ... The Dreadful Lemon Sky ... The Empty Copper Sea ... The Green Ripper ... Free Fall in Crimson ... Cinnamon Skin ... The Lonely Silver Rain.*

Landscapes in Book Titles

Landscapes have been a popular feature in book titles, especially popular fiction, throughout this century from *Beach Front Murders* and *Desert Sunrise* to *Mountain Meadows Massacre* and Jacqueline Susann's *Valley of the Dolls* which, in the twenty years since its 1976 publication, has sold over 26 million copies. Some other popular landscape-bearing titles: *On the Beach ... The Cliff Dwellers ... Woman in the Dunes ... Desert Solitaire ... Animal Farm ... The Onion Field ... The Old Forest ... No Highway ... Hill of Dreams ... The Green Hills of Africa ... Man from the Broken Hills ... The Jungle Book ... Fire in the Lake ... The Magic Mountain ... A Bend in the River ... A River Runs Through It ... The Burning Shore ... Streams in the Desert ... Valley of the Horses ... The Long Valley.*

Earth, Sun, and Moon as Titles

The earth, sun, and moon have been consistent book-title favorites over the years. Current titles starting with "Moon" number close to 250, while titles starting with "Sun" are in the hundreds. Some examples of such titles: *Earth Song ... Life on Earth ... The Good Earth ... Mother Earth ... The Sun Also Rises ... Sun Chief ... Two Under the Indian Sun ... Sun Dial Street ... Moon and Sixpence ... Moon Dance ... One Touch of Moon Dust ... A Moon for the Misbegotten ... Tell Me That You Love Me, Junie Moon.*

Chapter 8

Book Word Origins and Curiosities

Origin and Meaning of "Book"

"Book" comes from the Teutonic word which means writing tablet. Originally derived from the word "beech" because early writing tablets were made from the bark of the beech tree. The word was later extended to refer to a writing, a narrative, a record, a list, or a register.

The book has existed in some form for almost as long as it has been possible to trace any form of civilization. Books in the form of clay tablets with cuneiform inscriptions recorded decisions of the law courts of Babylonia. In early Egypt, books took the form of papyrus rolls covered with hieroglyphics, which date back to 4000 B.C. The recording of events on papyrus continued up until the thirteenth century. The Greeks gave papyrus the name of "biblos" from which the word "bible" is derived.

UNESCO defines a book as a printed and bound document with more than forty-eight pages. A book, however, can have many forms: a printed and bound document, a series of clay tablets, a set of wall panels, numbered and unbound sheets, microfilm or microfiche reproduction, a machine-readable disc, and more.

The ISBN: Its Purpose and Origin

An ISBN, an International Standard Book Number, appears at least twice in every book that has been published in the past quarter century. The ISBN is a unique 10-digit identifying number that usually appears on the back of a book's title page and also in some prominent position outside the book. On the outside it usually appears as a bar code, and above the bar code the number itself is reprinted in an Optical Character Recognition (OCR-A) font.

There are three sequences in each 10-digit ISBN number. The first digit is a "0" or a "1" if the book originates in the United States or another English-speaking country. Other language countries use "2" through "9" as the first digit. The second sequence of numbers identifies the publisher. The third sequence provides the individual publisher's numerical sequence of the book since the publisher started using the ISBN numbering system.

The ISBN system originated in England in 1967. It was adopted in the United States in 1968 and became international in 1969.

Preface, Foreword, and Introduction: How They Differ

In *I Love Books*,[1] John Snider described the function of the opening sections of a book: "We begin to know a book, or rather the man behind the book, as soon as we read his preface and the introduction. These tell us who he is, what he is, and why he has put his thoughts in book form."

The terms preface, foreword, and introduction are often used interchangeably. Yet, there are distinct differences between the three, as the following explanations will reveal:

Preface: A *preface* is an introductory statement in a book, usually about one to three pages in length. It is written by the author or editor to describe the scope, aims, and history of the work and, sometimes, the author's reasons for writing the book. The preface will focus on the book's subject matter, although it may also acknowledge help if there is no separate Acknowledgements section.

Foreword: A *foreword*, says the *Chicago Manual of Style*, is usually a statement from someone other than the author. Often the author or publisher will find an eminent person to write the foreword. In such cases, the eminent person's name may be added on to the book's title page as "With a Foreword by _____." The name of the writer of the foreword will usually appear at the end of the foreword. However, when the foreword is a lengthy one, the name may appear at the beginning. The foreword is not normally changed for succeeding editions.

Introduction: The *introduction* is a preliminary portion of a book dealing with its main subject matter. Considered an integral part of the book, it usually attempts to define the organization and limits of the book. Often, an introduction may carry page numbers the same as the main part of the book and serve as the first chapter rather than as preliminary matter leading up to the start of the book.

Origin of the Colophon

Colophon comes from the Greek, meaning "finishing touch." In the earliest days of bookmaking, medieval scribes placed their names, the date when a particular book was finished, and perhaps a note on the book or a prayer at the end. From this practice evolved the printer's colophon or tail-piece, which provided a wealth of useful information such as title, author, printer's name, place and date of printing, the patron who made possible the printing of the book, etc. It also included the printer's trade emblem, device, or logo. In current publishing practice, this identifying emblem, which usually appears on a book's spine and title page, is referred to as a *colophon*.

By about 1480, book printers started moving the information of the colophon from the back of the book to the front of the book. This marked the start of the title page in printed books. Much of the other information contained in the early end-of-book colophon has been expanded in present-day books to serve as the preface or introduction.

Impression and Edition: How They Differ

Edition: All copies of a book printed from substantially the same setting of type and in the same format. When changes are made in the text, the printing is called a new edition. When the edition of a book is mentioned, it is usually identified by number on the book's title page (for example, second edition). In lieu of a number, the word "Revised" is sometimes used. The number of an edition is also noted on the copyright page since each edition bears a new copyright date, which is the year of that edition's publication.

Impression: A reprinting of a book without change is called an *impression* or a *printing*. Since there may be a number of impressions within an edition, each impression or printing bears the copyright date of that edition. The favored method of identifying a book's impression number, or number of times the book has been reprinted, is the insertion on the copyright page of a series of ascending or descending numbers from 1 to 10 like this:

(ascending)   1 2 3 4 5 6 7 8 9 10

(descending)   10 9 8 7 6 5 4 3 2 1

Then, when a new impression is printed after the initial one is sold out, the book's manufacturer eliminates the "1," leaving the other numbers so that the numbers starting with "2" identify the book as a second printing.

Origin of the Word "Encyclopedia"

Although encyclopedias have existed as forms of extant scholarship for over 2,000 years, the word "encyclopedia" did not come into use until the 16th century. Scholars believe the first usage of the word in English was by the English scholar and diplomat, Sir Thomas Elyot (1490-1546) of Carleton, Cambridgeshire, who was widely known for his championship and use of English for subjects customarily dealt with in Latin. An *Encyclopedia Britannica* entry says of Elyot, "Both as a moral and political philosopher and as a lexicographer he endeavored to 'augment our Englysshe tongue' as a medium for ideas, and he added many new words to the English language."

The most likely first use of the word "encyclopedia" was by Elyot's 1538 *Dictionary* (Latin into English). In it, Elyot explains, "Encyclios et encyclia, the cyckle or course of all doctrines," and defines "Encyclopedia" as "that lernynge whiche comprehendeth all lyberall science and studies."

While the above origin by Elyot was given in the 14th edition of *Encyclopedia Britannica*, the 15th edition (1981) claims a later date with the statement, "Paul Scalich, a German writer and compiler, was the first to use the word to describe a book in the title of his *Encyclopedia; seu, orbis disiplinarium, tam sacrarum quam prophanum epistemon* (*Encyclopedia; or Knowledge of the World of Disciplines, Not Only Sacred But Profane*) issued at Basel in 1559.

Dictionary and Encyclopedia: How They Differ

It's a *dictionary* if the definitions are confined to information the reader must have to understand an unfamiliar word. The emphasis is on the word, and the information must bear directly on the meaning, pronunciation, use, or history of that word.

It's an *encyclopedia* if it contains articles essentially topical and deals with the entire subject represented by the article's title. An encyclopedia on religion, for example, does not merely say what "religion" means or has meant in the past, or how it is pronounced or used—an encyclopedia systematically describes the religions of the world.[2]

Novella and Novel : How They Differ

Originating in Italy around 1460, the term "novella" translates into "something new" or "new thing." Based on local happenings of political or humorous nature, the novella evolved into a short tale using a frame story that tied the various components into a common theme.

In modern times, *novella* is used to describe a medium-length work of fiction that is longer than a short story and shorter than a full length novel. A novella may run 30,000 words, contrasted with a novel which is likely to run 60,000 words or more. A novella may be published in a slim volume, or it may be combined with other short stories and issued in a more ample volume. The word "novel," the larger counterpart of the novella, is derived from a shortened version of the word.

The Coffee Table Book:
It Has Nothing to Do with Coffee or Tables

The *coffee table book* is a large, usually expensive, lavishly produced and illustrated book designed more for scanning and show than for reading. Such books are often displayed in the home in an eye-catching position (sometimes on coffee tables) intended to impress a visitor with the owner's depth of learning or good taste. In the book trade, coffee table books are sometimes referred to as gift books since they are often intended to be purchased as gifts rather than to be read.[3]

The Bookplate:
Its Meaning, Origin, and Introduction in Colonial America

The *bookplate* or *ex libris* is the label usually placed on the inside front cover of a book indicating ownership. The Latin phrase "ex libris," which is used synonymously with bookplate, means "from the library of." On a bookplate, the owner's name is usually filled or printed in.

Nearly as old as the printed book, the oldest-known bookplate dates back to 1480 in Buxheim, Germany. A gift of Brother Hildebrand Brandenburg of Biberach to the Carthusian Monastary in Buxheim, the date of the gift was recorded on the bookplate.

Virtually all the early woodcut book plates were found in large numbers in Germany, long before they began to be used in other countries. Bookplates have been found in colonial America bearing dates spanning the years 1642 to 1674. In Massachusetts, Henry Dunster, the first president of Harvard College (from 1640 to 1654), had three different bookplates which he brought from England. Also, a Stephen Daye bookplate, bearing a 1642 date, was discovered, but there has been no confirmation that it was printed in America. On the other hand, the John Cotton plate of 1674 is definitely known to have been printed in America. Two early American bookplate engravers were Nathanial Hurd and Paul Revere.

The Sponsored Book: What It Is, What Benefits It Offers

The *sponsored book* is a book issued by an established publisher in behalf of a company or organization with a special interest in having it published. Sometimes a payment is made to ensure the publisher against loss from the small sale through normal channels, or the sponsor may agree to buy a sufficient number of copies at an agreed-upon price to ensure profitable publication. The benefits of a sponsored book to a publisher are:

- There is little risk of loss to the publisher.
- The book is usually profitable on publication.
- The book is usually by an accomplished writer.
- Manuscript preparation costs usually are covered by the sponsor.
- The sponsor may also advertise and promote the book at its own expense.
- The publisher usually pays no royalty on sales to the sponsor.

University presses could not afford to fund a large number of important projects they normally undertake if they were not funded by grants from foundations, corporations, or individuals. Through such sponsorships, the fruits of much scientific and scholarly research is brought to light. In addition, numerous classic works are returned to print or brought into existence.

Often, there is extremely limited sales potential of a sponsored book to others than the sponsor. John Wiley, in the 1970s, published a sponsored book on a major chemical scientific development, sponsored by the corporation involved in its development. In exchange for Wiley publishing the book, the corporation agreed in advance to buy 10,000 copies at an agreed-upon price. The book, although well researched and professionally written, failed to sell more than a few hundred copies through normal book sales channels although given normal release and promotional treatment.

Origin and Meaning of Loose Leaf Publishing

Loose leaf publishing means the publishing of unbound books in loose sheets in a ring binder so that outdated or obsolete portions of the book can be updated periodically by the publisher. The invention of loose leaf publishing resulted from the publication of a book with an incorrect chapter. Unable to afford a reprint, the new book publisher, Prentice-Hall, reduced the incorrect book to sheets, replaced the incorrect chapter in each, and sold the loose-paged book in a ring binder.

Today, the practice of loose leaf publishing as a means of keeping publications up to date is in wide use. The idea of currency is crucial in the practice of law, as today's decision may overturn yesterday's rulings and set a new precedent in handling a legal problem. The need to be current with the latest information is also the reason for the wide use of the loose leaf format in the fields of medicine, scientific research, and business.

See also Chapter 3A — How a Disaster Led to Invention of the Movable Page in Book Publishing.

How Baedeker Became a Generic Term for Guidebooks

For over a century and a half, *Baedeker* has meant travel guide, and it is so defined in most dictionaries. This generic term for guidebook is also a series title and brand name for one of the oldest and largest selling travel guides in the world, but one with a humble beginning.

Baedeker travel books had their birth in Koblenz, Germany, in 1835 when 34-year-old Karl Baedeker, a second generation bookseller, decided to try his hand as a publisher with a regional travel guide in the German language. The title: *A Guide to the Rhine: A Rhine Journey from Mainz to Cologne.* When his first guide proved highly successful, Baedeker expanded the effort with additional guides, each dealing with a country or large city.

His travel guides were ultimately published in English, French, and German editions. In addition to establishing the practical travel guide, Baedeker is also credited with introducing the star rating system for evaluating inns and restaurants.

Origin of the Word "Almanac"

An *almanac* is a book containing the days, weeks and months of the year together with information about festivals, holidays, anniversaries, astronomical data, and often other useful information. The word "almanac" is of medieval Arabic origin, according to the *Encyclopedia Britannica*, and means the place where camels kneel. It later came to mean campsite or settlement, and, finally, the weather at the specific site. In modern Arabic, "almanac" is the only word for weather.

The term "almanac" as associated with a publication appears to have come into use in the 13th century. In 1267, Roger Bacon used the term in his encyclopedia, *Opus Maius*, for a table giving the movements of celestial bodies. By the 15th century, the name "almanac" was generally given to calendars of astrological, astronomical, and meteorological tables for periods of years and sometimes also for forecasts; also to church days, saint days, and other anniversaries.

The first standard almanacs were those produced in 1380 by John Somers and in 1386 by Nicolas de Lynne at Oxford, England. Scottish observers pioneered astrological almanacs during the 1500s and 1600s.

The first American almanac was printed at Cambridge, Massachusetts, under the supervision of Harvard College in 1639.

A popular almanac of the late 18th century was *The Lovers Almanac of 1799*, created and distributed by Mason Locke Weems, the Book Peddling Parson and biographer of George Washington.

America's oldest, largest-selling, and most-popular almanac, *The World Almanac and Book of Facts,* has been published annually since 1868. It was first published as *The World Almanac*, an adjunct to the New York City newspaper, *The World*, where it was used as a handbook by the paper's staff to provide background information. Also containing calendars, astronomical data, and advertising, it sold to the public for about 20¢. It consisted of 120 pages, contrasted with about 1,000 pages for the current edition.

Origin of the Word "Atlas" to Describe a Book of Maps

The dictionary defines an *atlas* as a book or bound collection of maps. This term originated with the Flemish cartographer and geographer Gerardus Mercator (1512-1594), considered the foremost geographer of the 16th century. When Mercator published his first collection of maps in 1569, on the title page of the collection he drew a figure of Atlas supporting the world on his shoulders (Atlas is the Titan in Greek mythology condemned by Zeus to support the heavens on his shoulders).

This 1569 collection was the first part of Mercator's great atlas in which he sought to describe the creation and history of the world. Although never completed, it was printed by his son in 1595 (a year after his death) with the title: *Atlas, or Cosmographical Meditations on the Structure of the World.* Mercator's *Atlas* was widely used by early explorers of the New World.

Origin of Incunabula: The First Printed Books

Printed books originated in 1450 with the invention of movable type by Johannes Gutenberg, a goldsmith from Mainz, Germany. When the so-called *Gutenberg Bible* was completed in 1456, the number of manuscript books in Europe numbered only in the scores of thousands. However, by the end of the year 1500, just fifty years after the invention of printing, there were more than nine million books in print.

Incunabula is the term now used to describe all books printed from 1450 through the year 1500. The term comes from the Latin words meaning "things in the cradle." As part of the English language, it has now come to mean the first states of anything or any artifact of an early period.

The largest collection of incunabula in the United States may be found in Washington, D.C. at the Library of Congress. It holds 5,600 such books.

Origin, Meaning, and Current Use of the Blurb

A *blurb* is a short sales pitch or review of a book usually printed on the jacket or in an advertisement. For paperbacks, the blurb is usually on the back cover. The term "blurb" was coined by Gelett Burgess* (1866-1951), a Boston-born humorist, author, and editor of a San Francisco literary review, *The Lark*.

Blurb evolved from a 1907 effort by Burgess to adorn the cover of his latest novel with the picture of a pretty young woman (pictures of young women on novel covers were a common practice at that time). In the advertising text accompanying the picture, he christened the woman, Miss Belinda Blurb. In a later effort to introduce the word into the language, Burgess used the word "blurb" in his 1914 book, *Are You a Bromide?*, to mean an advertising pitch for a book. The word caught on.

In present-day publishing, the jacket blurb for most general interest books are written by the publisher's publicity department. However, for some high level scientific and scholarly books, the author may be invited to write the blurb so that it accurately reflects the book's true content.

* Gelett Burgess, a conscious coiner of new words, was included in a 1930's list of America's ten leading coiners of slang that was compiled by W.J. Funk of Funk and Wagnalls, publishers of the *Standard Dictionary*.

First Use of a Publisher's Blurb in an American Book

Although the word "blurb" for a publisher's short sales pitch on the jacket or cover of a book was not yet introduced, the first publisher's blurb to appear in a book took place sometime around 1791. The writer of the blurb was George Washington. Here's how it came about.

Mason Locke Weems, an ordained clergyman from Arundel County, Maryland, and an itinerant book salesman, had also established himself as a publisher of books on upbeat religious and moralistic topics in association with the publisher Mathew Carey. Weems had published a highly-successful book by the Italian nobleman Luigi Cornaro, titled *Sure and Certain Methods of Attaining a Long and Health Life.*

Reissued in a new title, *The Immortal Mentor*, Weems sent a copy to Washington who responded with this comment: "I have perused it with great satisfaction and hesitate not to say that it is, in my opinion at least, an invaluable compilation. I cannot but hope that a book whose content does such credit to its title, will meet a very general patronage."

Weems had Washington's endorsement printed and pasted into existing copies of *The Immortal Mentor*, and in subsequent printings and editions the blurb became the Introduction to the book.

Origin of Block Books:
Books Printed From Hand Carved Wooden Blocks

The term *block book* is used for books in which all the words on a page were cut by hand on a solid block of wood. There is no record of any block book being printed until twenty years after Johannes Gutenberg's invention of printing from movable type. However, the history of block printing of illustrative matter from engraved wooden blocks predates the invention of printing from movable type by nearly 700 years. Almost certainly of Chinese origin, a block print bearing a dated inscription was produced in 77 A.D.

Bowdler's Contribution
to the Vocabulary of Book Publishing

When in 1818 Thomas Bowdler published the *Family Shakespeare*, the publishing event brought into being four new words which are now part of the vocabulary of book publishing. In his published version of Shakespeare's works, Bowdler removed all the words that he considered dirty, contentious, or blasphemous. The word-cleaning practice initiated by Dr. Bowdler (he had been trained as a doctor) spread to other areas of publishing and for several generations, both in England and America, cleaned-up texts of many literary classics were published that, because of changes, were inaccurate and misleading.

The term "bowdlerize" appears in most dictionaries today as a description for the prudish expurgation of a book. The specific practice has become known as "bowdlerization." The responsible publisher or editor is a "bowdlerizer" while the general practice is referred to as "bowdlerism."

Origin, Meaning, and Value of Bestseller

The most popular use of the term *bestseller* is to denote a book in current active demand in bookstores. The term is generally based on sales rank over a given period of time on one of the national indexes such as the *New York Times* or *Publishers Weekly* bestseller list.

The term bestseller "was coined and came into common use," wrote publisher Fred Melcher in 1946, "because it filled a need. A term was needed to describe what were not necessarily the best books, but the books that people liked best."

In *70 Years of Best Sellers,*[5] Alice Hackett wrote that "The term *best seller* is comparative rather than absolute. There is no fixed figure which a book's sales can reach in order for it to be considered a best seller. A book may be a best seller in one store or in one city. It may be the best seller over the whole country, for a month, a year, five years, or a century."

Of the bestsellers on the national lists, Carole Sinclair, a former marketing head at Doubleday Publishing, wrote in 1985,[6] "The best thing that a publisher can say about any book is that it is a best-seller. Once the word appears in an ad headline, it generates a whole new market: those people who read best-sellers, but little else."

The longest duration on the *New York Times* bestseller list has been for *The Road Less Traveled* by M. Scott Peck, which had its 648th week on the paperback nonfiction list as of April 14, 1996. Chances are that it will continue on that list for many weeks to come.

An Understanding of Grain,
or Why a Book Sometimes Won't Stay Closed

Paper used in books has a definite grain, which means it tends to fold more easily in one direction than the other. Grain results from the way the fibers tend to align themselves as the pulp is laid in the paper manufacturing process.

Books are normally printed on sheets containing many pages. The pages are laid out so, when the sheets are folded, the grain for each page runs up and down, rather than crossways. Books printed on pages with the grain running vertically tend to stay closed. If, however, a book is printed with the grain running crossways (as is sometimes done), the book has an unpleasant springy feel and tends *not* to stay closed.

Origin of Writing and Printing with Ink

The earliest reported use of ink is about 2697 B.C. when hollow reeds were used for writing pens. The early inks, used in both China and Egypt, consisted of lampblack (carbon) mixed in a solution of water and lamp oil. This combination was used for many centuries until the invention of movable type in the fifteenth century. About 1440, inks started being made by mixing varnish or boiled linseed oil with lampblack to speed the ink-drying process and, thus, increase printing production.

Origin of the Word "Parchment"

Parchment, which made possible the making and binding of books due to its capability of being folded, came into wide general use in the second century B.C. because of a dispute between the rulers of two ancient countries. As the story goes, Eumenes II*, king of Pergamum in Asia Minor, incurred the ill will of the Ptolomies, then rulers of Egypt, who imposed an embargo on the exportation of papyrus from Egypt to Pergamum.

As a substitute writing material, the people of Pergamum reverted to the use of dressed and prepared animal skins. In fact, they so refined the process that the substitute writing material they created became an exportable commodity. As the improved writing material was more durable than the fragile papyrus, it was exported into the Roman world, where it became known from its place of origin as *pergamena*, from which the name in time found its way into English as *parchment*. Parchment was the dominant writing material in Europe until the advent of paper.

Origin of Signature to Denote a Section of a Book

A *signature* is the folded printed sheet that forms one section of a book. Used since the earliest days of book printing, the term was originally used by the printer as an aid in identifying the printed sheets during the binding process. The "signature" was a distinguishing mark, letter, or figure placed at the foot of the first page of each form or printed sheet of a book for the purpose of showing the order of that sheet's appearance in the book. The term came to also identify the form or sheet on which the mark was placed.

Another use of the term "signature" dates back to the early days of printing when book signatures were folded by hand. The folders had to initial or place their signatures on their own work so that errors could be traced.

* It was under the same king that there was founded at Pergamum the celebrated library that for a long time rivalled the great Alexandrian Library in Egypt. With 100,000 volumes, the library at Alexandria housed the greatest collection of books in the world before the invention of printing.

A book signature commonly consists of sixteen or thirty-two pages, although any multiple of four is possible. The actual term *signature* has been traced back to 1656, although books assembled from folded sheets date back to the fifth century.

Origin of Italics, Compact Books, and Cardboard Covers

Italics are sloping types, as distinct from roman types. The idea behind the design of such a face was its space-saving properties which allowed the Greek classics to be reprinted in small, compact editions.

Aldus Manutius (1449-1515), the great scholarly printer who established the Aldine Press in Venice in 1490, came up with the idea for the design of italics. Most of his early productions were Greek texts or Greek grammars, but it was his desire to be able to produce copies of the great classics in small, compact, and affordable editions that traveling scholars could easily carry with them in their saddlebags.

In 1500, Aldus had his typefounders make a font of the new italic type based on the form of handwriting known as *chancery* script, from its development in the Vatican chancery. The type was made from punches cut by Francesco Griffo of Bologna, a goldsmith then resident in Venice. The new type was first introduced in a few words of a woodcut illustration in the *Epistole* of Saint Catherine of Siena, which Aldus published in 1500. The first book completely set in the new italic typeface was the *Virgil* of 1501.

Aldus made a number of other important contributions to the progress of book publishing and book production, including the production of books in compact, affordable editions. In addition, he was also among the first book producers to use cardboard for the covers of books, cardboard being a new and lighter material that gradually replaced wood covers.

Bibliomania —
Origin of Term and History's Greatest Example

The dictionary defines *bibliomania* as "an exaggerated liking for the acquisition and ownership of books." Although certain people had been displaying a madness for the ownership of books in earlier centuries, bibliomania did not come into widespread use as a word until 1809. That year, the Reverend Thomas Frognall Dibdin (1776-1847) popularized the word in a published work titled, *The Bibliomania; or, Book-Madness; containing some account of the History, Symptoms, and Cure of This Fatal Disease.*

In a 1966 psychiatric journal article, Dr. Norman S. Weiner of Philadelphia characterized the bibliomaniac as a person with an "inordinate desire" for books who will "pursue a volume in an active or seductive way; he will use intrigue and stealth; he will hazard his fortune, and he will journey around the world, or even marry for the gain of a coveted book."

The greatest bibliomaniac of the 20th century was Stephen Blumberg of Ottumwa, Iowa. Over a 20-year period ending when he was caught in 1990, he had stolen some 23,600 books weighing over nineteen tons and valued at $20 million, from libraries in forty-five states, the District of Columbia, and two Canadian provinces. To gain access to these libraries, Blumberg had stolen the identity of a University of Minnesota professor.

At his 1991 trial in Omaha, Nebraska, Blumberg's attorneys used an insanity defense. Conceiving himself a Victorian man, Blumberg thought of his ill-gotten collection as a resource library for studies in Victorian Americana. Among the books stolen were a first edition of *Paradise Lost*, sheet music from the 8th century, Anton Koberger's hand-printed 1480 *Biblia Sacra*, and a 1493 history of the world, the *Nuremberg Chronicles*, written in Latin.

Found guilty of theft, he was sentenced to five years and eleven months in prison, plus fined $200,000. On December 29, 1995, Blumberg was released from prison, but soon fled the half-way house where he was staying. Captured again, he was later released to the custody of his father, Dr. Henry Blumberg, on April 26, 1996.[7]

Biblioclast — History's Most Notorious Example

The term *biblioclast* means mutilator of books. The word comes from "biblio," or book, and "clast," modeled after the word iconoclast which means breaker or destroyer of images.

The most infamous iconoclast in history was the British rare book collector, John Bagford (1650-1716). He amassed sixty-four large volumes containing the mounted title pages he had torn out of 25,000 books.

Bagford, a shoemaker by trade, intended the collection of 25,000 book title pages for a history of printing which he never wrote. Bagford's collection may be seen in the British Museum where it is classified as the Bagford Fragments.

Jailed Bibliomaniac: Can Prison Library Be Safe?

One very recent case of book mania resulted in the theft and destruction of more than 600 scholarly books from the Widener Library at Harvard University. Before "the library slasher" was caught, he had stolen or mutilated many books, including valuable texts in Latin and Greek as well as rare books on early Christianity in Icelandic and other languages.

Leaving notes threatening anyone who tried to stop him, Stephen J. Womack, a 41-year-old temporary worker at Harvard's Widener Library, turned his $5-an-hour job into a one-man theft ring. According to his court testimony, Womack was only seeking revenge against authorities who had sentenced him to a state mental hospital after unrelated convictions for malicious destruction and exposing himself.

On March 14, 1996, Womack was sentenced to seven to ten years in prison. Will that stop him? Who knows? Just after his arrest, he asked an investigator the following "dead-up serious" question: "If I go to jail, do you think they'll let me use the library there?"

The Complete Guide to Biblio Words

Biblio — A prefix from the Greek meaning "of or pertaining to books."

Bibliobibuli — Those who read too much.

Biblioclast — One who mutilates or destroy books.

Bibliodemon — A book fiend.

Bibliogenist — A producer or publisher of books.

Bibliognost — One who knows books and bibliography.

Bibliographer — One who writes about books.

Biblioklept — One who steals books.

Bibliokleptomaniac — One with an obsessive impulse to steal books.

Bibliolater — One with extreme devotion to, concern with, or dependence on books.

Bibliolestes — A book robber.

Bibliology — An account of books or book lore.

Bibliomancy — Prophecy by books or by verses of the Bible.

Bibliomania — A passion for collecting books.

Bibliomaniac — One with an exaggerated liking for acquiring and owning books.

Bibliopegy — Bookbinding as a fine art.

Bibliopegist — A bookbinder.

Bibliophage — One who devours books; an ardent reader or bookworm.

Bibliophile — A lover of books; a book collector.

Bibliophobe — One who fears books.

Bibliopole — A dealer in books; a bookseller; sometimes a second-hand or rare book dealer.

Biblioriptos — One who throws books around.

Bibliosopher — One who gains wisdom from books.

Bibliotaph — One who hides or hoards books.

Bibliothec — A librarian.

Bibliotheca — A library; a collection of books.

Chapter 9

Innovative Book Promotion and Exploitation

The Advertisement that Started
the Mass-Market Paperback Revolution in America

Although there had been several waves of paperback book publishing in the United States in the preceding 100 years, the birth of mass-market paperback publishing, as it exists in America today, began when Robert Fair de Graff launched a revolutionary publishing plan called Pocket Books that was designed to make bestselling books available in unabridged form at 25¢ a copy. On June 19, 1939, Pocket Books placed a full-page advertisement in the *New York Times* over the headline:

The new Pocket Books that may revolutionize
New York's reading habits

Today is the most important literary coming-out party in the memory of New York's oldest book lover. Today your 25¢ piece leaps to a par with dollar bills. Now for less than the few cents you spend each week for your morning newspaper you can own one of the great books for which thousands of people have paid from $2 to $4.

These new Pocket Books are designed to fit both the tempo of our times and the needs of New Yorkers. They're as handy as a pencil, as modern and convenient as a portable radio—and as good looking. They were designed specially for busy people—people who are continually on the go, yet who want to make the most of every minute.

Never again need you say "I wish I had time to read" because Pocket Books gives you the time. Never again need you dawdle idly in reception rooms, fret on train or bus rides, sit vacantly staring at a restaurant table. The books you have always meant to read "when you had time" will fill the waits with enjoyment.

First Publisher Ad Designed to Benefit Booksellers

In the earliest centuries of book publishing, the printer, publisher, and bookseller were one and the same. By the early eighteenth century, the retail book trade in Europe was becoming better organized and the separation between publisher and bookseller more evident. According to the 15th edition of the *Encyclopedia Britannica*, the first advertisement ever by a publisher claiming that his books were "available in every bookshop" was made by a publisher in Leipzig, Germany, in 1717.

Some 19th Century Approaches to Book Advertising

Advertising for general interest books was slow to get off the ground in the United States. Prior to the Civil War, publishers did not consider advertising as their responsibility. Instead, they required authors, by contract, to pay for any promotion outside of the publisher's catalog listing.

A *New York Times* editorial in 1885 stated that "publishers have no real conception of the art of advertising," although the editorial conceded "that at least one publisher has learned how to conduct business." That publisher, credited with knowing how to do business, had sent *sandwich men* out on the street advertising a new novel.

In the last decade of the 19th century, publishers began experimenting with various advertising formats in the newspapers—one going so far as to advertise one letter each day of a book's title until the entire title had been spelled out.

According to John Tebbel in *Between Covers*,[1] "In 1896, Funk & Wagnalls became probably the first publiser to use card advertising in streetcars displaying the merits of its *Standard Dictionary* tucked in between displays of skirt binding and baking powder."

Start of Newspaper Book Review Supplements

Book review supplements first began appearing in newspapers in the early 1900s. About that time, book publishers had begun buying advertising space in newspapers to exploit their major titles. Mindful of this potential source of advertising revenue, newspapers added book departments to attract more such advertising. One of the earliest leaders among the book supplements was the *New York Times Saturday Book Review Supplement*.

Beginnings of Innovative Book Advertising

The decade of the 1920's was notable for the spread of book advertising to a variety of new media. Billboards across the country were used to tout major new works such as *Elmer Gantry* and *Sorrell and Son*. New York's

Fifth Avenue buses began carrying advertising. In addition, outdoor electric signs appeared in this country to advertise new books.

The most innovative book advertising of the decade occurred in 1928 when skywriting was used for the first time to advertise a book titled *Murder?*. An airplane wrote "Murder" in the skies over New York City with tie-in newspaper advertising the following day. On subsequent days, the airplane's messge to New York City skywatchers was "Read Murder."

Mail Order Advertiser Who Sold Over 500 Million Books

The book industry has had its share of successful direct mail geniuses over the years, but none can compare with Philadelphia-born Emanuel Haldeman-Julius, publisher of the Little Blue Book series in Girard, Kansas, from 1919 to 1951. Haldeman-Julius (Haldeman was his wife's maiden name) concocted wild, often erratic advertisements that helped sell a reported 500 million copies of his 2,000 titles over the years through the mails at an average price of 5¢ a copy (minimum order: 20 copies).

His first advertisement for the little paper-covered, stapled, pamphlet-like books of about sixty-four pages each (measuring 3½" x 5") produced 5,000 orders. A second ad, for which he paid $150, produced an added $1,000 in orders. Sensing that he was on to a good thing, he was off and running with his combination publishing/advertising campaign under the headline: "Would You Spend $2.98 for a College Education?"

Known as Little Blue Books because of their semistiff blue cover stock, most titles were scaled-down reprints of the classics that were in the public domain.

Among the respondents to his mail order advertising campaigns were the Emperor of Ethiopia, Haile Selassie, who wrote for a complete list of Little Blue Books; Admiral Richard E. Byrd, who took a complete set of Little Blue Books with him during his exploration of the South Pole; and Franklin P. Adams, a regular on the panel of the nationally-popular *Information Please* radio show.

There was wide opposition to Haldeman-Julius's advertising tactics, centered primarily among the clergy and religious people. His merchandising methods were roundly denounced, and efforts were made to stop some of them.

Introduction of Publisher Jacket Blurbs
Sparks Wodehouse Book Sales

In the years prior to World War I while he still lived in England, the English humorist and writer, P.G. Wodehouse had written numerous books, but each sold only about 2,000 copies. In 1917, Wodehouse switched to a new British publisher, Herbert Jenkins. To stimulate sales of the books he published, Jenkins had started printing a synopsis of each book on the book's jacket under the heading: "This Story Is About..." With these blurbs added to the jackets of Wodehouse books, the average sale went from about 2,000 copies to 9,000 copies.

Wodehouse was likened to Mark Twain as a humorist and is best remembered for his creation of the character Jeeves. He churned out more than seventy novels during the ninety-four years of his life (1881-1975), and his books have sold more than 30 million copies in countless translations.

Little known, even to Wodehouse fans, is that he also collaborated as a lyricist on various Broadway musicals with George Gershwin, Jerome Kern, and Rudolph Friml, among others. Wodehouse wrote the song "Bill" for the musical "Oh, Lady, Lady," but the show opened February 1, 1918, without it because it didn't suit the voice of the leading lady. When it was revived nine years later as a ballad in "Show Boat" for Helen Morgan, it became a nightly show-stopper.

Massive Book Ad Campaign Had Surprise Ending

The editor at a mass market paperback house had been ignoring a hardcover book sent in weeks earlier for possible reprint consideration. All of a sudden he began seeing the hardcover publisher's ads for the ignored book in subways and buses all over New York City. The ad surprised the editor. He knew the hardcover publisher was a small house not given to expensive advertising campaigns. So he concluded there had to be something special about the book or they wouldn't be pushing it so hard.

So the editor read the book, loved it, and purchased the reprint rights at a very modest fee from the hardcover publisher. Subseqently he honored a request from the author of the book for a luncheon get-together. The author appeared not that well off and, based on the hardcover sales, he couldn't have earned more than $3,000 in hardcover royalties. So the editor asked the author: "What do you do for groceries?"

Replied the author, "I work for Transit-Ads."

Marketer Turns to Phone Book for Hero's Descendants

Talk to any veteran book marketing manager, and he will recount some bitter lessons learned by experience. A good case in point is the experience some decades back of one of McGraw-Hill's most seasoned mail marketing managers.

He had the responsibility for the direct mail promotion of a forthcoming book on Robert E. Lee, chief general of the Confederate armies during the Civil War. While considering direct mail possibilities, he had a brainstorm: Why not mail a promotion to all the people named Lee in the various telephone directories?

After locating a mailing list source that was able to access and supply all the "Lees" listed in telephone directories, he sent each name an attractive brochure on the great general. The mailing failed.

Subsequent investigation for the mailing failure provided a simple answer: The vast majority of Lees taken from the phone directories were either proprietors of Chinese laundries (or related to them) and had little interest in the distinguished Civil War general!

Strange New Market For Books:
Losing Lottery Ticket Buyers

Here's a book promotion aimed only at lottery ticket buyers—but only those who lost. The sponsor was the government of the Canadian Province of Ontario, which runs a weekly lottery for $1 a ticket. What the Ontario government did, during several periods in the late 1970s and 1980s, was to establish a time interval during which losing lottery tickets could be used as cash toward a purchase of a book by a Canadian author.

When first tried for three months in 1978, losing Wintario lottery tickets could be used as 50¢ cash, up to four tickets per purchase, to buy any Canadian-authored book, hardcover or paper. In subsequent promotions in the early 1980's, losing lottery tickets could be used to buy only Canadian-authored paperbacks, with a limit of $1 per book. Over 95% of Ontario's booksellers honored the losing tickets as cash, for which they were reimbursed from lottery proceeds by the Ontario government.

Using Magazine Subscriptions to Sell Books

Among the more oddball book promotion stunts was the one launched in the fall of 1992 by the publisher of Sidney Sheldon's *The Stars Shine Down*. William Morrow, the New York publisher, arranged in August of 1992 to have bookstores hang Reservation Boards in their stores so potential buyers of Sheldon's book could reserve a copy of the book in advance of publication. When they later returned and bought the novel, they were given a free three-month magazine subscription of their choice to one of three popular magazines published by a sister company of Morrow.

Bestseller List Created Advertising Market for Local Paper

In the early 1980's, the Sunday Book Review section of the *San Francisco Chronicle* was practically without book advertising. Instead, the national advertising money of big publishers seemed to go directly to the *New York Times Book Review* and to the book trade journal, *Publishers Weekly*. The editor of the *Chronicle* supplement, Patricia Holt, decided to do something about it.

As a first step, she instituted a local bestseller list, which appeared weekly in the *Chronicle* book supplement next to the *New York Times* bestseller list. In addition, the local Northern California Booksellers Association was encouraged to buy a volume of advertising space in the Sunday book section which it made available at its greatly-reduced local rates to local booksellers. The booksellers, in turn, used cooperative advertising money offered by many publishers to advertise books with good local sales potential.

As a further incentive to build publisher book advertising, the *Chronicle* also alerted the publisher's local reps to upcoming reviews that would be given major coverage. The reps, in turn, would call their sales managers in New York urging them to place tie-in advertising to coincide with the appearance of the review.

Best Spot for Publisher Book Advertisement

Publishers have found that the ideal spot for advertising their books is in the book's title. The title must carry an advertising message—especially an information-oriented book—that will immediately capture the attention and imagination of the potential buyer and also identify with the book's logical audience. One of the outstanding examples of a reference book that aptly portrays its content is the 1992 third edition of the *Random House American Heritage Dictionary of the English Language* which shows the word dictionary in its title on the book cover and spine thus:

dic•tion•ar•y

Gimmicky Spot for Publisher Book Spiel

When Dutton published *Bogart: In Search of My Father* by Stephen Bogart in the summer of 1995, it sent phone cards good for five minutes of free long distance phone time to each of its top 500 bookstore accounts. Each time a bookseller used the phone card, he or she first got a short promotional spiel on the Bogart book before their call was put through.

First Use of Book Chapter
to Advertise Book in Consumer Magazine

On January 10, 1996, when *Days of Drums* by Philip Shelby went on sale, the book's publisher, Simon & Schuster, inserted a chapter sampler in that week's issue of the million-circulation *Entertainment Weekly* magazine. The *New York Times* reported on that day, "This was the first time a chapter from a trade book has been included as an advertisement in a consumer magazine." It cost Simon & Schuster $400,000 to insert the book chapter into the magazine.

Chapter 10

Some Personal Publishing Recollections

Books in First Neiman Marcus Christmas Catalog

The annual Neiman Marcus Christmas catalog is usually a news-making event because of its unusual selections. For example, in 1992, the thirty-third annual catalog contained 484 items highlighted by a His and Hers selection costing $35,000—a pair of vintage motorcycles with sidecars.

Reading about the 1992 catalog in the *New York Times*[1] brought to mind my involvement in the first Neiman Marcus catalog in 1959, in which books were an important component. I was then sales manager of Baker & Taylor, the country's largest wholesale bookseller, located in Hillside, New Jersey. One day, I received a phone call from Texas with the caller identifying himself as Stanley Marcus.

"We're putting together a Christmas catalog," Marcus told me, "And I understand that you can supply us with an assortment of good books for that catalog."

I assured Marcus that we could and asked what books he had in mind. He told me he had no specific books in mind but would like Baker & Taylor to send him a suggested list of gift books priced at $25 and higher. This was at a time when most bestselling fiction and nonfiction was priced at $2.95.

One of my assistants, Jerry Corbut, put together such a list, and I dispatched it to Neiman Marcus. Most were found acceptable and, thus, the first Neiman Marcus Christmas catalog was partially a book catalog.

In the years and catalogs that followed, the catalog aimed at news-making entries. One year it was a pair of matching Beechcraft airplanes, another a fully-operative solid-gold miniature train carrying rubies, diamonds, sapphires, and emeralds. Then, too, there was a mummy case, a pair of ostriches, and a Chinese junk at a bargain price of $11,500 delivered from

Hong Kong. But, most likely, none of the thirty-six catalog offerings that followed that first one were as bookish as the one in 1959 with all the coffee table books Baker & Taylor provided from dozens of American publishers.

How Scientific Publishers Mirror Research Advances

The earliest results of scientific research usually are published in various scientific journals. Consequently, the publishers of advanced scientific journals frequently are the first to publish break-through books that result from such advanced research.

For many years, I was associated with one of the world's foremost publishers of advanced scientific journals, Elsevier Publishing Company of Amsterdam, Holland. During that time, I worked in the New York office of its American affiliate.

In the early 1960s, Elsevier airmailed to me a book just off the presses by L.M.V.U. Salton titled *The Bacterial Cell Wall*, so I would have it in time to display it at a meeting of scientific researchers (FASEB) in Atlantic City. In the publisher's book display at the meeting, the book drew scant attention.

The following year at the same Atlantic City meeting of scientific researchers, attendees lined up at the Elsevier book display to inspect this same book. That year, the book was our No. 1 seller at the meeting. A year later, the book's third year of display at this particular meeting, the book was hardly looked at and sales were nil.

Puzzled by this phenomenon, I questioned the Elsevier science editor from Holland, Dr. Jacques Remarque, who gave this reply: "Two years ago, scientific research had not yet reached the cell wall, so the book was too early. Last year, research had arrived at that point, so the book was 'hot.' This year, research has advanced beyond the cell wall, so the book is passé."

Famed Dictionarist's Strange Source of Inspiration

As a marketer for some thirty years in the book industry, I came in frequent contact with authors, and I found it often eased conversation to ask how they started writing books. Perhaps the strangest reply I ever received to this question came in the 1960s from an internationally-recognized compiler of multi-lingual technical dictionaries.

"How did you get started writing dictionaries?" I asked the noted European scholar when we were having lunch during a New York visit.

Without hesitation, he offered this unusual reply: After his first wife had died, he'd gotten himself locked into a bad second marriage. To avoid conflict with his second wife, he developed the habit of going to sleep early in the evening. As a consequence, he told me, he arose very early as well.

"And what can you do in the middle of the night?" he added, "So I started writing dictionaries."

Achieving the Impossible:
Monumental Dictionary Accomplishment

If it is possible for an author to achieve the impossible—and under impossible conditions—I know of only one author in my 30-plus years in publishing who accomplished it. His name was Ernest Klein. In Toronto, Canada, where he made his home, he was known as the rabbi of the orthodox Congregation Beth Yitshak.

His authorship was something special. He created the first wholly new major dictionary of English language etymology to appear in this century. His work, now called *Klein's Comprehensive Etymological Dictionary of the English Language*, was first published by Elsevier Publishing Company in two volumes in 1965 and 1967. In 1971, it was reissued in a large format single-volume edition (when the name "Klein" was also added to the title).

To begin with, the undertaking of a major etymological work of the English language from the beginning would have been a monumental task even for a large staff of scholars and researchers. But Dr. Klein's etymological work of nearly 50,000 entries was strictly a one-man effort.

And so good was that effort, that on publication virtually all the reviews were raves (*up-to-date...valuable...accurate...meticulous...superb...comprehensive...scholarly...immense*). In addition, the American Library Association judged it "the best reference work of the year."

What made Dr. Klein's undertaking more incredible is that, in order to accomplish it, he had earlier mastered all forty languages—both spoken and extinct—in which the English language is rooted. Even more remarkable, he was working in a foreign language (English was not his native tongue) and was, for part of the time, under threat of instant death in a Nazi concentration camp.

Dr. Klein received his Ph.D. at the University of Vienna, after having left his home in Nove Zamky, Czechoslovakia. In 1944, while rabbi of the Jewish congregation in Nove Zamky, he was interned along with his wife, child, three sisters, and parents in the Auschwitz concentration camp and later the Allach-Dachau concentration camp. It was during this period that he started his work on etymologies. When the concentration camps were liberated by American troops in 1945, Klein settled in Toronto with his sister and her husband—the only surviving members of his family.

In Toronto, Klein completed his monumental etymological dictionary, each word with its etymology on a single piece of paper, patiently written by hand. Eventually, when the Canadian Council for Culture was made aware of his project, they gave Dr. Klein a grant to have his manuscript typed in a form that could be submitted to Elsevier.

The dedication in Dr. Klein's monumental *Dictionary* is a reminder that the human spirit can flourish and survive, even under the most adverse conditions, and still produce works of greatness:

Dedicated to the Sacred Memory of the Best Parents
My Dear Mother
Who After a Life of Self-Sacrifice Died in Szatmar in 1940
and My Dear Father
The World-Renowned Rabbi and Scholar
Rabbi Ignaz (Isaac) Klein of Szatmar
Who Died a Martyr of His Faith in Auschwitz in 1944;
and to the Sacred Memory of My Wife
and of My Only Child, Joseph (Hayyim Israel)
who also Fell Victims to Nazism in Auschwitz in 1944

How *A Stress Analysis of a Strapless Evening Gown* Became a Bestseller

For a generation up to the 1970s, Professor Robert L. Weber stimulated and inspired his physics students at the University of Pennsylvania by giving them examples of parodied and misapplied concepts of physics, symbolic logic, and mathematics that would make physics learning more fun. He used such examples as "A stress analysis of a strapless evening gown" ... "The inertia of a broomstick" ... "Heaven is hotter than hell" ... "When does jam become marmelade" ... and many more.

Ultimately, when Professor Weber had assembled several hundred of these examples, he put two hundred of his favorites (including the above) into an anthology which he titled *A Random Walk in Science.*

He first offered the manuscript to the publisher of his widely-used introductory college physics text—McGraw-Hill—since they had published a number of widely-adopted editions. But McGraw-Hill told Weber, "No."

Weber's book was subsequently turned down by thirty-five more publishers, despite his solid national reputation as a physicist, teacher, published author, and reviewer for the American Institute of Physics. Not one to give up, Weber decided to make one more try.

On the strength of his reputation, Weber had been given a membership in the British society of physicists, the Institute of Physics, which conducted an active book publishing program at its Bristol headquarters. The Institute's first reaction was to turn his anthology down, but then the Institute's business manager, Martin Beavis, said, "Wait! We have our 100th anniversary coming up. *A Random Walk* will make a good item to offer as a special centenary volume."

The Institute of Physics printed enough sheets of *Random Walk* to produce 4,000 books—and then started to get cold feet. Beavis phoned an American publisher friend, Ben Russak, head of Crane, Russak & Company, a small independent publishing company based in New York. He told Russak about Weber's book, adding that he felt it would have at least some sales potential in the United States. Would Russak take 1,000 copies at 55% off British list price for exclusive North American rights? Ultimately, Russak accepted, and the books were dispatched to Crane, Russak from England.

When an advance sample bound copy of *Random Walk* was airmailed to Crane, Russak in New York, it was directed to my attention as marketing manager. I was captivated by the wildness and variety of the selections.

Since I knew that Brian Vanderhorst, writer of the popular "Scenes" column at the *Village Voice*, was an avid science buff, I sent the advance copy to him via messenger. In the next week's column, Vanderhorst gave the book a rave review. Since the *Village Voice* was the "in" New York paper and read by many publishing people, the review generated many advance orders and inquiries of interest from three book clubs—even before the books arrived in New York City.

From the early publicity and similar breaks, book club rights were sold, first to the Macmillan Book Club as a Library of Science main offering and later to the Book-of-the-Month Club as an alternate selection.

Russak's original 1,000 copies were quickly depleted but the Institute of Physics told Russak they would not part with any additional copies of their original 3,000 copy inventory. As a consequence, Russak had to go to press with a reprinted American edition of several thousand copies, joined in the same press run by a second printing of the Macmillan Book Club selection and a first printing of the Book-of-the-Month Club alternate selection.

The *Random Walk* publicity also caught the attention of the IP's sister organization, The American Institute of Physics, which began offering copies of *A Random Walk* to its membership through *Physics Today* by special arrangement with Crane, Russak, which filled all the member orders.

Encouraged by highly favorable reviews as well as radio and television interviews, Professor Weber produced a second volume some years later.[2]

How Two Publishers Treated Historic Publishing Decision

Although the seeds for printed circuitry, the invention that sparked the electronic revolution and the computer age, were first planted in World War II, it wasn't until well after the end of that War that printed circuitry slowly evolved through the combination of science and printing technology.

One of the early pioneers in the birth and development of printed circuitry was an RCA engineer, Abraham Pressman, who wrote the first book on printed circuitry, *Design of Transistorized Circuits for Digital Computers*, in the early postwar years. Pressman's thinly-paginated but heavily illustrated book quickly became the bible of America's engineers who were members of the IRE (Institute of Radio Engineers, the precursor to the IEEE, Institute of Electrical and Electronic Engineers).

The lucky publisher was John F. Rider, Publisher, founded and run by John Rider, a pioneer in American electronic publishing and himself the author of numerous books on the subject. Rider's managing editor was Jerome Kass, an electronic engineering genius who had written extensively on his subject for leading encyclopedias and who had been editor of an electronics magazine as well. Rider, who reprinted the Pressman book frequently under steady and growing demand, often told visitors to his 14th Street premises in New York City "with pardonable pride" that Kass was the man "who discovered Pressman."

While attending a meeting of scientific and technical publishers in the late 1970s, I engaged in a conversation with Eugene Falken, a former technical publishing manager at McGraw-Hill. When Kass's name came up, I recalled Rider's oft-repeated claim about Kass and told Falken, "Yes, Jerry Kass was the guy who discovered Abe Pressman."

Instead of acknowledging my remark, Falken responded, "That's not quite how it really happened. Pressman first brought his book to me at the old McGraw-Hill building on 42nd Street. It seemed very small, and I recall asking Pressman what he thought the sales potential of his book might be. He told me sales might go as high as 3,000 copies. I told Pressman that McGraw wasn't interested in anything under 5,000 copies. Why not take it down to John Rider on 14th Street? He'll publish anything."

Achieving Success in Computer Books:
Inside Look at Co-Publishing

In the early 1970s, Crane, Russak of New York had a vigorous publishing program in the sciences and technology. Almost all titles on its list were co-editions of British books for which Crane, Russak got North American or American rights by importing as few as 500 copies of published books.

Having not previously been into computer books, Crane, Russak signed with one British publisher who was in production with a four-volume set in the computer sciences. Crane, Russak had obtained North American rights to the set with an agreement to purchase 500 sets on publication. (This is a fairly common practice in publishing; many English publishers often cannot afford to publish an edition for the tiny U.K. market without first finding a U.S. partner to share production costs.)

Midway into production of the set, the British publisher informed Crane, Russak that for budgetary reasons it was forced to cancel the computer book project. But, if Crane, Russak wanted to publish the set on its own, the British publisher would buy back 500 sets of the American edition.

Crane, Russak did publish. As promised, the British publisher bought back 500 sets. In addition, an American engineering book club bought a like number of sets for its members, thus enabling Crane, Russak to break even on production costs before the first outside copy was sold.

Chapter 11

Publishing Miscellany

The Truth at Last! —
Sherlock Never Mouthed Those Famous Words

Sherlock Holmes is best identified with untold millions of fans around the globe by his famous remark to his physician friend, Dr. John H. Watson: "Elementary, my dear Watson."

In truth, in all of the words penned by Arthur Conan Doyle—four novels and fifty-six short stories—Doyle never put those words in Sherlock's mouth even once! So where did this most famous of Sherlockian lines originate? The answer: In Hollywood from the lips of Basil Rathbone, the South African-born English actor who played Sherlock Holmes in a continuing series of Hollywood movies that spanned the decades of the 1930s and 1940s. Rathbone died in 1967 at the age of 75.

Here's a Secret! —
World's Bestselling How-to Book Was Never Completed

Dale Carnegie's masterpiece, *How to Win Friends and Influence People*, has sold more than fifteen million copies since first published in 1936. Yet, the book was never completed.

Here's why: At the end of each copy, Carnegie included space for the intended ending by providing two blank pages with the heading below.

My Experience in Applying the Principles Taught in This Book.

Thus, each copy that was sold was intended to be completed in real life by the buyer.

Pool Hustler Adopts Fictitious Name
Used to Describe Him in Novel

The legendary Minnesota Fats, the most famous pool hustler in the 500-year history of the game, was actually Rudolf Wanderone, a native of New York. He practiced his art under his nickname, New York Fats, until the publication of the novel, *The Hustler*, by Harper in 1958. In that novel, the main character, Minnesota Fats, closely resembled him.

When *The Hustler* became a movie in 1961, the 5'10", 300-pound Wanderone adopted the sobriquet, Minnesota Fats, as his own and used it for the remaining decades of his life. He died on January 18, 1996, just a day before his 83rd birthday.

Author Told Not to Attend Publishing Party for His Book

When a party is held to celebrate the publication of a new book, its author is usually the center of attraction. But not so in 1991 when the author of a new book was excluded from his own party.

The book was about Indonesia, so the party was scheduled to be held at the Indonesian consulate. But someone in the consulate happened to read the book before the party took place and discovered that the author had taken a couple of swipes at Madame Suharto, wife of the Indonesian president, calling her "Madame Tien Percent" among other things. Shortly afterwards, the author received a letter informing him that, due to unavoidable circumstances, his invitation to the party had been cancelled. But it was too late to call off the party itself, which went on as scheduled.[1]

Publisher Who Turned Away Book
Pays Royalties to Author

The author provided an acceptable outline, signed a publishing agreement, and obtained a comfortable advance on a publishing project. When he turned in the completed manuscript, although it followed his outline, the publisher's editor rejected it out of hand commenting, "I just don't like it; it doesn't feel right."

The editor then demanded return of the advance, but the author refused. The editor then told the author he wouldn't release the author from the publishing agreement for the book. Deciding to take a chance anyway, the author sold the book to another publisher.

Upon publication, his publisher immediately sold the book club rights to a book club owned by the publisher who had originally turned down the book. The author never repaid the advance to the original publisher. And, for years, he earned book club royalties on a publishing project the book club's owner had rejected and still legally owned.

Rejected Benchley Rejects Club That Rejected Author

When the Harvard Club in New York City blackballed a man named John Macy on charges of radicalism because he had written a book about socialism, Robert Benchley was quick to defend Macy. Benchley pointed out to the club powers that there was little in Macy's book to endanger the spiritual well-being of the Harvard Club membership. It was an unfair rejection, he told them, and to show his upset, he was sending in his resignation.

The Harvard Club promptly responded to this effect: "You can't resign; you've already been suspended for nonpayment of dues."

Mother Writes Book to Help Deal with Son's Allergy

Second only to the Bible in sales, cookbooks are said to be the steadiest bestsellers since the advent of printing. Of the various reasons for creating a cookbook, at least one of the estimated 400 that entered the market in 1992 was created to fill an important need.

When Phyllis Potts of Oregon City, Oregon, learned that her son was allergic to foods containing wheat, she set out to find a recipe book for wheatless breads and foods. When she could not find such a book, she searched out or created some 250 recipes for wheatless foods and published her own book: *Going Against the Grain: Wheat-Free Cookery.* Such has been the popularity of her wheat-free recipe book that, in 1994, she published a second volume, *Still Going Against the Grain: Wheat-Free Cookery.*

Evaluations of Writing Clarity of Century's Bestselling Authors

Did the topselling authors of this century write clearly? Is there a simple way to measure the clarity of their writing?

The answer to both of these questions is "yes." The measurements are readily attainable by a simple yardstick called the Fog Index.

The Fog Index was created by Robert Gunning, head of a writing clinic and advisor to thousands of writers. The concept is based on a simple formula which determines the level of any piece of writing based on the length of sentences and the number of words (per 100 words) that contain three or more syllables. According to Gunning's Fog Index formula, Dr. Benjamin Spock's *Baby and Child Care*, which has sold over 20 million copies, was written at the eighth grade reading level.

Here are the reading levels, according to Gunning's Fog Index formula,[2] for some of this century's best-selling novels:

Erskine Caldwell, *God's Little Acre* (6th grade reading level)

D.H. Lawrence, *Lady Chatterley's Lover* (6th grade)

Harper Lee, *To Kill a Mockingbird* (5th grade)
Grace Metalious, *Peyton Place* (5th grade)
Harold Robbins, *The Carpetbaggers* (5th grade)
Mickey Spillane, *I, the Jury* (5th grade)

In his book, Gunning cited John Steinbeck's novels as being written in extremely simple language, testing at the 5th, 6th, and 7th grade levels. Other leading novelists of this century with low reading level scores included Sinclair Lewis, J.D. Salinger, John Cheever, Ernest Hemingway, Somerset Maugham, and Truman Capote.

How Publishers Said "No" When Rejecting Famous Books

The following rejections have been adapted from *Rotten Rejections* with the permission of the publisher, Pushcart Press.[3]

* *The Good Earth*, Pearl Buck (1931) — "Regret the American public is not interested in anything on China."
* *The Ipcress File*, Len Deighton (1963) — "Author tends to stay too long on non-essentials ... is enchanted with his words, his tough style, and that puts me off badly."
* *Madame Bovary*, Gustave Flaubert (1856) — "A heap of details which are well done but utterly superfluous."
* *Lord of the Flies*, William Golding (1954) — "You have (not) been wholly successful in working out an admittedly promising idea."
* *Catch-22*, Joseph Heller (1961) — "A continual and unmitigated bore."
* *The Spy Who Came in From the Cold*, John le Carre (1963) — "le Carre — he hasn't got any future."
* *The Razor's Edge*, W. Somerset Maugham (1944) — "I do not find the thing good of its kind.... I think it is distasteful."
* *The Jungle*, Upton Sinclair (1906) — "It is fit only for the wastebasket."
* *Lust for Life*, Irving Stone (1934) — "A long, dull novel."
* *The Time Machine*, H.G. Wells (1895) — "Not interesting enough for the general reader ... not thorough enough for the scientific reader."
* *Look Homeward, Angel*, Thomas Wolfe (1929) — "Marred by stylistic cliches ... has all the faults of youth and inexperience."
* *Poems*, William Butler Yeats (1895) — "Absolutely empty and void ... does not please the ear, nor kindle the imagination."

How to Locate Any of 1.5 Million American Books in Print

There are currently approximately 1.5 million American book titles in print, available from more than 40,000 different publishers. All 1.5 million may be quickly located by title or author in a fat ten-volume annual titled *Books in Print* which consists of about 17,000 four-column pages. By comparison, the first *Books in Print* published in 1948 provided author and title information for 85,000 titles in a single-volume reference book.

A copy of *Books in Print*, published by the R.R. Bowker Company of New York, can be found in most libraries. An annual supplement or companion reference, titled *Subject Guide to Books in Print*, lists all entries in *Books in Print* under their subject headings. *Books in Print* is a primary reference tool of librarians and booksellers in helping them to locate any book by title, author, or subject.

The *Books in Print* family is also now available on CD-ROM under the title, *Books in Print PLUS*. The CD-ROM version is more likely to be found only in larger libraries because an annual subscription currently costs $1,095.

Books in Library of Congress Would Stretch from D.C. to Oregon

If all the books in the Library of Congress were laid backside down from end to end, they would form an unbroken line stretching from Washington, D.C. to beyond Portland, Oregon. The Library of Congress, the world's largest library, has more than 80.7 million holdings, which includes more than 22.5 million books and 30 million manuscripts. It was founded in 1800 with a grant of $5,000.

Many early Library of Congress materials were lost in a fire in 1814 during a bombardment of Washington D.C. by a British fleet. However, the collection was re-established through the acquisition of the library of Thomas Jefferson.

The Library of Congress was founded with the primary purpose of serving as a reference source for members of Congress and other offices of the Federal Government. In addition to its vast holdings, the Library of Congress also houses the National Union Catalog, a record of the books contained in 2,500 libraries.

How American Book Pricing Has Grown Since 1930

In the spring of 1930, three young but successful publishing houses announced books at what were then considered revolutionary low prices. Simon & Schuster said it would offer six of its fall fiction titles, originally priced at $2.00 to $2.50, to be sold at $1.00 in paper covers. Coward-McCann offered a similar plan with its Premier Fiction series also priced at $1.00. And Farrar & Rinehart said it would offer a dozen fiction titles in hardcover at $1.00. Doubleday quickly followed, offering at $1.00 popular novels originally priced at $2.00 and $2.50. Crime Club mysteries then reduced its price to $1.00.

By contrast, prices for hardcover fiction has been gradually escalating, except for 1992 and 1993). Compare these average annual prices for popular hardcover fiction over the years 1977-93 as reported in *The Bowker Annual*:

1977	$10.09
1989	18.69
1990	19.93
1991	21.88
1992	20.39
1993	20.35

Trade paperback fiction prices have escalated comparably in recent years, from $4.20 in 1977 to $11.32 in 1990, $12.17 in 1991, $13.68 in 1992, and $13.59 in 1993.

A breakthrough in popular fiction pricing occurred in 1992 with Random House's release of Norman Mailer's 25th book, *Harlot's Ghost*, at $30.00. It was the first work of popular fiction ever to be priced at the $30.00 mark. With 1,310 numbered pages, Random House said that the book was underpriced, even at that level.

Story Behind Those Astronomical Gutenberg Bible Prices

On October 22, 1987, a copy of the *Gutenberg Bible*, printed in 1455 by the craftsman and inventor, Johannes Gutenberg of Mainz, Germany, was sold for $5,390,000 to the Japanese bookselling firm, Maruzen. It was the highest price ever paid for a printed book.

Earlier in 1978, within the span of four months, three other copies of the famed *Gutenberg Bible*, containing the Old Testament (from Genesis to the Psalms) were sold. Each also was sold at a record-breaking price, with each sale breaking the previous record high. Here is how these three sales went:

- In March 1978, $1,800,000 was paid for a *Gutenberg* by the Gutenberg Museum of Mainz, Germany.
- In April 1978, $2,000,000 was paid for a *Gutenberg* by the West German Library in Stuttgart.
- In June 1978, $2,400,000 was paid for a *Gutenberg* by the University of Texas.

What makes the *Gutenberg* so valuable? Well, for one thing, its rarity. A worldwide census of known copies taken in 1950 revealed forty-five copies in existence on vellum and paper in various states of completion. Here is the known distribution in 1950 by country:

- 12 in the United States
- 11 in Germany
- 9 in Great Britain

- 4 in France
- 2 each in Italy and Spain
- 1 each in Austria, Denmark, Poland, Portugal, and Switzerland

By comparison to the high figures noted on the previous page, here are some of the prices paid for *Gutenberg Bibles* between 1898 and 1949:

- 1898 — Imperfect copy, £2950 (approximately $14,750), purchased by Dr. Eugene Augustus Hoffman.
- 1923 — Perfect copy, £8500 (approximately $42,500), purchased by Carl Pforzheimer.
- 1924 — Imperfect copy (17 leaves missing), $46,000, purchased by John H. Scheide.
- 1926 — Perfect copy, $106,000, purchased by Mrs. Edward Harkness who presented it to Yale University.
- 1937 — Imperfect copy (250 of 317 leaves, £8,000 (approximately $40,000), purchased by Arthur A. Houghton, Jr.
- 1949 — Imperfect copy, $150,000, purchased by Mrs. Edward Doheny.

The First Gutenberg to Enter the United States

In 1845, on a commission from the New York millionaire book collector James Lenox (1800-1880), Henry Stevens, a celebrated American book hunter living in England, purchased a *Gutenberg Bible* in London for £600 (approximately $2,900). Lenox was so furious at the amount paid for the Bible (a "mad" sum in those days) that he at first refused to pay the customs duties when the book arrived in New York. This *Gutenberg* is currently part of the Lenox collection at the New York Public Library.[4]

Almanacs in America Since the Colonial Era

Almanacs have been popular in America since the British colonial era when they were sold in the printing establishments where they were produced as well as in scattered towns and villages by country peddlers.

At one point, Milton Drake of New York City undertook the task of compiling a bibliography of almanacs published at various times in the United States. In twenty-five years, he came up with 14,000 almanacs held in various collections in the fifty states.

Published in two massive volumes titled *Almanacs of the United States*, Drake's compilation showed the various locations of the 14,000 almanacs, currently held in 558 institutions, 36 state libraries, 38 state university libraries, 39 state historical societies, 47 public libraries in the 50 largest cities, the Library of Congress, the American Antiquarian Society, the Boston Athenaeum, and 40 leading private almanac collections.[5]

Origin of Tijuana Bibles

When erotic books come up for auction (sale of publication rights), they are often described in a variety of discreetly suggestive terms, such as "amatory" and "esoteric." In the United States, a frequently used term has been "Tijuana Bibles."

Why this name? Because, at one time, Tijuana in Mexico was the porn Mecca for Americans unable to obtain erotic works locally.

Why Authors Once Sold Dedications in Their Books

In ancient Rome, books were individually produced by hand and, thus, had very limited circulation. Consequently, this meant little income for their authors. Probably as a result, it was common practice for authors to dedicate their written works to friends or patrons who were expected to reciprocate with payment in coin or kind.

The ancient custom of selling book dedications by authors survived at least into the 18th century. This is evidenced in the work of the British religious leader and novelist, Laurence Sterne (1713-1768) who, in one of his published volumes, in the space usually used for the dedication, published this message: "To be let or sold for fifty guineas."

An Insider's Look at Self-Help Psychology Books and the People Who Publish Them

In a 1992 *Newsweek* article,[6] the acquisitions editor for a small publisher of self-help psychology books talked about the impact of such books on herself and others in the same publishing establishment. The self-help books that this publisher "churned" out ranged from "the gauzily spiritual and embarrassingly naive to ... no-nonsense professionally acceptable stuff." About half of the publisher's output sold to psychologists who pass the books out to clients. The other half sold direct to consumers who would rather do it themselves for $13.75 than pay out $75 an hour once a week.

"You would think," the acquisitions editor said, "that people who work for such a company would be well adjusted."

This does not happen to be so, according to the *Newsweek* article in which the editor vented her opinion. She added some details of in-house problems to reinforce her view. They included two department managers who had to work in separated areas because they couldn't stand each other, a boss who got so excited during phone calls that he fell out of his chair onto the floor, and two in-house authors of a book on stress who were on the verge of suing each other. Further, she related, the publisher's bestselling book on phobias lacked a cover photo of the author because the author had a phobia about having his picture taken.

The acquisitions editor ended her comments with this statement: "I'm looking for a self-help book for editors of self-help books."

After telling all about her colleagues, we couldn't help but wonder if she also didn't wind up look for an acquisition editor's job elsewhere.

How Horror Books Help Readers
Overcome Real-World Problems

"Horror tales," says Neil Barron, a former academic librarian, "have a hidden and important function beyond entertaining." In his introduction to *Horror Literature: A Reader's Guide*,[6] Barron adds, "It's reassuring to suffer a solid fright and to survive. It's also healthily edifying to our subconsciouses. For if we can find the psychological coin to get past a fictional slasher assault, or alien body-snatching expedition, or insidious satanic possession, then perhaps we also have the resourcefulness to deal with real-world problems that seem so impervious to solution."

Unschooled Youth Who Learned From Books:
How the Lessons Paid Off

He was born in a log cabin in the Midwest and grew up without schooling. As a youth, he clerked at a country store and found friendship in books that helped him envision a world outside that he had never seen or known about. He told his neighbors, "The things I want to know are in books. My best friend is the man who'll git me a book I ain't read."

He widened his circle of book friends and educated himself. Eventually, his "friends" helped him acquire the knowledge that elevated him to the highest office in the land. His name was Abraham Lincoln.

Statewide Literary Hall of Fame for Million Copy Authors

The only statewide literary hall of fame in the United States is the New Jersey Literary Hall of Fame, which honors and installs authors who were born, lived in, or produced their written works in New Jersey. Currently, to qualify, authors' works must also have sold over a million copies.

Founded in 1976 by English professor Herman Estrin at the New Jersey Institute of Technology, its headquarters, it is currently headed by journalist Gordon Bishop. Inductees receive a "Michael," a plaque named after its designer, Princeton architect and artist, Michael Graves.

Distinguished New Jersey authors inducted posthumously include: James Fenimore Cooper (1789-1851), author of *The Last of the Mohicans* (1826), born in Burlington; William Dunlap (1766-1839), America's first professional playwright and author of *History of the American Theatre* (1832), born in Perth Amboy; and Stephen Crane (1871-1900), author of *The Red Badge of Courage* (1895), born in Newark.

Television Evolving as Major Bookselling Outlet

Recent research studies have largely overlooked the evolution of television as a major bookselling outlet. Yet, this medium is a growing factor for getting certain types of books into the hands of bookbuyers, as the following statistics indicate. The home shopping television channel, QVC, reported in a December 1995 trade publication that it sold more than 2.3 million books in 1995. On its strongest bookselling day (November 14, 1995), QVC sold more than 60,000 units of a particular book that was priced at $23.34, plus $5.22 for shipping and handling.

How You as a Reader Should Evaluate an Author

The following is adapted from John D. Snider's *I Love Books*:[7]

In reading ... you should search until you find an author who talks to you as a friend in language you can understand. I do not mean you must always agree with a writer. But you must be willing to meet the author rather than insist that he meet your point of view.

You should be friendly, trustful, attentive, respectful, and open of mind. Otherwise, you are discourteous and unfair to him. You must of necessity enter his thoughts before you can rightly evaluate them.

The Job Rewards of Working in Book Publishing

One of the more pleasant aspects of a job in book publishing is that there is a thin line between work and play in many publishing positions. According to one psychotherapist, "publishing insiders report a difficulty of maintaining a clear distinction between work and leisure; many describe themselves as 'always thinking about work'."

Richard Snyder, chairman of Simon & Schuster, summarized it this way:[9] "The thrill of publishing a bestseller is not one that happens every day, but there is everyday joy of another kind—the kind that comes from working with creative, talented people, literate people who love books, who share books and ideas."

John Sargent, publisher of children's books at Simon & Schuster, offers this added thought: "Producing books provides great satisfaction.... At the end of the day you have been involved with the making of something of intrinsic worth. That and the people you end up working with make publishing a hell of a lot of fun."

If you're thinking of entering book publishing, take heed of this advice from Lisa Healy, executive editor of the Philip Lief Group.[10] She says, "There has never been a more exciting time to enter the profession of book publishing.... Although recent advances in computer technology are radically changing the nature of book publishing, it seems reasonable to expect that much of the basic trade lore will remain essentially unchanged.... The only common denominator among tens of thousands of people working in publishing is a love of books."

The Financial Rewards of Working in Book Publishing

Having read about some of the joys of publishing, perhaps you, too, may one day want to consider a career in this captivating field. But, if you're interested in entering book publishing for the money, forget it!

Because of the intense competition for entry-level positions, salaries tend to be very low. As the late Curtis Benjamin, one-time head of the McGraw-Hill Book Company once noted, "Every summer eager graduates flock to New York and the few other major publishing centers, each yearning to become part of the glamorized literary scene."

At virtually every level of publishing, salaries tend to be more modest than their equivalent counterparts in business and industry. Samuel Vaughan, senior vice president of Random House, summed up publishing pay scales this way: "The pay is poor at the bottom, middling in the middle, and rarely rich at the top. The hours are nonsensical ... and the rewards are mostly hidden. But if you don't mind living vicariously off others' fame ... strongly desire to be underpaid and overworked ... you may find your niche."

The Financial Aspects of Starting Your Own Press

A survey of thirty-one independent publishers[11] who had founded their own presses revealed that most had started by utilizing personal income. Where a married couple started a press, it generally was with the arrangement that one spouse worked outside to support the press (and the household) while assisting the other who worked fulltime on the press. Several had financed their book publishing operation with inherited income or the return on investments.

The Financial Aims of University Presses

The more than 100 university presses in the United States are all non-profit publishing establishments that function, for the most part, as subsidized departments of the universities to which they are attached. They exist primarily for the purpose of publishing books that would not succeed in the commercial market.

University presses specialize in two types of books: scholarly materials, purchased mainly by scholars and libraries, and regional-interest books, purchased mainly by consumers and libraries.

The largest university press is the University of Chicago Press, founded in 1891. Currently publishing about 350 new titles every year, the Press has approximately 4,500 titles in print.

Smallest Publisher to Win an Award

The smallest publisher ever to win an award, according to *Publishers Weekly*,[12] was Evelyn Kaye of Blue Penguin Publications in Boulder, Colorado. Blue Penguin won the Silver Award given by the National Nature Media Awards Program for the best travel book for 1992.

How small is Blue Penguin Publications? According to Ms. Kaye, she writes, edits, publishes, stores, packs, and unpacks books in one room of her house. Ms. Kaye, a past president of the American Society of Journalists and Authors, has written thirteen travel books as well as numerous articles in *Travel & Leisure*, *New York Times*, and other major publications.

World's Oldest Free Municipal-Library

Founded in 1852, the Boston Municipal Library System is believed to be the world's oldest free municipal library system. Housing between four and five million books, one of the library's earliest acquisitions was the famed anti-slavery novel by Harriet Beecher Stowe, *Uncle Tom's Cabin*, published that same year.

World's Oldest Library Still in Existence

The world's oldest library still in existence, according to *The Smithsonian Book of Books*,[13] is The Biblioteca Capitolare in Verona, Italy, which was founded in the sixth century. The library's collection consists largely of religious, literary, and historical manuscripts, including those of the classical writers Pliny (23-79 A.D.) and Catullus (84-54 B.C.).

World's Slowest-Selling Book

The world's slowest-selling book, according to the 1995 *Guinness Book of Records*, is David Wilkins's translation of *The New Testament* from Coptic into Latin. Published by Oxford University Press in 1716 with a press run of 500 copies, the book finally sold out in 1907 after remaining in print for 191 years.

Smallest Town to Get Own History

Jean Zipser, a former journalist and mayor of Pahaquarry, New Jersey, is writing a book about the history of her 19-square-mile town, located in the northwest corner of the state. What makes the author of the Pahaquarry history so special is that she represents half of the town's total permanent population of two residents. The other half of the town's population is township committeeman Harold Van Campen, a descendent of the town's original settlers, Dutch copper miners who arrived in the 1600s.

Besides the town's two permanent residents, Pahaquarry is also home to two National Park Service employees and their two children. The town's population peaked in 1860 when it had 465 residents.[14]

Short Life of Book Club Membership

According to a December 1995 published report, the average life of a book club membership in the United States was twelve months for clubs offering current popular fiction and nonfiction (with special-interest book clubs having considerably longer life spans). In Great Britain, the book club life span was also twelve months. By contrast, in continental Europe, book club membership life span was five to seven years.

Worldwide book club membership exceeds 25 million members, according to Bertelsmann AG of Germany, owner of numerous book clubs around the world, including the Doubleday Book Clubs and Literary Guild in the United States.

American Publishers Quick to Reject James Bond —
History Proves Otherwise

James Bond made his first appearance in *Casino Royale* on April 13, 1953. Ian Fleming's first book, published by Jonathan Cape with a printing of 4,750 copies, sold out in six weeks.

Fleming's agent then approached several American publishers, all of whom quickly turned Bond down. Doubleday returned it to Fleming's agent without comment. It then went to Norton who turned it down with the comment, first "Very English cross between early Ambler and Mickey Spillane." Next Knopf turned it down because "its excesses outweigh its readability."

But Ian Fleming's initial effort, *Casino Royale*, and its eleven successors did get published in the United States. And in 1977, twenty-four years after first publication and thirteen years after Fleming's death, here are the sales results for various James Bond novels:[15]

1953	*Casino Royale*	3,307,253
1954	*Live and Let Die*	2,883,400
1955	*Moonraker*	2,877,500

1956	*Diamonds Are Forever*	2,648,411
1958	*Dr. No*	3,239,500
1962	*The Spy Who Loved Me*	2,798,400
1963	*On Her Majesty's Secret Service* . . .	3,438,700
1964	*You Only Live Twice*	3,283,000
1965	*Thunderball*	4,211,700
	Total for nine titles:	28,366,800

Record Book on the *New York Times* Bestseller List

The record run for a hardcover fiction book on the *New York Times* bestseller list was 162 weeks set by *The Bridges of Madison County* by Robert James Waller. The three-year plus run lasted until September 17, 1995. The book first made the bestseller list on August 16, 1992.*

Judge's Action in Loud-Snoring Case
Catapults Book to Success

A book on how to stop snoring was going nowhere until the author noticed a short newspaper item in which he read about a wife filing for a divorce because she could no longer stand her husband's loud snoring. The author quickly sent off a copy of his book to the judge hearing the case. On reviewing the book, the judge announced in court that he felt the book could save the couple's marriage.

The judge's action made the local news, was later picked up by the wire services, and subsequently resulted in feature articles—all, of course, mentioning the book. We don't know if the judge's action saved the marriage, but the book went into four printings.[16]

Publishing After Retirement

The following poem was written by William J. McGlothlin and published in the March, 1978 issue of the *Bulletin of the American Association of University Professors.*[17]

Old Scholars retire, but never say die
for print they eternally cherish
They'll comb the Great Lib'ry up in the sky
and publish long after they perish.

* Coincidentally, it was on August 16th that the two main characters in the romance novel first met. In the novel, Robert walked up to Francesca's house on August 16, 1965, to ask for directions to one of the bridges. She invited him in for lemonade. The rest, as they say, is history.

Phrase Coined for Book Title Now Word in English

When Joseph Heller's World War II protest novel was published in 1961, he gave it the title *Catch-22*. The title so caught on with the American public that it worked its way into English-language dictionaries as the definition for any difficult situation or problem whose seemingly alternative solutions are logically invalid.

Catch-22 was the result of an odd coincidence. Heller had originally titled his book *Catch-18*, but the number "18" conflicted with Leon Uris's novel *Mila 18*, which was being published about the same time. So Heller raised the "18" to "22" to avoid conflict.

Bookseller Permanently on the Shelf

James Edwards (1757-1816) was an English bookseller who achieved both fame and riches traveling throughout Europe buying and selling books. At his death in 1816, in accordance with his wishes, he was buried in a coffin of wood made from his own bookshelves.

His burial was at St. Mary Harrow-on-the-Hill, a little parish church on a prominent hill in Middlesex, England. "He lies there to this day," wrote Michael Olmert in *Smithsonian Book of Books*,[18] "permanently on the shelf, but definitely out of circulation."

Jacqueline Kennedy Onassis Estate Catalog Scores Big

Perhaps the most sought-after higher-priced book issued in the first half of 1996 was the *Jacqueline Kennedy Onassis Estate Catalog*, which preceded the estate auction sale held at Sotheby's auction galleries in New York City on April 23 to 26, 1996. The 100,000-copy Special Edition ($100 clothbound, $55 softcover) quickly sold out. Its 584 pages featured a list of paintings, furniture, decorations, jewelry, and books—some used by President John F. Kennedy—as well as candid family photographs and interior views of the Onassis Fifth Avenue apartment.[19]

Notes

Chapter 1

1. *A Candid Critique of Book Publishing* by Curtis Benjamin (R.R. Bowker, 1977).
2. *Eighty Years of Best Sellers* by Alice Hacket and James Henry Burke (R.R. Bowker, 1977).
3. *In the Company of Writers* by Charles Scribner, Jr. (Macmillan, 1990).
4. *Studies in English* by LaRocque DuBose (University of Texas Press, 1953).
5. *A Gentleman of Broadway* by Edwin P. Hoyt (Little, Brown, 1964).
6. *Dreams in the Mirror: A Biography of E.E. Cummings* (Liveright, 1980).
7. *Robert Frost, The Later Years 1938-1963* by Lawrence Thompson and R.H. Winnick (Holt, 1976).
8. As adapted from the second volume of *Pearl S. Buck: An Autobiography* by Theodore Harris (John Day, 1971).
9. *In the Company of Writers* by Charles Scribner, Jr. (Macmillan, 1990).
10. *The Autobiography of William Carlos Williams* by William Carlos Williams (Random House, 1951).
11. *Agatha Christie: An Autobiography* by Agatha Christie (Dodd, Mead, 1977).
12. *Dukedom Large Enough* by David A. Randall (Random House, 1969).
13. *Screening History* by Gore Vidal (Harvard University Press, 1992).
14. *The News and Observer*, Raleigh, NC (September 17, 1989).
15. *A Sort of Life* by Graham Greene (Simon & Schuster, 1971).
16. *The World's Best Books* by Asa Don Dickinson (Wilson, 1953).
17. *Dr. Seuss & Mr. Geisel* by Judith and Neil Morgan (Random House, 1995).
18. *How to Write Books That Sell* by L. Perry Wilbur (Wiley, 1987). Adapted with permission of the author.

Chapter 2

1. *On the Wild Side* by Martin Gardner (Prometheus Books, 1992).
2. *In the Company of Writers* by Charles Scribner, Jr. (Macmillan, 1990).

3. As told to the author by Ed Langlois on August 13, 1992.
4. *The Business of Book Publishing* edited by Elizabeth Geiser and Arnold Dolan (Westview Press, 1985). Frederick Praeger was a prominent figure in American book publishing for 50-plus years before his death in 1944. Founder of Praeger Publishers in 1950 and Westview Press in 1975, he is estimated to have published close to 10,000 titles.
5. *Publishing Lives* by Jerome Gold (Black Heron Press, 1995).
6. *A Moveable Feast* by Ernest Hemingway (Scribner's, 1964).
7. *Between Covers* by John Tebbel (Oxford University Press, 1970).
8. *What Is an Editor?* by Dorothy Commins (University of Chicago Press, 1978).
9. *ibid.*
10. *My First Year in Book Publishing* edited by Lisa Healy (Walker & Co., 1994).

Chapter 3A

1. *Distinguished Classics of Reference Publishing* by Catherine Seybold (Oryx Press, 1982).
2. Reprinted from *Against the Grain*, February 1992, a newsletter for librarians and publishers as written by the author.
3. From R.R. Bowker databases, *Publishers Weekly* (March 20,1995).
4. *Between Covers* by John Tebbel (Oxford University Press, 1987).
5. *Where the Bluebird Sings* by Wallace Stegner (Random House, 1992).
6. *New York Times* (November 20, 1995).

Chapter 3B

1. *Early American Books and Printing* by John Winterich (Houghton Mifflin, 1935).
2. *Guinness Book of Records* edited by Peter Mattews (Sterling, 1995).

Chapter 3C

1. *New York Times* (December 19, 1995).

Chapter 3D

1. *The Art and Craft of Lexicography* by Sidney Landau (Scribner's, 1984).
2. *Publishers Weekly* (September 20, 1985).
3. According to David Randall, head of Scribner's Rare Book Department in *Dukedome Large Enough* by David Randall (Random House, 1969).

Chapter 4

1. *Between Covers* by John Tebbel (Oxford University Press, 1987).
2. *In the Company of Writers* by Charles Scribner, Jr. (Macmillan, 1990).
3. *Book Peddling Parson* by Lewis Leary (Algonquin Books, 1984).
4. *The Private Life of Sherlock Holmes* by Vincent Starrett (Mysterious Press, 1988).
5. *The Truth About Publishing*, 8th Edition, by Sir Stanley Unwin (Academy Chicago Publishers, 1986).
6. *Bookselling in America and the World* by John Tebbel (Quadrangle, 1975).

Chapter 5

1. *Story of J* by Terry Garrity (Morrow, 1984).
2. *Book Industry Word-Finder and Writer's Guide* by Nat Bodian (not yet published).

Chapter 6

1. *Typefounding in America* by Rollo Silver (University Press of Virginia, 1965).
2. *Publishers Weekly* (November 1, 1991).

Chapter 7

1. *Now All We Need Is a Title* by Andri Bernard (W.W. Norton, 1994).
2. *I Wanted to Write* by Kenneth Roberts (Doubleday, 1949).
3. *A Fragment of Biography* by John Gunther (Harper & Row, 1962).
4. *How to Choose a Winning Title* by Nat Bodian (Oryx Press, 1989).
5. *New York Times* (April 25, 1991).
6. *New York Times* (July 17, 1991).

Chapter 8

1. *I Love Books* by John D. Snider (Review and Herald, 1960).
2. *How to Choose a Winning Title* by Nat Bodian (Oryx Press, 1989).
3. *Bodian's Publishing Desk Reference* by Nat Bodian (Oryx Press, 1988).
4. *ibid.*
5. *70 Years of Best Sellers* by Alice Hackett (R.R. Bowker, 1967).
6. *The Business of Publishing* edited by Elizabeth Geiser and Arnold Dolan (Westview Press, 1985).

7. *A Gentle Madness* by Nicholas Basbanes (Henry Holt, 1995).

Chapter 9

1. *Between Covers* by John Tebbel (Oxford University Press, 1987).

Chapter 10

1. *New York Times* (September 15, 1992).
2. Adapted from an award-winning presentation by the author to the Professional Publishers Marketing Group, Rockefeller Center, New York (June 1983).

Chapter 11

1. Source: Richard Morris, former Director of COSMEP.
2. *The Technique of Clear Writing* by Robert Gunning (McGraw-Hill, 1968).
3. *Rotten Rejections* by Andre Bernard (Pushcart Press, 1990).
4. *A Gentle Madness* by Nicholas Basbanes (Henry Holt, 1995).
5. *America and Her Almanacs* by Robb Sagendorph (Little Brown, 1970).
6. *Newsweek* (August 31, 1992).
7. *Horror Literature: A Reader's Guide* by Neil Barron (Garland Publishing, 1990).
8. Adapted from *I Love Books* by John D. Snider (Review and Herald, 1960).
9. *Book Publishing Career Guide*, 4th Edition, edited by Ronald Fry (Career Guides, 1989).
10. *My First Year in Book Publishing* edited by Lisa Healy (Walker & Co., 1994).
11. *Publishing Lives* by Jerome Gold (Black Heron Press, 1995).
12. *Publishers Weekly* (October 19, 1992).
13. *Smithsonian Book of Books* by Michael Olmert (Wings Press, 1992).
14. *New York Times* (October 27, 1995).
15. *Eighty Years of Best Sellers* by Alice Hacket and James Henry Burke (R.R. Bowker, 1977).
16. *1001 Ways to Market Your Books*, Fourth Edition, by John Kremer (Open Horizons, 1993).
17. *Bulletin of the American Association of University Professors* by William J. McGlothlin (March, 1978).
18. *Smithsonian Book of Books* by Michael Olmert (Wings Press, 1992).
19. *USA TODAY* (April 22, 1996).

Bibliography

Academic American Encyclopedia, International Edition, 1994

American Heritage Dictionary, 2nd College Edition, 1982.

American Heritage Dictionary, 3rd Edition, 1992

Anderson, Charles B., Editor, *Bookselling in America and the World*, 1975

Barron, Neal, Editor, *Horror Literature: A Reader's Guide*, 1990

Bartlett, John, *Familiar Quotations*, 14th Edition, 1981

Basbanes, Nicholas A., *A Gentle Madness*, 1995

Benjamin, Curtis G., *A Candid Critique of Book Publishing*, 1977

Berg, A. Scott, *Max Perkins: Editor of Genius*, 1978

Bodian, Nat, *Bodian's Publishing Desk Reference*, 1988

Bodian, Nat, *Book Industry Word-Finder and Writer's Guide* (not yet published)

Bodian, Nat, *Book Marketing Handbook*, Volume 1, 1980

Bodian, Nat, *Book Marketing Handbook*, Volume 2, 1983

Bodian, Nat, *Copywriter's Handbook*, 1984

Bodian, Nat, *How to Choose a Winning Title*, 1989

Bruccoli, Matthew, *The O'Hara Concern: A Biography of John O'Hara*, 1975

Canfield, Cass, *Up & Down & Around: A Publisher Recollects*, 1971

Carrington, C.E., *The Life of Rudyard Kipling*, 1955

Cerf, Bennett, *At Random: The Reminiscences of Bennett Cerf*, 1977

Chicago Manual of Style, 13th Edition, 1982

Christie, Agatha, *Agatha Christie: An Autobiography*, 1977

Commins, Dorothy, *What Is an Editor? Saxe Commins at Work*, 1978

Concise Columbia Encyclopedia, 1983

Coser, Lewis A., et al., *The Culture and Commerce of Publishing*, 1982

Dickinson, Asa Don, *The World's Best Books: Homer to Hemingway*, 1953

Donaldson, Gerald, *Books*, 1981

Doran, George, *Chronicles of Barabbas*, 1884-1934, 2nd Edition, 1952

Encyclopedia Americana, 1993

Encyclopedia Britannica, 14th Edition, 1941

Encyclopedia Britannica, 15th Edition, 1981

Exman, Eugene, *The Brothers Harper*, 1965

Fischel, Daniel N., *A Practical Guide to Writing and Publishing*, 1984

Fisher, Leonard, *The Papermakers*, 1965

Fisher, Leonard, *The Printers*, 1965

Freedman, Russell, *Jules Verne: Portrait of a Prophet*, 1965

Fry, Ronald, *Book Publishing Career Guide*, 4th Edition, 1989

Fyvel, T.R., *George Orwell, A Personal Memoir*, 1982

Gaskell, Philip, *A New Introduction to Bibliography*, 1972

Geiser, Elizabeth, Editor, *The Business of Book Publishing*, 1985

Gold, Jerome, *Publishing Lives: Interviews with Independent Book Publishers*, 1995

Greene Graham, *A Sort of Life*, 1971

Gruber, Frank, *Zane Grey*, 1970

Gunning, Robert, *The Technique of Clear Writing*, 1968

Gunther, John, *A Fragment of Autobiography*, 1962

Hacket, Alice, *Seventy Years of Best Sellers*, 1967.

Hacket, Alice, and James Henry Burke, *Eighty Years of Best Sellers*, 1977.

Harris, Leonard, *Upton Sinclair: American Rebel*, 1975

Hart, James, *Concise Oxford Companion to American Literature*, 1986

Healy, Lisa, Editor, *My First Year in Book Publishing*, 1994

Heller, Steven, and Seymour Chwast, *Jackets Required*, 1995

Hemingway, Ernest, *A Moveable Feast*, 1964

Hirsch, Carl, *Printing From a Stone*, 1967

Horne, David, *Boards and Buckram*, 1980

Hoyt, Edwin P., *A Gentleman of Broadway*, 1964

Kane, Joseph Nathan, *Famous First Facts*, 1975

Kennedy, Richard S., *Dreams in the Mirror*, 1980

Kiefer, Marie, *Book Publishing Resource Guide*, 1996

Kiefer, Marie, *Directory of Book Printers*, 1995

Kipling, Rudyard, *Something of Myself*, 1937

Klein, Ernest, *A Comprehensive Etymological Dictionary of the English Language*, 1964

Knight, G. Norman, *Training in Indexing*, 1969

Kremer, John, *Book Marketing Made Easy*, Report Series, 1996

Kremer, John, editor, *Book Marketing Update* newsletter, 1986-1996

Kremer, John, *Celebrate Today*, 1996

Kremer, John, *Complete Direct Marketing Sourcebook*, 1992

Kremer, John, *50 Best Ways to Promote Your Books*, 1997

Kremer, John, *1001 Ways to Market Your Books*, 4th Edition, 1993

Kyle, David, *A Pictorial History of Science Fiction*, 1976

Landau, Sidney, "Editorial Preparation of the International Dictionary of Medicine and Biology," *Science and Technology Libraries*, Spring 1989

Latham, Harold S., *My Life in Publishing*, 1965

Leary, Lewis, *The Book-Peddling Parson*, 1984

Lee, Marshall, *Bookmaking*, 1966

Lippincott, J.B., *The Author and His Audience*, 1967

MacMillan Everyman's Encyclopedia, 4th Edition, 1959

Matthews, Peter, Editor, *Guiness Book of Records*, 1995

Maugham, Robin, *Somerset and All the Maughams*, 1966

McArthur, Tom, *Oxford Companion to the English Language*, 1992

McCormack, Thomas, Editor, *Afterwords: Novelists on Their Novels*, 1969

McMurtrie, Douglas, *The Book: The Story of Printing and Bookmaking*, 1943

Morgan, Judith and Neil, *Dr. Seuss & Mr. Geisel*, 1995

New York Public Library Desk Reference, 1989

New York Times Index, 1971 and 1972

O'Connor, Maeve, *The Scientist as Editor*, 1979

Olmert, Michael, *The Smithsonian Book of Books*, 1992

Onions, C.T., Editor, *Oxford Universal Dictionary on Historic Principles*, 1955

Parsons, Nicholas, *The Book of Literary Lists*, 1987

Pattis, S.W., and Robert A. Carter, *Opportunities in Publishing Careers*, 1995

Pearson, John, *The Life of Ian Fleming*, 1966

Perry, L. Wilbur, *How to Write Books That Sell*, 1987

Peters, Jean, *The Bookman's Glossary*, 4th Edition, 1961

Peters, Jean, *The Bookman's Glossary*, 5th Edition, 1975

Peters, Jean, *The Bookman's Glossary*, 6th Edition, 1983

Pilpul, Harriet, and Theodora Zavin, *Rights and Writers*, 1960

Pocket Pal, International Paper Co., 1979

Poynter, Dan, *Self-Publishing Manual*, 7th Edition, 1995

Proudfit, Isabel, *Noah Webster: Father of the Dictionary*, 1942

Randall, David A., *Dukedom Large Enough: Reminiscences*, 1969

Rettig, James, *Distinguished Classics of Reference Publishing*, 1992

Roberts, Kenneth, *I Wanted to Write*, 1949

Robertson, Laurie, *Melville: A Biography*, 1996

Romano, Frank, *The TypEncyclopedia*, 1984

Ross, Marilyn and Tom, *Complete Guide to Self-Publishing*, 1994

Sagendorph, Robb, *America and Her Almanacs*, 1970

Scribner, Charles, Jr., *In the Company of Writers*, 1990

Sencourt, Robert, *T.S. Eliot: A Memoir*, 1971

Silver, R.G., *Typefounding in America 1787-1825*, 1965

Silverman, Al, Editor, *The Book of the Month*, 1986

Sinclair, Andrew, *Jack: A Biography of Jack London*, 1977

Skillin, Marjorie, and Gay, Robert, *Words into Type*, Revised Edition, 1964

Stein, Jess, Editor, *Random House Unabridged Dictionary of the English Language*, 1968

Suskin, Steven, *Show Tunes*, 1905-1985, 1986

Teachout, Terry, Editor, *A Second Mencken Chrestomathy*, 1994

Turner, Mary C., *The Bookman's Glossary*, 4th Edition, 1961

Unseld, Siegfried, *The Author and His Publisher*, 1980

Unwin, Sir Stanley, *The Truth about Publishing*, 7th Edition, 1952

Vizetelly, F.H., Editor, *Practical Standard Dictionary of the English Language*, 1924

Wind, Herbert Warren, *The World of P.G. Wodehouse*, 1972

Winterich, John T., *Early American Books & Printing*, 1981

Wood, J.P., *The Man Who Hated Sherlock Holmes*, 1965

General Index

Book Title Index

About the Author

Nat Bodian is the author of eleven books on publishing and direct marketing, including *Book Marketing Handbook*, Volumes 1 and 2, *Bodian's Publishing Desk Reference, The Publisher's Direct Mail Handbook, The Copywriter's Handbook*, and *How to Choose a Winning Title.*

Bodian's thirty-plus years in the book industry include former marketing management positions with John Wiley & Sons, American Elsevier Publishing Company, Hayden Book Company, Crane Russak & Company, and the Baker & Taylor Company. For twelve years, he was the marketing head for the professional and reference product lines and encyclopedias in the Sci-Tech Division of John Wiley & Sons. Now retired, he still shares his font of knowledge and experience as an independent publishing consultant and writer on publishing topics.

He is currently a monthly columnist for the *Book Marketing Update* newsletter, a contributing editor to the periodical *Against the Grain* (for publishers and librarians), and a contributor and book reviewer for *Publishing Research Quarterly* and *Logos, the Professional Journal of the Book World.*

Book industry recognition has included nominations for the Publishing Hall of Fame in 1986 and for the Association of American Publishers's prestigious Curtis Benjamin award in 1984. He has also won two awards from the Professional Publishers Group.

He continues to write books about the publishing industry, including the not yet published *Book Industry Word-Finder and Writer's Guide.*